Live from Jordan

Live from Jordan

*Letters Home from My Journey Through
the Middle East*

Benjamin Orbach

AMACOM

AMERICAN MANAGEMENT ASSOCIATION

New York • Atlanta • Brussels • Chicago • Mexico City • San Francisco
Shanghai • Tokyo • Toronto • Washington, D.C.

This publication is designed to provide accurate and authoritative information in regard to the subject matter covered. It is sold with the understanding that the publisher is not engaged in rendering legal, accounting, or other professional service. If legal advice or other expert assistance is required, the services of a competent professional person should be sought.

The views present in this book are those solely of the author. They do not reflect the position of the U.S. Department of State or of the United States government.

Library of Congress Cataloging-in-Publication Data

Orbach, Benjamin.
　　Live from Jordan : letters home from my journey through the Middle East / Benjamin Orbach.—1st ed.
　　　　p.　cm.
　　ISBN-13: 978-0-8144-7427-3
　　ISBN-10: 0-8144-7427-6
　　1. Orbach, Benjamin—Travel—Middle East.　2. Jordan—Description and travel.　3. Middle East—Description and travel.　I. Title.

DS153.2.O73　2007
956.05'4092—dc22
[B]　　　　　　　　　　　　　　　　　　　　　　　　2007001140

Printing number

10　9　8　7　6　5　4　3　2　1

For my Parents
Alex and Linda Orbach

Contents

Live from Jordan

Introduction

PEEKING AROUND the corner into a small white room, I watched six older men gather around a standing microphone. They wore knitted white skullcaps and button-down shirts, neatly tucked into gray or brown trousers. One man stepped forward and sang out, *"Allahu Akbar!"* and the group repeated the call to prayer in unison. A balding man with a gray mustache stepped into the room. Amid smiles, the semicircle smoothly opened and he slid between two friends and joined in the group's singing. On Fox News Channel, "Allahu Akbar!" or "God is greatest!" is a terrorizing war cry. In the heart of Damascus's old city, inside the Umayyad Mosque, it is a graceful call of beauty and devotion.

My exhaustion and stomach problems forgotten, I stood by the doorway of this little room inside the Umayyad Mosque, mesmerized by the voices of those older men singing out the *adhan*, the call to prayer. I'd spent the past four weeks backpacking through Turkey and Syria and was looking forward to returning to my apartment in Amman, Jordan. Living off of Syrian street delicacies and various Turkish delights had taken a toll. I went to the Umayyad Mosque that evening out of a sense of obligation. You can't go to Paris and skip the Mona Lisa, and you can't travel to Damascus without a trip to the Umayyad Mosque, no matter how sick you feel.

The Umayyad Mosque is the first great architectural construction of Islamic history. It served as a symbol of power as the Islamic Empire expanded westward from Arabia. The mosque stands on ground cherished as sacred for more than a couple thousand years. At the beginning of the eighth century, when Damascus was the seat of the Islamic Empire, the mosque was built alongside the Cathedral

1

of St. John. Before Christian rule, the site was occupied by the Roman temple of Jupiter, which had replaced another pagan temple even before that.

The mosque compound is also the resting place of a legend: Salah al-Din, the Muslim general who liberated Jerusalem from the Crusaders in the twelfth century. Though not an Arab—he was of Kurdish ethnicity—his victory over the Crusaders and his reconquest of Jerusalem make him one of the great heroes of Arab history. Eight hundred years after his death, his legacy remains relevant to the struggles of Arab heroes who fight foreign powers. Over the last thirty years, leaders such as Yasser Arafat, the late chairman of the Palestinian Liberation Organization (PLO), and Saddam Hussein, the former president of Iraq, have sought to claim the mantle of a modern-day Salah al-Din. These leaders built popular followings among the Arab masses by vowing to liberate Jerusalem and to rid Palestine of what they claimed were the latest incarnation of the Crusaders, the Israelis.

In addition to being a piece of Islamic and Arab history and a tourism site for Muslims from all over the region, the Umayyad Mosque continues to serve the faithful. Earlier that evening, a group of young Iranian men proceeded through Damascus's famous covered market to the mosque's compound. They were led by a young bearded man wearing a collared black shirt and blue jeans. He sang lamentations into a microphone while two larger men carried speakers on their shoulders behind him. The leader, the speaker-bearers, and most of the fifty-person group of young Shia Muslim men wept openly and uncontrollably. They were mourning the martyrdom of the Prophet Muhammad's grandson Hussein, the son of Ali. Ali was the Prophet's son-in-law, and the term "Shia" is short for "Shiat Ali," or the partisans of Ali. Hussein was killed in the year 680 at the Battle of Karbala, in what is today Iraq. The martyrdom of Hussein is a seminal moment in Shia history and is observed on the day of Ashura, the tenth day of the month of Muharram.

The public display of emotions by the Iranian pilgrims was a startling contrast to the mosque's peaceful and sprawling outdoor marble compound. Below three towering minarets, children ran about freely, worshippers washed their hands and feet in preparation for prayer, and tourists snapped pictures of the detailed tiled facade. Yet it was inside the mosque, beyond the lavishly carpeted floors and the ornate handwork, that my emotions were touched. The private affection and fellowship of those older men in that little room inside the mosque spread over me like the reassuring warmth of Thanksgiving among family and childhood friends, but with an added religious element that felt spiritual.

Pure religious devotion combined with hundreds of years of history generates an intoxicating and addictive feeling. I yearned to be a part of it—to stay and pray—but when the adhan ended, and the mosque had filled with worshippers, I remembered that it wasn't my place and that it was time for me to go. I stepped into the sunset pinks and oranges of the expansive marble courtyard and exhaled. That call to prayer in Damascus's old city was only one of many times that the siren songs of the Arab world beckoned me closer and offered me a chance to see beyond newspaper headlines and the explosions of the nightly news.

From July 2002 until August 2003, I lived in the Middle East, first in Amman, Jordan, and then in Cairo, Egypt. I left the United States ten months after the 9/11 attacks and returned four months after the fall of Saddam Hussein's regime. On a graduate school fellowship, I studied Arabic at two different universities, at two different language institutes, with a private tutor and with several different language partners. More than Arabic, though, I set out to learn as much as I could about life in the Arab world and the Arab relationship with America. I sat in coffee shops; I spoke with anyone who would speak back to me; and I walked a pair of size 13 Rockports to that shoe store in the sky. My journey included travel throughout the Middle East, from Morocco to Oman, highlighted by that four-week trip across Turkey and Syria.

The stories that follow are from the worlds that I discovered for the first time. They come from a part of the "Arab Street," the Middle Eastern equivalent of "Main Street," that does not make the nightly news. Living in Amman and Cairo, I met people like Salah, an Egyptian cook who confronts authoritarian power every day with a smile; Sundos, a *muhajiba* or head-covered Jordan University freshman who digs surfing the Web; and Fadi, a Palestinian dreamer who loves Mariah Carey but hates George W. Bush. Day in and day out, Salah, Sundos, Fadi, and countless others shared with me their beliefs, fears, and dreams.

As narrator of their stories, I am obliged to introduce myself. Over the thirteen months detailed in this book, I claimed, under sometimes difficult circumstances, to be the grandson of a Turk, the son of a Kyrgyz refugee, a Canadian, and even an Iraqi Kurd, but I was always Ben, a twenty-seven-year-old from Pittsburgh.

Though I had lived in the Middle East before, this was my first extended experience in the Arab East—my own term for the countries of the Middle East and North Africa where the people's primary language is a dialect of Arabic. The distinction between the "Arab East" and the "Middle East" is that the Arab East does not include Israel, Turkey, or Iran. As a junior in college, I studied Middle Eastern history at Hebrew University in Jerusalem for half a year. Propelled by the intensity of a peace process that competed with bus bombs and having lived amid thousands of years of indigestible history, I chose a path that led me to learn Arabic, attend graduate school to earn a masters degree in Middle East studies, and spend what I thought would be a year in Jordan.

I first tasted the Arab East the summer before I started graduate school. In 2000, while President Clinton, then Israeli Prime Minister Ehud Barak, and PLO Chairman Arafat convened what were to be failed peace negotiations at Camp David, I spent the summer in Cairo studying Arabic and playing dominoes in Egyptian coffee shops. It was my first opportunity to see the Arab East for itself, outside the context of a country's relationship with Israel and the oil contours of American foreign policy. While I couldn't understand a lick of Arabic, I was thrilled by the superficial beat of daily life— the coffee shops, the open markets, the water pipes, the buses that you had to chase to climb on and ride, and the generosity of people that seemed present at almost every turn. I left Cairo that summer wanting more and saw that I would only get it by learning Arabic.

After two years of graduate-level study of the Middle East, economics, and Arabic, I accepted a year-long fellowship that put me in

Amman to further study Arabic and to conduct a research project on the success of a Jordanian-American trade program. This fellowship was a chance to expand my budding language skills from the Modern Standard Arabic taught in the United States to the Shami dialect which is spoken by Jordanians, Palestinians, Lebanese, and Syrians.

Modern Standard Arabic (MSA) is a modernized form of classical Arabic, the Arabic of the Koran, and it is taught in universities across the United States. Arabic teachers and others like to say that MSA is spoken across the Arab East, but dialects of Arabic are different at least by country, if not by city or village. There are of course similarities, but a Kuwaiti would have a difficult time understanding an Algerian speaking in dialect. Because of Egypt's film and soap opera industries, Egyptian colloquial is the most widely understood Arabic.

While my stated goal was to improve my Arabic and to complete my research, I decided that my year in Jordan was really to be a mission of nobler calling. Fresh out of graduate school and ready to negotiate a peace treaty (or so I believed), I decided to anoint myself America's secret diplomatic weapon. My quixotic objective was to confront stereotypes, correct false perceptions, and find some common ground between Americans and Arabs on a personal level. I wanted to give Arabs who were critical of America a living double take—to force them to reconsider the ideas that they had formed based upon what they saw on their news, read in their papers, and watched in American movies. In short, I was going to open up my own personal front in what has been dubbed the "battle for heart and minds."

I left JFK airport in New York on July 16, 2002, accompanied only by my baggage. There was no one waiting for me in Amman, I had no place to live, and I certainly did not speak Shami Arabic. My mission was an act of devotion to my naive ideas about how I thought things should be. It would be my own personal contribution to the goal of reaching a mutual understanding between my country and the part of the world whose mention elicited anger, fear, and confusion among most Americans that I knew.

That was how I drew it up, the idealistic plans of an ambitious graduate student seeking to leave a positive mark. Well, a mark was left, but whether I did right by anyone besides myself remains a gray area. Instead of dictating terms, an activity familiar to American foreign policymakers, I immediately found myself on a journey that tested my patience, my sense of humor, my ideas, and even my identity. My ability to adapt to my surroundings became as important as my persistent idealism.

In the end, my experiences, my travels, and, most important, the people I met along the way left me learning more lessons than teaching them. Some of my opinions evolved, like my thoughts on Palestine. In other cases, however, such as with my feelings on what the United States and Americans have to offer the people of the Arab East, my experiences and the stories and lives of the people who I met bolstered my pre-arrival views and perspective.

This book is a compilation of the stories of the real people I met, the places I traveled to, and the understanding I gained from living the American-Arab relationship twenty-four hours a day for a year. These tales are recounted through the words that I wrote home to my family and friends and that I wrote to myself in my journal at night as my head spun and I questioned so many dearly held notions. They are presented here in letter form.

When I moved to Jordan, there was considerable skepticism on the part of my family as to what I would do, why I was going, and how safe I would be. Following the September 11th attacks, many among my family and friends found it strange that I would choose to live in a part of the world that seemed full of people directing an unbound fury at America and Americans. As such, I wrote home frequently and in great detail. There were the "Dear Mom and Dad, I'm fine" kind of e-mails, and then there were longer "Live from Jordan," type letters where I described the people I was meeting, what I was doing, and the clash of preconceptions versus reality that I was living. Over thirteen months, I wrote thirteen of these letters. With each letter, my distribution list expanded gradually— eventually to include professional colleagues in Washington, D.C., grad school classmates from Johns Hopkins, and college friends from the University of Michigan. In turn, the number of replies that I received multiplied. With so many follow-up questions and so much interest in issues greater than my own personal misadventures, I realized there was a human story about the joys, struggles, and taste of everyday life that wasn't being told.

So I took on the responsibility of providing my distribution list a different context by which to view developments in the Middle East. To reach more people, I began to write op-eds about the world I lived in and its connection to home. Many of these op-eds went unpublished, but a couple appeared in my hometown newspaper, the *Pittsburgh Post Gazette*. These were "letters" of a different variety, and I distributed them to my list, too.

At the same time, I wrote voraciously in my journal. Days passed in Jordan and Egypt and throughout my travels where I didn't have a substantive conversation in English. All of my thoughts, observations, fears, and ridiculous stories were poured into my journal, which became a stream-of-consciousness about my life on the Arab Street. All of these pieces—the letters, the op-eds, and the fit-to-print highlights of my journal—are brought together here in this collection of letters home.

These letters are different from the average rainy day, Camp Tioga effort. They are longer, and they include conversations. In the cases in which I was interviewing people for my research, the interviews were mainly held in English and I was able to take notes. For most of the conversations recounted in my letters, however, discussions were in Arabic and in an informal setting. When you're hanging out with friends in a coffee shop, you can't take notes. Some conversations were seared into my brain; I remember them today. In other cases, whether due to translation or because I was only able to record the events later that night in my journal, word choices may not be exact. For Arabic words that don't translate easily or that repeat throughout these stories, I've compiled a glossary, found in the back of the book.

Until recently, the direction of Middle Eastern winds meant little to our daily lives. Popular interest in the Middle East did not extend beyond gas prices and peace in the Holy Land. Today, though, with U.S. soldiers and taxpayers' dollars entangled in Iraq and the threat of terrorism lurking at home, we are all grasping at Middle Eastern straws. Many of us wonder about the effects of our war in Iraq, or what impact the absence of peace has on our lives, and certainly about the consequences of being hated. Na'el the barber, Jihan the diva, Ramis the factory owner, and all the other ordinary people that step out from these letters offer a different context, a more personal and human context, with which to view this faraway world and these very real problems that have arrived on our front stoop with such an impact.

Part One

The Arab Street

Letter

1

Head First, Lost in Amman

July 27, 2002

Dear All,

Imagine walking home from work, a tall foreign-looking man approaches you and asks, "I beg your pardon, my good sir, but I just arrived in your country. And in actuality, I do not possess a place of residence, nor do I possess much currency. Can you please assist me with locating a furnished flat?"

Please don't hurry past or roll up your window—that's me asking the question, and I need help! I don't know anyone, I don't speak the language, I don't know where anything is, and even if I did, I don't know how to get there. Oh, I should also mention that when people find out where I'm from, they want to know whether my country is going to invade the country next door, destroy the local economy, and kill innocent people. My first week in Jordan hasn't quite gone as smoothly as I had hoped.

Classes started at the university, but I spent most of the past week walking the streets of Amman, looking for an apartment. It turns out that the housing market is tight in the summer because rich vacationers from Persian Gulf countries like Saudi Arabia, Kuwait, and Qatar drive on over to enjoy Amman's summer breeze. Amman isn't the Tropicana, but 95 degrees with an evening breeze beats 130-degree temperatures in the still desert.

While all of the Middle East may appear on TV to be a hot and dusty scene out of *Ishtar*, Jordan really is a desert country. Carved out by the British after World War I as a reward to the Sharif Hussein bin Ali (great-great-grandfather to Jordan's King Abdullah II) for his support against the Turks and the crumbling Ottoman Empire, Jordan lies between the Jordan River to the west, Syria to the north, and the Iraqi and Saudi deserts to the east and south. While the Sharif's third son, Faisal, received the lush Kingdom of Iraq from the British, his second son, Abdullah, received a swath of desert that was called Transjordan at the time. When Abdullah arrived in Amman in 1921, he found his inheritance to be a poor desert country populated by a combination of Bedouin nomads and farmers. Today, Amman is a Middle Eastern hub, and Jordan is a quickly developing country of 5 million people whose literacy rate is greater than 90 percent. In 1921, though, a quarter of a million people inhabited the four districts of Transjordan, and social communities and laws were largely determined by tribal affiliation.

Wadi Ram.

Jordan's growth and history have been marked and complicated by the Arab-Israeli wars of 1948 and 1967. As a result of each war, a wave of Palestinian refugees crossed the Jordan River and took up residence, setting the stage for a contentious relationship between the Bedouin shepherds and farmers on the one hand and the displaced and discontented new arrivals on the other. In 1970, this complicated relationship erupted into civil war. The demographic difficulties of the Jordanian-Palestinian relationship were compounded further in 1991, when Jordan experienced a third major wave of immigration as 300,000 Palestinians and Jordanians were expelled from Persian Gulf countries as retribution for PLO Chairman Yasser Arafat siding with Saddam Hussein against Kuwait and Jordan's King Hussein (father of King Abdullah II) remaining neutral in the 1991 Gulf War.

Many of these 300,000 people sent money home regularly and had been a key source of income for Jordanian and Palestinian families in Jordan. In a heartbeat, they went from meal ticket to unemployed uncle and landed jobless in Jordan. At the same time, Jordan lost critical donor support in the Gulf and the West. International isolation and the influx of new refugees put an economic strain on Jordan, a resource-poor country. This economic despair was a key factor in King Hussein's choice to pursue peace with Israel and its accompanying promises of Western financial support.

While I generally find these sorts of political fault lines fascinating, it's finding a place to live that has me most concerned these days. I spend my days walking around, asking people for help, and looking for agencies that rent furnished apartments. Walking isn't the most efficient means of getting about, but I haven't figured out how to take the buses. Theoretically, I could take a cab, but I don't know where I would tell the driver to take me. So, that leaves me trudging through Amman's streets, searching for white signs with red Arabic letters that advertise furnished apartments. These signs stand out against the Amman skyline and beckon me forward, like the flashing lights of the dollar store at a strip mall. I pick my way through side streets and traffic jams, making my way toward the elusive promise of unpacking my bags.

Along the way, I stop people and, in Modern Standard Arabic, ask for help. Though some ignore me, most people are friendly and curious to know who I am, where I've come from, and what I'm doing in Amman. These encounters end in smiles and a friendly point toward another magic place off in the distance that holds the answers to all of my problems. Many times, though, there is more. Yesterday, someone offered to rent me his basement. After a visit to the apartment, I decided to pass; the boiler was in the "living room."

Others have offered their phone numbers and told me to call if I need help. The pay phones here take phone cards, though, not coins. So I bought a phone card the other day and have now memorized the Arabic-speaking operator's message for "the number that you have dialed is not correct; please hang up and try again." There is no reason to believe that people are giving me wrong numbers. Rather, I think I have my own issues as far as figuring out how to use the phone.

My number-two activity, which I frequently get to do while I'm looking for an apartment, is walking up hills. Amman is a bridgeless city of winding roads carved into little hills that I'm always ascending. I thought that walking around with Lonely Planet's travel guide to Jordan would land me an apartment and be the best way to figure out how to get around the city. Either Lonely Planet's maps are the cartographic version of creative writing, or Amman suddenly added more streets in the past year. A tip for aspiring cartographers— details count; include all the streets.

Buses zip past me as I sweat through shirts and walk up Amman's hilly streets, lost. Their existence suggests a reprieve from further uphill exercises in futility, and I long to hail down one of those buses, but I just don't know what to say. Besides, my not knowing the bus routes, I don't have a clue about my own destination. Complicating the problem, if the bus did stop for me, I would probably end up saying something like, "Pardon me, my good man, but will you be embarking on a voyage to the center of this fair metropolis? I desire to travel with you, sir."

Not knowing the Jordanian dialect is definitely a problem. With my Modern Standard Arabic (MSA) grad school training, I can explain in Arabic the impact of globalization on developing countries, but I don't know how to ask for the check at a restaurant. I struggle to express myself in the context of daily needs and everyday life, and my small talk is as fluid as a stuttering Frenchman at an Ebonics convention. I would give all my dry shirts for some sort of magic decoder ring that lets me make the transition from MSA to dialect.

To be fair to my grad school Arabic teachers, most people do understand me when I speak. My words lead to a combination of looks of disbelief, big smiles, and the occasional "you need a shower" face scrunch. My problems actually begin when I stop speaking, have to listen, and am expected to respond. At that point in the conversation, I hit the canvas, lights out, a first-round Mike Tyson knockout—i.e., I don't understand much. As words float by (like butterflies), I ponder whether I've really been studying Arabic continuously for the past two years. And, if so, who decided to drop dialect from the curriculum? Ten out of ten lost white guys in the Middle East agree: bad choice.

At the end of a day of being lost and not understanding the world around me, I retreat to Safeway, the air-conditioned palace that is a cross between Whole Foods and Target, but with an Internet café, too. Back home, the closest thing to Amman's Safeway is the Meijer store, that marvel of Midwestern one-stop shopping where you can fill your cart with fresh pears, cargo shorts, and a chain saw. Unlike the Sunday-morning Meijer crowd, though, the people at Safeway don't have bed-head and aren't wearing sweatpants. Safeway is where Amman's elite go to shop, and they dress for the occasion. Besides the university, it is the only place where I see women walking around unaccompanied by their menfolk or family. In the air-conditioned wonderland of Safeway, I people-watch, browse the aisles for my favorite foods, and check prices. Everything costs a lot less than at home, except for name-brand Western products. Heinz ketchup costs about $6! Not a big concern for me right now, but that's outrageous.

Even better than Safeway—and my favorite thing about Amman so far—is the Nefertiti Hotel, my temporary home. The Nef is a low-budget hotel that caters to Palestinians and Iraqis who have come to Amman for work or to get away from the stresses of life in the West Bank or Iraq. I stumbled upon the Nef during one of my apartment hunts and decided to stay there after Issa, the twenty-five-year-old receptionist and driver, welcomed me warmly. At $12 a night, the hotel is within my price range, and the people there are very friendly. Even better, they don't speak English, which means I can practice my Arabic all the time.

In my short time at the Nef, I've taken on a sort of mascot-like status. Mascot might not be the best description; I'm more like a novelty act than the San Diego Chicken. I'm similar to a street performer that people are inexplicably drawn to for a moment, before moving along about their business. There are so few foreigners here, and the ones that do come generally stay in places like the Hyatt or other luxury chains. So, for the non-elites, and in particular the Iraqis and Palestinians that stay at the Nef, I'm a curiosity: an American who came to Jordan for a year to study Arabic at Jordan University.

When I come home from Safeway, I sit in one of the many chairs of the TV room lobby of the Nef and wait for Issa, his older brother Mohammed, and friends of the neighborhood to stop by and visit. Other guests come and go, sit and watch the news, and pepper me with a sequence of questions that usually include:

"Where are you from?"

"When did you arrive?"

"What are you doing in Jordan?"

"Why are you studying Arabic?"

"What is your religion?"

"What is your *asl*—your (genealogical) roots?"

This last question may seem odd, but it makes sense here. When I respond and, in kind, ask people where they are from, most declare, "I'm of Palestinian descent, but a Jordanian citizen."

Clearly, they feel the importance of making such a distinction. If they said "Jordanian," then I might think that their family is from

Jordan and that they are trying to hide their Palestinian identity, of which they are proud. And if they answered "Palestinian," I might confuse them as someone who doesn't have citizenship. Many of the Palestinian-Jordanians who ask me this question seem eager to recount their own personal stories of injustice and to assert their Palestinian identity. At times, I've felt that I'm asked about my asl solely due to the questioner's nationalistic need to share his own personal narrative, rather than out of real curiosity about my otherness.

It is also possible, however, that by asking me to explain my roots, my new acquaintances are affording me the courtesy of asserting exactly who I am. I don't have to just be an "American"—I can be an Italian-American or a Lebanese-American. In any case, I've had several long conversations about where I am from. Because of my goatee, short dark hair, and choice to come live in the Arab East, most people think that I have an Arab parent. When people hear my name, though, if they are educated, they suspect that I come from Jewish roots. In this regard, Benyamin Netanyahu, Israel's former prime minister, is turning out to be one of the more influential people in my life. "Benyamin" or "Benjamin" has become a well-known Jewish name in the Arab East. Telling people that my name is "Ben" isn't really an option since it means "son" in Arabic and is not a name. Bin Laden means the "son of Laden." So, I introduce myself as "Benja," which is good for confusing the educated and noneducated alike.

Because hostility toward Israel is plainly obvious here, I don't feel comfortable telling people that I meet on the street or at the university that I am Jewish. For the most part, I've told people that I come from a mixed Muslim, Christian, and Jewish background that involves ancestors from Turkey and Poland. This story has gotten complicated at times, and I actually wrote the whole narrative down in my journal to keep it straight. I'm not proud of lying, but I don't want my religion to become the centerpiece for all of my conversations.

In addition to being curious and full of questions about who I am and what I'm doing here, the people at the Nef are incredibly generous. Whenever Issa, Mohammed, or Fayez—a journalist who works nearby—have something to eat, they insist on sharing their meal with me, no matter how hard I protest that I'm not hungry. Frequently, we sit on the patio in front of the hotel and drink tea. A few times, Fayez and others have taken me to a local coffee shop to sit outside in the summer breeze, smoke a water pipe, and drink more tea.

On the patio or at the coffee shop, Fayez, Issa, Mohammed, and others speak with me in MSA, rather than dialect, so that I can understand them. Beyond the oft-repeated basic questions, the hot topics that interest my friends at the Nef are religion and American foreign policy, with a heavy emphasis on Israel and Iraq. Whether it is sitting at a coffee shop with Fayez, a water pipe in hand, or reclining in the passenger seat of the Nef's white Fiat parked in front of the hotel while Issa plays with the radio dial, I am bombarded with questions concerning American foreign policy:

"Why does America confront Iraq?"

"Why does America sell F-16s to Israel to use against the Palestinian people?"

"Why does America condemn Palestinian resistance against Israel but veto United Nations resolutions that condemn Israeli terrorism against Palestinian civilians?"

"Why doesn't America organize an international coalition to expel Israel from occupied Palestine the way it expelled Iraq from occupied Kuwait in 1991?"

"Why does America hate Muslims and wage war against Islam?"

"Why can't Arabs obtain visas to enter the United States? Is it true that Arabs are attacked on the street in America because of September 11?"

Frequently, I feel like an American spokesperson scrambling for answers, seeking to make logical arguments that will make the point that America is not at war with Islam in the aftermath of the September 11 attacks. The Israeli-Palestinian issue is tougher to address. Almost everyone that I've met so far at the Nef, on the street, or at the university identifies themselves as Palestinian in some way. Their parents or grandparents came to Jordan in the 1948, 1967, or 1991 waves of Palestinian immigration. The continuing Israeli occupation of the West Bank and Gaza is also a factor in the flow of Palestinians to Jordan. As a result, the majority of the people living in Jordan are Palestinian or of Palestinian ancestry—estimates range to as high as 60 percent of the population. Not surprising, these displaced Palestinians have strong and emotional opinions on the Arab-Israeli conflict, a topic that I'll have to take up in a future letter.

I should probably say something about the university, the reason why I'm here. I've been to a few of my classes so far and already realize that the university setting itself, home to about 30,000 students, is much more interesting than the content of my classes. The campus is the size of a few city blocks, fenced in, and lined with trees. On my first day, I showed the guard my passport, entered the main gate, and stepped into a different universe. Feelings of disorientation have characterized my past week, but I experienced sensory overload at the university; it felt like I was wearing a wool sweater in August.

When I walked through the main gate and down the central artery, a wide stone pathway surrounded by tall evergreen trees and administration buildings, I felt as if all eyes were upon me. I scanned the crowd for a familiar face, but of course there wasn't one—I am in Jordan, and everyone I know lives at the Nefertiti Hotel. On the main walkway, hundreds of students milled about or sat on notebooks (to keep their clothes from getting dusty) under the shaded cover of towering trees.

As usual, I had no idea where to go, but I continued straight along the stone walkway toward the clock tower in the center of campus. I walked past men wearing tight Euro-style jeans and short-sleeved collared shirts, and women who could have stepped out of *Vanity Fair* ads, with designer jeans and shirts. Other women were dressed more conservatively, with gray or white *hijabs* and blue, green, gray, khaki, or black *jilbabs*. A hijab is an Islamic head scarf and a jilbab is a shapeless button-down or zip-up outer garment that looks like a painter's smock. It covers a woman's clothes from her collar to ankles.

I passed the library and, with moving lips, read the names of other buildings, looking for one that might house the language center. I thought about asking for directions, but I didn't know who to approach. While I have no problem with strangers on the street laughing at me, for some reason, I'm sensitive about serving as the butt of students' jokes. I even felt reluctant to make eye contact with female students, not knowing what would be culturally acceptable and what might be misinterpreted. I think I might be overly sensitive to not wanting to offend people. Eventually, I found the language center.

Despite my limited attendance so far (I've spent most of my time lost and looking for a place to live), it's clear that classes are horrendous. There are about twenty other students in my Arabic class—the second most advanced level—who I've divided into three groups: the Lawrences, the princes, and the true believers. The Lawrences, who I've nicknamed after the British Arabist played by Peter O'Toole in *Lawrence of Arabia*, are Western academic types who study Arabic because of their interest in Arab history or culture. Their presence at the university and their study of Arabic is an affair of the mind; they want to gain a skill set valuable to professional development and achievement. Based upon their political persuasion and interpretation of history, Lawrences are classified, in a black or white way, as either "Arabists," if they love all things Arab, or "Orientalists," if they are critical of aspects of Arab history or culture. In our class, we have a few Lawrences: a Korean-American, a British guy, a couple of Italians and Spaniards, and me.

The princes (and princesses) are Arab-Europeans or Arab-Americans who speak either good Arabic, because their parents spoke their native language to them as children, or no Arabic, because their parents chose to speak only their new tongue upon immigrating to America or Europe. Our class has a French-Palestinian and a French-Iraqi who both speak Arabic almost to the level of fluency, but struggle to read and write the language. Their study of

Arabic is an affair of the heart; they seek to complete a missing part of their identity.

Lastly, there are the true believers who are religious Muslims from Chechnya, Indonesia, and Turkey. They read from the Koran masterfully but can't speak Arabic at all. Their study of Arabic is an affair of both the heart and the mind; knowledge of Arabic will allow them to achieve spiritual fulfillment. Together, we make quite a combination, both socially and academically. Though on the social front, my classmates so far share a common trait of not wanting to speak with me. Maybe it's because I missed the first week of school and the icebreaker games.

It's not this group of Lawrences, princes, and true believers that makes classes difficult though—it's my teachers. I have four teachers, and all but one comes across as lazy or disinterested. My grammar teacher has devoted the first fifteen minutes of each class to talking about how much he hates Israel's prime minister, Ariel Sharon. He then spends half of the class answering questions from Austin (the Korean-American) regarding grammar minutia. The other day we spent twenty minutes on the pronunciation of female plurals in the dual set. That's not going to help me find a place to live and is as relevant as a fifth-grade English class back home practicing the spelling and pronunciation of Polish last names. "M-U-R-K-O-W-S-K-I, now say it again, class!"

After grammar, our reading teacher, "the Cartoon," takes over. The Cartoon has a spiky blond mullet haircut and bulging eyes. He is kind of like a helmetless hockey player who has just been checked against the boards. The Cartoon spends half of class looking out into the hallway at students passing by, and the other half reading the text out loud, asking us what words mean, and behaving like Bugs Bunny. He doesn't actually explain vocabulary words or offer synonyms. Instead, he acts out the words. Since I only know vocabulary that deals with globalization, occupation, and weapons of mass destruction, I never know the answers to his questions. The texts we've read so far have been about marriage, sickness, and camels. The Cartoon frequently curls his upper lip, theatrically snarls "no" to the answers students give, and then acts out words and phrases such as "virus," "camel with two humps," and "wedding engagement." Strangely, it is always the same pantomime routine. Both he and the Sharon-hating grammarian answered their cell phones in class today.

The best part about class is the break. Between grammar and reading, I sit outside, eat oranges, and people-watch for thirty minutes. Yesterday, while I was eating an orange, a student with her head covered approached me. Usually, I try not to let Jordanians speak to me in English by playing the game of answering English questions in Arabic. I was so taken aback by her forwardness, though, that I would have spoken with her in pig latin had she asked. Nadia, the girl, wanted to practice English. She told me that she was a Jordanian of Palestinian descent and asked me about my roots, sure that I was a prince. We ended up talking about religion. She told me that just because people were religiously observant didn't mean that they were good people. Nadia was very appreciative of my willingness to speak with her, which I found funny. She doesn't know that I don't really have any friends to speak with, except for my bewildered associates at the Nef.

From Nadia, to the group at the Nef, to the people I've met on the street, I'm impressed by the little acts of generosity and hospitality strangers have offered me so far. My prearrival fears of encountering hatred and anger toward Americans were pretty off. As Jordanians and Palestinians give me directions, welcome me to their country, and make suggestions as to where I might find a place to live, they say to me that as an American, I am welcome.

People, they tell me, are different from their governments. We are all human beings and the same everywhere, regardless of our nationality. Governments, however, are evil. Since no one here has a say in choosing their government, Jordanians and Palestinians have sympathy for Americans. To them, my government is an international bully and liar, and not reflective of the positive stereotype of American people being honest and well meaning. (There are, of course, negative stereotypes, which I'm discovering, too—a story for later.) They don't hold me responsible for American foreign policy—I'm just a simple citizen, like them, who has nothing to do with my government's choices. I can't help but wonder whether this sentiment will change as I continue to defend U.S. policies in discussions about Iraq, the war on terrorism, and the Arab-Israeli conflict.

It's been quite a beginning, hope you all are well. More to come soon—

Love,
Benja

Letter

Palestine, Palestine, Palestine

August 7, 2002

Dear All,

The signs here read "Amman," and there are billboards with the slogan "Jordan First," but I'm sure that I've stumbled into some sort of *Twilight Zone*–like Palestinian dimension. I've met a legion of Palestinian Jan Bradys. Instead of "Marcia, Marica, Marcia!" they holler "Palestine, Palestine, Palestine!"

My own Palestinian Jan Brady is Fadi, a thirty-one-year-old fellow I moved in with a week ago. We live in an apartment across from the university that doesn't have an address. It isn't that the number fell off of the building or that the building is located on an obscure alleyway—it is on a major thoroughfare. There is just no address. When I went to register with the police for my residency card, the officer wrote down the following description in a big gray binder: "The first apartment on the first floor of the building next door to the card store, on the street across from the north entrance of the university." Street names and addresses aren't so big here;

landmarks are more important to finding your way around, as I've found from my adventures of being lost.

Fadi entered my life by way of a "roommate wanted" sign at the university's language center. He isn't the traditional university flat mate in that he is not a student, he's not regularly employed, and he's not a Jordanian citizen. I was desperate to unpack my bags and do a wash, and he seems like a nice guy. He's already taught me how to ride the bus, helped me register with the police, and taken me to buy a used cell phone. Other foreign students have lived in the apartment before me—a British one is actually there now, too—and the location is ideal. At worst, this situation is only for a month, until the end of my summer classes.

The apartment does have some limitations, however, like no hot water. If we want hot water, we have to buy diesel fuel to heat it. Fadi told me he wasn't interested because there are summer water shortages, and we shouldn't waste water on hot showers. I reacted skeptically, unable to fathom turning on the kitchen faucet and not having water at least dribble out. Dry pipes seemed like an urban legend, until it happened on Sunday. Three minutes into my four-minute cold shower, the trickling stream of water sputtered to a stop. Our water is pumped on Thursday, and I had washed two loads of sweat-stained clothes shortly after moving into the apartment.

That evening, Fadi patiently explained to me that showering was a waste of water, laundry water had to be reused no matter what color it turned, and we needed to flush the toilet selectively. He then showed me a new way to wash the dishes, soaping them first and then rinsing them in a basin full of still water. When the sun had set, he went up to the roof and used a hose to siphon some water from our neighbors' tanks. Needless to say, I now consider my cold four-minute shower every other day a treat.

Since I no longer need to look for a place to live, I'm developing new activities. Some effort is going into my homework, but I spend a lot more time walking around different parts of the city. I speak with people and attempt to build relationships by hanging out or eating at the same places and trying to become a regular. I also spend time with Fadi and his cousin Marwan. Chatting with them in

Arabic is good practice, and they've opened a window for me into the Palestinian school of hard knocks.

Fadi is searching for work, a process made more complicated by the fact that he is a Jordanian resident rather than citizen. Fadi moved to Jordan from the West Bank a few years ago. Previously, he worked as a driver and handler for a Japanese businessman, a very good job. The businessman treated him with dignity, appreciated his efforts, and paid him well. Because of the pressures related to the Palestinian *intifada* raging across the Jordan River and the shadow of potential war in Iraq, however, the Japanese businessman returned to Japan, and Fadi has not worked regularly since.

Fadi's life is marked by waiting. He waits for his Japanese golden goose to return one day, but more important, he waits to meet his one true love. Fadi's dream is to get married and to have a daughter. He is in love with the idea of being in love; he sings along with Mariah Carey on the radio in our kitchen while he cooks dinner. Fadi speaks frequently about his dream of living in America, where he would work hard for the minimum wage and speak American slang. A few times now, I've sat down on the couch next to Fadi, and he has eagerly asked me, "What's up?" The other day, with genuine curiosity, he asked, "Should I say 'What's up nigga or bro?' when I meet African-Americans?"

Also in his dream life in America, Fadi imagines coming home from a long day of work to a nice dinner and a little daughter who

Fadi and Marwan.

would meet him at the door with a hug. Fadi wants a daughter rather than a son because girls are more loving than boys. A girl will be excited to see him when he enters the house, while a boy will only be interested in "playing video games and hanging out with his friends."

Some serious obstacles stand between Fadi and the fulfillment of his dreams. He has no money, no apartment (he lives rent-free as long as he can find foreign flat mates for the landlord), and no citizenship. While not having a job or an apartment are each show-stoppers, not being a citizen is a killer. In most Arab countries, citizenship passes through the father, so even if Fadi marries a Jordanian citizen, his kids will not be Jordanian citizens and will not have equal status here. If he returned to the West Bank, he'd have the same financial problems, with a worse economic situation, and still face citizenship problems, since there is no official Palestinian state with accompanying paperwork. On top of that, he would have to worry about his safety, too.

So Fadi tries to meet foreign students and their friends, hoping for an opportunity to meet an American, British, or European Palestinian princess he can fall in love with and marry. He imagines returning to her home and leading a Muslim life with all the Palestinian traditions, happily tucked into the diaspora and never returning to Jordan, a country he hates for all the official and social discrimination that he faces as a Palestinian noncitizen.

Fadi's best friend is his twenty-four-year-old cousin Marwan. Everyday, Marwan comes over to hang out, drink coffee on the balcony, and watch TV. He is home for the summer from medical school in Bulgaria and has one more year before completing his degree. Marwan and Fadi talk a lot about the issues surrounding Marwan's Bulgarian girlfriend, who awaits his return to Sofia. Unlike Fadi, Marwan is a Jordanian citizen. His family worries that he will marry his non-Arab girlfriend and stay in Bulgaria. Marwan is close to his younger brother and his parents and is clearly conflicted about the predicament with his girlfriend. Fadi is the only member of the family who tells Marwan that he should do what will make *him* happy. In fact, perhaps projecting his own dreams, Fadi encourages Marwan to marry his true love and to stay in Bulgaria.

Marwan and Fadi make an odd couple. On the one hand, Marwan moved to Bulgaria by himself when he was eighteen. He didn't speak Bulgarian, nor did he know anyone there. While there are obvious difficulties to adjusting to a new life within a different culture far from home, the experience sheltered Marwan from many of the hardships of life in Jordan. On the other hand, Fadi faced all of these professional and social hardships as he has bounced back and forth between the West Bank and Jordan over the past ten years. In addition to his citizenship and job problems, Fadi is always ready with a story of abuse that he suffered at the hands of either Israeli or Jordanian soldiers.

Fadi's parents have passed away, and he is estranged from most of his family except his sister and an aunt in the West Bank. In most conversations about social issues such as marriage, the role of women, and religious coexistence, Fadi references lessons from the life of the Prophet Muhammad. Fadi also goes to the mosque on Friday to pray and certainly doesn't approve of premarital sex. He holds very clear opinions on what is right and what is wrong. Marwan has no interest in prayer or the mosque, but he too has high moral standards. His kindness and generosity are clear as he sits for hours each day on our living room couch and listens to Fadi speak of his frustrations and dreams. Yet, in Bulgaria, Marwan lives with his girlfriend, and I've yet to see or hear Fadi questioning him on the details of that situation.

While I've entered this world of Fadi's and Marwan's personal struggles, there are national struggles that also run through their lives, which at times dominate life here or, at a minimum, exacerbate preexisting feelings of frustration. The other evening, Fadi and I were watching al Jazeera, the flamboyant Arabic satellite TV news station. We've watched a few times this week, and Fadi helps me out with new words. I've done the same for him a couple of times with the American movies that the Jordanian channels show at night. It's a good trade, Yasser Arafat for Keanu Reeves.

This night was different, however. The Israeli army assassinated a Hamas leader earlier that day and, in the process, leveled a building in Gaza, killing nine people, including little children, and hurting 150 others. Al Jazeera was live at the scene, showing wounded and dead children, people in the hospital with blood running from wounds, the rubble of the building, and horrified women screaming in the street. They showed earlier funeral coverage of a two-month-old baby who had been killed. An adult, maybe the baby's father, held the wrapped dead infant above the crowd.

I told Fadi that I didn't want to see this, that it was too much. Instead of changing the station, he turned the volume up. He demanded in English, "You have to watch it!"

With a finger pointed at the television, turning back and forth between the graphic images that filled the screen and me, he cursed Israel and America. He yelled, "America sells them weapons and fighter jets, and look what the Israelis do! They kill children! And tomorrow at the U.N. Security Council, when there is a resolution, America will veto it! When Hamas kills children at a pizza place, you call it terror! Tell me why you call this a 'hot operation' and not terrorism? The Israeli government is terrorist! Sharon is a terrorist! Do you know how many Palestinians he has killed?"

Images of rubble and wailing *muhajiba*, or head-covered, women flashed across the screen, Fadi continued to yell, and I felt hopeless. A hundred logical arguments weren't going to take away the fact that children had been killed and that the full details were displayed before us. Americans and Israelis are worried about indoctrination, incitement, and the nature of the Arab media. But there wasn't anything that wasn't true in that media coverage. Al Jazeera didn't make that story up; they just reported its gory details, feeding into preexisting frustrations and anger. ABC or CNN would not have shown the dead baby or a corpse covered in blood, but that doesn't mean that it didn't happen and that the incident wasn't another footnote in the ongoing Arab-Israeli conflict.

The conflict is more than one brutal continuing news story. Before I came here, I knew that there were differences in perspective on the same events, but I didn't realize that there were two different stories—two different truths—that share the same dates and actors. That night, Fadi railed on about killings, deportations, and the destruction of a people. Israel had attacked every one of its neighbors: Egypt in 1956 and 1967, Syria and Jordan in 1967 as well, Lebanon in 1982, and the Palestinians repeatedly over the last fifty years. Israel had invaded and occupied its neighbors' lands, and all in the name of "defense." Israel did not want peace. If it wanted peace, it would follow the U.N. resolutions, which Fadi claimed specified a withdrawal to 1948 lines. All the Israelis did was attack and kill.

Fadi spoke of a home in Jaffa, now part of Tel Aviv, and of family members who were run out under threat of rape and murder in 1948. He recounted, "They took our land, and they kicked us out to places like this, to Jordan. The soldiers are killers. They use 'dumb dumb' (hollow-tipped) bullets, kill babies, and break children's arms and legs. You like [former Israeli Prime Minister Yitzhak] Rabin, the 'peacemaker'? He said to break our bones. He told the soldiers to break children's bones. Do you know what happens at the check-points? Nineteen- and twenty-year-old soldiers embarrass men in front of their children. They throw them to the ground and kick them. They make them beg just to go to work. The Israelis treat non-Jews like animals."

I began to object. "Come on, they . . ." but Fadi interrupted.

"No? Then why do the Israelis trade Arab prisoners for dead bodies?"

In the past, the Israeli government has exchanged prisoners for the remains of Israeli soldiers, so the soldiers might be given a proper Jewish burial. Fadi raged on, his eyes wide and forehead creased, "Are a few dead Jews equal to a hundred live Arabs?"

I remained quiet, and then he asked me rhetorically, "Do you want to know why we have no water? The Israelis steal Jordanian water from the Sea of Galilee. They bombed the dams in Jordan and Syria. They took the Golan Heights from Syria. They demand water from an underground source shared by Saudi Arabia and Jordan, and they also want water from Egypt's Nile, too. They go swimming in their pools in the settlements, and we have no water to wash the dishes!"

Obviously, some of these stories are not true; others are truths that Israelis now must live with; and others are lore, part of a larger narrative. Events have occurred, and the way that they are viewed, reported on TV, or retold over generations is a matter of interpretation.

In Washington policy circles and on Capitol Hill, the contents of Palestinian textbooks is an issue of concern. There is a feeling that peace would be possible if Palestinian textbooks were changed to recognize the existence of Israel, with Israel named on maps, rather than referring to the whole area of Israel, the West Bank, and Gaza as "Palestine." These kinds of changes to textbooks are an important step, but the differences are much more complex than those reflected in the formal education taught in schools. There is a whole history and interpretation of events that is accurate, or is believed to be accurate, in the eyes of the Arab East. In the case of the Palestinians, how can a people searching for recognition, justice, and an acknowledgment of wrongdoing ever walk away from their historic claims? These same historic claims sustain them through their daily problems and define their identities. A national dream, for some, is also personal deliverance.

There is a cultural aspect here that just can't be understated, either. *Asl,* or roots, are a principal component of a person's identity. People here want—no, need—to tell you that they are Palestinian. No matter what state of wealth or poverty they are in, being *Palestinian* is part of their core being. A few nights ago, Tara, a friend of a friend from graduate school who has worked here on a consulting job for a year, took me to a club. Before going there, we stopped by the apartment of her Canadian co-worker, Tracy. We had a drink with Tracy and her Palestinian-American boyfriend, Munir, a flashy guy who works for his father's export business.

After half an hour, Munir's very attractive twin cousins arrived. They had studied in Montreal for the last six years and had Canadian passports, but were actually born in Dubai. They both had dark smooth skin and sharp features, and they were dressed in sexy close-fitting outfits. They were on their way to a concert at a club. I later found out that the club was about a half-hour away and had a

$40 cover charge. Fadi could probably buy a month's food with $40. When I asked where they were from, they replied, "Palestine."

"Where in Palestine?"

"Haifa." Haifa is a Mediterranean port and Israel's third largest city.

"Really, were you born in Haifa?"

"No."

"Did you grow up there?"

"No."

"Have you ever been to Haifa?"

"No. But our father is from there, and it goes by where you father is from."

"I'm sorry, let me get this straight. One day, *in sha'Allah*, when you have children, where will they be from? Palestine?"

"If their father is from Palestine, yes."

"But what if their father is Egyptian or French?"

"Then they will be Egyptian or French, but Palestinian, too."

So not only are Palestinians furious about what Israelis have done and are doing to them, but there is also a continuous chain of passing on Palestinian nationality to children, grandchildren, and great-grandchildren, regardless of where they were born or where they live. Munir told me that there are 12 million Palestinians in the world. I'm not sure where he got that number since there are roughly 4 million Palestinians living in the West Bank and Gaza, while the United Nations has registered another 2.5 million refugees living outside of the Palestinian territories. Being Palestinian has taken on an almost religious quality for the diaspora. It has become a transcendent nationality that people keep, along with the nationality of the country in which they have citizenship.

Tara and I proceeded to a club, though not the $40 one (thank God), where we met a couple of her Jordanian friends. Since it was

Thursday night and the beginning of the weekend, there was a singer and a band. The crowd was a well-dressed group, and Tara and I were the only foreigners. There was lots of singing, and people danced at their tables. If the music hadn't been in Arabic, it could easily have been a night out in a European country.

On the way home at 2:15 A.M., in my cab ride back to the other side of Amman, where the pipes sometimes run dry, I again encountered the unending claims of Palestinian heritage. The cab driver who picked me up was in his mid-twenties. He had dark skin, jet-black gelled hair, and a chinstrap beard. After riding in silence for a block, I continued my quest to speak as much Arabic as possible and asked him how he was doing. He said "God is blessed," and our conversation took the usual turn.

"Where are you from?" I asked.

"From Palestine."

"Where in Palestine?"

"Tel Abib, Yaffa."

"Were you born there?"

"No."

"Was your father born there?"

"Yes, but he is dead, may God watch over him."

"So, where were you born?"

"Syria, in Latakia."

We talked some more, and I found out that his family still has the key to their home in Jaffa. He also told me that he was getting married next summer and asked me if I would still be here. I could come to the wedding.

So, on a Thursday night in Amman, I came face-to-face with a thirty-one-year-old unemployed Palestinian sitting at home waiting for *Die Hard* to come on TV, twenty-two-year-old Palestinian-Canadian playgirl twins dancing the night away at a club on the outskirts of the city, and a twenty-five-year-old Palestinian-Syrian, from "Tel Abib," driving around the city at two in the morning, perhaps carrying a key to a home that no longer exists. "Palestine" is everywhere; it is not just a place but also a legend.

In some ways, the legend of "Palestine" is similar to that of *Andalus*, or Andalusia, in southern Spain. Andalus was the capital of the Islamic Empire during the period considered the golden era of Islamic rule. It was a center of intellectual thought, where scholars made advances in the fields of philosophy, medicine, and astronomy. The Andalusian period was a time not just of achievement, but of religious tolerance and coexistence with Christian and Jewish minorities—who were persecuted elsewhere in Europe—participating socially and economically in society. Arab elites in both the Arab East and the West romanticize the golden era of Andalus, perhaps as a result of the present-day situation in places like Egypt, Syria, and Iraq. No longer are Cairo, Damascus, and Baghdad progressive centers of world-leading and academic and cultural achievement. They are Arab capitals characterized by authoritarian, corrupt, and at times, brutal rule.

Similarly, "Palestine" is its own legend of happiness and fulfillment for a Palestinian diaspora that struggles to cope, in the face of a difficult status quo, with a home that has been lost but not forgotten. The sweet memories of "Palestine" have become even sweeter in the face of displacement, a homeland occupied, and second-class (social or official) rights in neighboring countries. It is a powerful insult to many diaspora Palestinians, from Fadi to Munir, that the world refuses to correct the injustice they have been dealt and to officially recognize that their home exists.

But this is where the comparison falls short: Andalus really existed, while it is difficult, intellectually, for me to accept the existence of "Palestine." I'm sympathetic to the heartfelt stories and personal narratives about Palestinian life that I hear everyday, yet before Israel became a state in 1948, there was a Palestinian mandate under British rule. Prior to that, it was the Ottoman Empire that ruled the Holy Land for several hundred years. Before the Ottoman era, there were periods of Islamic, Christian, Jewish, and pagan rule. There was never a "Palestine," ruled by Palestinians.

Beyond the overwhelming nature of Palestinian historical narratives, the day-to-day turbulence of Palestinian affairs and politics plays a prominent role in people's lives. "Palestine" dominates conversations, whether at the university, with strangers, or with my people over at the Nef. It's possible that because I'm an outsider, people feel as if they need to get on the record and express their views, but the percentage of time that people talk about Palestinian issues surpasses anything I've ever seen. The closest comparison I can make is to Pittsburghers talking about the Steelers during the playoffs.

The other night, I swung by the Nef to check in with my former hotel roomies. I don't want them forgetting me—those guys have known me longer than anyone else in Jordan. Fayez the journalist was there, and he and his friend Ghazi took me to a nearby coffee shop to smoke a water pipe and drink tea. After discussing Ghazi's upcoming wedding for fifteen minutes, we spent the next four hours speaking about the Arab-Israeli conflict and Palestinian rights. Fayez reviewed the entire history of the conflict for me, going back to Theodor Herzl and the birth of Zionism.

Following the history lesson, we negotiated a peace treaty. Fayez stressed the necessity and desire for a just and full peace between two equal states. Their opening position was a return to 1948 lines, but in the end the three of us agreed on the 1967 borders proposed in the Saudi peace deal and offered at the Arab summit in Beirut earlier this year. The Saudi deal offered full normalization of relations between Israel and Arab countries in return for full return of land captured by Israel in the 1967 War, to include compromises on Jerusalem. This was all part of a regular "night out" with the boys.

At the university, conversation topics related to "Palestine" are dominant as well. Ali, my grammar teacher, who begins almost every class by bashing Ariel Sharon, is thirty, married, and has one child. He has a good job, is educated, and I frequently see him drinking coffee with friends or joking around with colleagues between classes. The other day in class, as part of a grammar lesson, he started talking about the village that his family is from in Galilee, in

Israel. He told the class his family was driven out in 1948, and he has never visited there. He described, in dramatic fashion, the sweetness of the village bread and the richness of the coffee. One time, he explained, he saw a video of the village: "It was green and the people laughed and were happy." With a grimace, he continued, "But they weren't my people. . . . They were Israelis, and they took it from us."

Every year at the University of Michigan, my alma mater, students award the Golden Apple to the teacher they judge to be the teacher of the year. Adnan, my oral expression teacher at the university, wouldn't contend for the Jordanian version of the Golden Apple. He spends most of our class sitting on the teacher's desk and pontificating about life. Iraq is obviously on people's minds, and the other day the class meandered into a discussion about whether Saddam has weapons of mass destruction. In the middle of this debate about weapons, Adnan launched into a monologue about the Jews of Iraq and their betrayal of Iraq's Muslims and Christians. Prior to Israeli statehood in 1948, Iraq had one of the largest Jewish populations in the Middle East.

Rocking back on the teacher's desk, Adnan, a thirtysomething portly guy with thinning hair and a wispy goatee, gave us a history lesson. He told us that "the Jews in Iraq, they never had it so good."

He held his hands apart, as if describing the size of a fish he had caught, and said, "They were fat, sitting on the Euphrates River. They were merchants, trading goods and making money. Then the European Jews came to Palestine. They stole land from the Palestinians"—at this point, Adnan made a grabbing motion—"and told the Jews from the Arab countries to come to Palestine."

Adnan grew animated. While making a thrusting gesture with his right arm, he continued: "So, the Iraqi Jews stabbed their neighbors, friends, and business partners in the back. They moved to Palestine and did it to the Palestinians, too."

He then looked directly at me and added, "The Palestinians were betrayed like the Indians in America who helped the European settlers. Palestinians helped the European Jews when they first arrived.

They didn't know the land, and they got sick. And the Palestinian reward was war. They were pushed from their land and became refugees."

All of this came from a conversation about Saddam and weapons of mass destruction.

For many, the topic of Palestine is always lurking beneath the surface, ready to pop out in any conversation. Ghazi the groom, who mostly restricted himself to nodding sagely during the four-hour peace negotiation with Fayez, unknowingly offered me some insight as to why. In the context of discussing the future status of Jerusalem and Muslims' access to the Al-Aqsa Mosque—the third holiest site in the world to Muslims—and the Dome of the Rock, Ghazi interrupted Fayez to state, "The most important thing in the world is respect."

"Sah," or "correct," Fayez agreed as he nodded his head.

The Palestinians and Palestinian-Jordanians that I've met in Jordan, including Ali and Adnan, have not received the respect they covet from Israelis, Americans, Jordanians, and the rest of the world. The need for respect here is rooted in questions of identity, perpetuated by an ongoing narrative of discontent and injustice, and reinforced and exacerbated by the conflict's daily strife and, for some, dissatisfaction with daily life.

While Americans, Europeans, and Israelis might seek ways to formally end incitement among Palestinians, we need to start understanding that the diaspora Palestinians here, to varying degrees, haven't moved on and don't accept that others have. Some don't have Jordanian citizenship, and others feel slighted within their living environment. Even those who are settled and happy have deep sympathies for family members who continue to struggle against Israeli occupation. They also don't understand, or at least won't admit, that they are not returning to previous homes in Jaffa or Haifa.

Whereas we in the West wonder how Palestinian and Arab leaders could leave their people as refugees in the Palestinian territories, Jordan, Syria, and Lebanon for more than fifty years, Palestinians here wonder how the international community has allowed such thievery, murder, genocide, and occupation to last so long without intervening. People here are still holding claims to homes that other people have lived in for generations. There is a stubborn lack of acknowledgment that at a certain point, it's a different place and can no longer be considered their home. Of course, not having their own place as compensation deepens this misery.

For these diaspora Palestinians and Israelis to move forward on anything, they would have to agree to start from the present reality, not from their differing historic narratives. This is difficult to begin with, but when children are killed, and Palestinians see it displayed so explicitly, how can they even do that? How could Amman's Palestinians possibly see Israelis' humanity if all they feel is that Israelis took everything from them? And now, people like Fadi face a situation of living in a country where they don't have equal rights, a home, or realistic prospects for an improved situation. The problem is indeed pervasive if Palestinian-Jordanians with jobs, like my teachers or the guys at the Nef, have these feelings, too, and are vulnerable to the festering infection of the conflict.

These are individuals' stories, not a scientific study, but that's the point. Different narratives and interpretations of the exact same events form the reality of life here. It is a reality that conflicts with what many people in the West believe to be true. I think it is impossible to reconcile some of these differing narratives, but that doesn't mean that there isn't value to becoming intimately familiar with their details. Knowing them offers a better understanding of the difficult road ahead.

I also see that the people I've met so far appreciate that I actually listen. With Fadi, the guys at the Nef, or even in the meetings and interactions that I have with strangers on the street, we can argue and discuss, and I'll make it clear that I don't agree, but there is no negative personal impact. A day after Fadi finished yelling at me about the attack in Gaza, he prepared some *maqlubeh*, a traditional Palestinian rice and chicken dish, and was adamant that I join him and Marwan for dinner. It was delicious. I ran into Adnan on the street a few days after his Native American comparison, and he stopped me, shook my hand, and insisted on talking for a few minutes. After our negotiating session, despite every objection, Fayez and Ghazi paid for my tea and water pipe, then drove me home.

This could be the result of discussions held in a tone of mutual respect, or it could be a testament to the importance that people here place on good hospitality. Or there very well could be more. I'm almost sure that there is an appreciation for real discussion and the exchange of ideas with an American, as the United States takes center stage in this showdown with Iraq, and as we are considered the major player in controlling the Israeli-Palestinian conflict. While political discussions are the norm here, being heard on matters considered to be of life and death by someone of perceived authority or importance—mistakenly me, in this case—is something unique.

Much more to come, I hope you all are well.

Love,
Ben

3

Three-Minute Showers and the Heinz Ketchup Eaters

August 18, 2002

Dear All,

Treasure your Heinz ketchup and those fifteen-minute hot water showers! Only now, as I eat watery imitation-brand ketchup and face the continued prospect of shaving with boiled water in a coffee mug, have I come to appreciate life's luxuries.

I've adjusted my hygiene standards to the realities of the water shortage situation. Shaving has now become an activity, something to plan out and prep for when I know I'll have the time. It is a process that entails boiling water in a *finjan*—a little metal pot with a long handle that is used to make coffee—soaking a washcloth in a steaming mug of water, wetting my face with the scalding cloth, lathering up, dipping my Gillette Sensor into the boiled water, and then hacking away at stubble.

On a more frequent basis, about every other day, I shower. While the term "shower" implies that I am cleaning myself, it's really more like I am wetting my body with water. I'll flip on the icy water for ten seconds so that I can soap up and shampoo. Once I'm lathered up, I turn the water back on and squirm for about two minutes, rinsing off. It's an unsatisfying ritual that ends in goose bumps and me boiling a cup of water in the finjan, this time for tea. On my nonshower days, I fill a salad bowl with bottled water and wash my face. I then dunk my head in the bowl, wet my hair, gel it into place, and head off to the university.

With this sort of water situation a daily reality, I've developed another new activity: afternoon trips to five-star hotel lobby bathrooms. The Hyatt is my favorite. The key to accessing five-star bathrooms is pretending that you are meeting someone in the lobby. Because I'm a Westerner, I can get away with busting a little attitude as I walk through the hotel's front doors and past the countless staff milling about. Once in the lobby, I make my best "annoyed and confused" face as I scan the room for my long-lost business partner, cousin, or childhood friend. As suspicious lobby guardians try to judge whether I belong in five-star Amman or not, I sometimes find it tough to hide my excitement at being only moments away from hot water. I'll meander around the lobby, searching faces for my cousin that I haven't seen since I was eleven years old, slowly gravitating toward the bathrooms hidden away from the general public. Amman's hotels never run out of water, and they always have the deluxe option of hot or cold. So, it is in Amman's five-star hotel lobby bathrooms that I wash my face, brush my teeth, and think deep thoughts.

The water situation isn't as bad as it sounds, just something to get used to. Case in point: Last week, after returning home from an all-day trip to the Roman ruins of Jerash, I found a "dry" apartment. It turned out that we had run out of water in the late morning, but Fadi hadn't called the landlord or the water company. Dusty and tired, I grew frustrated and irritated as Fadi told me not to worry and drank coffee with Marwan and Dean (a Palestinian-American student from the university who Fadi hopes will introduce him to a Palestinian-American princess). It was about 9:30 P.M., and Fadi showed no sign of understanding that I wanted to shower or at least wash my face before going to the university the next day. As I watched a 1960s black-and-white Egyptian film about romance in Cairo and did a slow burn, Fadi finished his coffee and went out.

To my surprise, he came back ten minutes later and told me that a water tanker truck was down the street and that we could buy four cubic meters of water (a lot) for about $20 (which is a lot of money here). We would have water as soon as the guy threw the hose up to our roof and filled the tanks. The water tanker was just hanging around on a Saturday night. I thought about the problems of getting a twenty-four-hour locksmith on the American equivalent of a Sunday night and laughed.

While on the subject of personal hygiene and grooming, I got a fantastic haircut last week. Bad (and cheap) haircuts at the Hair Cuttery and Supercuts have been an ongoing saga for me over the past few years. Recent memories of "the mullet" and "the lightbulb" ran through my head as I worried about getting a "bad fade," i.e., a bowl cut, with sharp rather than blended lines shaved into my head. Instead, I got my best haircut in years. Beforehand, I rehearsed with the ever-patient Fadi what I would say and learned the word for a "fade," literally in Arabic *tadreej*, or levels. I then walked down the street to the barber shop he recommended, one of the ten salons in the area. There are about 3.4 barber shops on every block here. The plethora of salons must have something to do with the water shortages and the inconvenience of shaving with scalding water in a coffee cup.

I explained to Na'el, the barber, who didn't speak any English, that I wanted a tadreej and not to look like Kojak. He nodded sagely, leading me to believe that he understood my reference to the striking looks of Telly Savalas. He first shampooed me and then spent thirty minutes cutting my hair, trimming my goatee, and talking with me about the possibilities of working as a barber in the United States. After he finished cutting my hair, he then shampooed me again. For someone with no hot water, limited showering opportunities, and who has been reduced to sneaking around Amman's finest hotel lobby bathrooms, this was a bonanza. Na'el then gelled my hair for three minutes, taking individual strands and putting them in place. He actually put so much gel in my hair that it looked exactly the same when I woke up in the morning. I could have broken off the few pieces of hair that were out of place. As it turns out, Na'el did know some English, because when he finished gelling my hair, he smiled and said "spiky." The whole experience cost about $4.25. I'm not exaggerating when I say that it is a great haircut, really a skilled piece of work.

On the walk home, pleased with my haircut, I pondered his situation as a barber working in a developing country and began to understand better some of the international trade theory that I studied for the past two years in grad school. In particular, given how little Na'el had just made for a job well done, it became clearer to me why low-income workers like him might not benefit from the perks of "free trade."

Economies all over the world are connected by international trade, whether it is the trade of raw materials like cotton, which are used as an input to make long-sleeve dress shirts, or an already-finished good, like an oak bedroom furniture set. In the big picture, consumers everywhere benefit from international trade because they gain more choices—of both cheaper goods, like Indian cotton shirts, and more expensive luxury items, like Lexus sedans.

With free trade (i.e., trade that is free of quotas and hidden costs), an outside force like the U.S. government or the Jordanian government does not prevent or limit certain products from entering the market. For example, the Jordanian government doesn't put high tariffs on importing Italian jeans or set a quota for the number of jeans that may be imported from Italy. Either of these actions would make Italian jeans ultra expensive in Jordanian stores and protect Jordan's own nascent jeans industry from foreign competition (if they had a jeans industry). The Jordanians might choose this tariff or quota route for cultural reasons, too; for instance, if some authority decided that Italian jeans are too tight-fitting and they don't want Jordanians wearing them. So, as I was brainwashed to repeat in grad school, free trade is good because it means more choices for all consumers, the "haves" and the "have-nots."

With free trade, all goods, from the cheapest T-shirt to the most expensive Rolex watch, become available to everyone. The market—i.e., the preferences of everyday consumers—determines whether an item will sell in a specific place. Elites, or the "haves," can head to Safeway and browse the aisles for luxury items they never knew existed or that they only came to appreciate while abroad. They can buy the products they like and the store will continue to import more. The "have-nots" benefit from a greater selection too. For example, they can buy those cotton shirts imported from India that are of high quality and that are also cheaper than locally produced goods.

These same principles of free trade benefit entrepreneurs that run export businesses, too. A Jordanian olive oil producer can export Jordanian olive oil to Texas, earning a profit by providing a high-quality product to a new market, and perhaps underselling competition from Greece. If there are no quotas and only meager (or even no) tariffs on exporting olive oil, then the Jordanian producer can sell as much to Texans as the local market will bear.

For the "have-nots" like Na'el, though, the impact of free trade is a bit more complicated. On the one hand, free trade enables Na'el to shop for lower-priced goods that are now available. On the other hand, the new problem is that while his wife is comparing prices, she'll notice out of the corner of her eye that Safeway is now selling New York strip steaks right next to local Jordanian lamb. In Jordan, beef is both exotic and expensive. The high price and presence of steak in Safeway's meat section could cast a shadow over locally produced and more common lamb, and make the lamb less desirable. Since the prosperity of the elites has either increased or remained the same, they are able to buy the exotic import. Yet, Na'el and his wife will look at the new import and only see that they can't afford it. So, while a Safeway bag boy carries the elites' packages of strip steak and bottles of Heinz ketchup out to their Lexus sedan, the have-nots continue to gather up their same groceries and walk down the street to the bus stop. It is possible that they didn't even know about things like strip steaks, Heinz ketchup, and Lexus sedans before free trade brought them cruising by their homes (and their line of sight).

Unlike the elites who are involved in the export industry or the sale of imports, Na'el does not see an immediate salary increase. In every economy, there are workers who produce goods like cars and others who deliver services, like teachers, waiters, and barbers. A haircut is a "nontradable" good or service, meaning that it is something that is purchased but cannot be traded internationally, like a Power Ranger action figure. A barber's salary isn't directly dependent upon the cost of raw inputs or the impact of tariffs or quotas on a good's price. The price of haircuts and the salaries of barbers don't rapidly adjust with a country's import and export flow. And, unlike a private-practice doctor or other elites whose wealth has remained constant, Na'el does not have a reservoir of savings that he can dip into to buy whatever new product has caught his or his wife's eye. Na'el still makes the same small amount of money, but the opportunities to spend it have increased. His world and means have not changed, but the world around him has.

Technically, Na'el isn't any worse off than before the changes in the local economy, but psychologically, he now knows what he can't reach. Since he can now afford less of what is being offered, he perceives that the cost of living has gone up. It could grow worse, though, when his son asks him for an American bicycle. At that point, Na'el will crash against the possibilities that are unavailable to him. If Na'el takes the plunge and decides to spend beyond his means, he will either sacrifice some sort of necessity or he will fail to save whatever income was leftover and intended for the future. Ultimately, he has to choose whether to go into debt for "luxuries" that are beyond his means, or figure out how to deal with the fact that there are a lot of new products that he can look at but not touch.

So Na'el continues to toil away at the same wage, with his salary buying less and the "cost of living" going up. Na'el couldn't have made more than a dollar on a half hour's worth of very good work on my hair. But a bottle of Heinz ketchup costs about $6, water reinforcements cost $20, and my rent is $200 a month for a bedroom in a three-bedroom apartment that has no phone in a neighborhood with water shortages. What this leads to is the number-one reason people want to come to the United States. People want their hard work to lead to economic mobility and the opportunity for self-sufficient dignity. Young men want to marry and start families. Until they can buy or build a home, and demonstrate that they can be financially secure, most continue to live in their parents' homes, often sharing a room with siblings.

There are two levels of living in Jordan. On the one hand, there are the "bus riders," the people from both the tradable and nontradable industries alike who work long hours, struggle to make a living, and can never save. On the other hand, there are the "ketchup eaters." They are the wealthy people: the Jordanian and Palestinian upper class who can afford to purchase luxuries like Heinz ketchup, expatriates like Tara and Tracy who can pay the cover charges of nightclubs, and the tourists taking hot showers at the Hyatt. It is almost impossible to make the jump from bus rider to ketchup eater. The bus riders live month-to-month and they have little hope of saving enough to buy a small business and making the leap to middle class, thereby bridging the gap between themselves and the ketchup eaters.

Samer, another of my "friends," is a bus rider, too. He works at the local Internet café from 10:00 A.M. to 10:00 P.M., six days a week, and always has a smile on his face. He takes a bus from his home in Mafraq to the bus station and then a second bus to Amman (roughly an hour-long ride). He leaves his home at 8:00 in the morning and typically returns between 11:00 and midnight. He is married—his wife doesn't work—and has a one-year-old son he plays with for an hour before going to sleep. He earns 150 Jordanian dinars (JD) a month, which is about $200, and has asked a few times about the best way to get a visa to the United States, where he can work a minimum-wage job.

Then there is Fadi, who speaks English well, has experience working with a foreign company, is highly competent and respectful, and possesses unquestionable moral integrity—aside from siphoning water from our neighbors' tanks. He is also unemployed and not a Jordanian citizen, which doesn't help his employment prospects. Because he has no money, he took a job last week as a driver for a Palestinian-American family of ketchup eaters visiting from California for the summer. He expected to be paid the standard of 10–15 JD ($14–$21) for a twelve- to thirteen-hour workday. Instead, the ketchup eater's brother in-law, a local big shot, told them that they only needed to pay Fadi 5 JD, or about $7 a day. This did not include the 1.5 JD it cost him to get to and from work and to pay for his meals. Fadi could not negotiate because there is always someone here willing to do the job for less.

In addition to paying an insulting wage, the ketchup eaters sat in the back of the car, demanded that Fadi open and close the car door for them, and expected Fadi to carry their groceries and other purchases. Fadi determined that the $5 that he was clearing for a thirteen-hour day was not worth such insults or his time, so he quit. The irony of the situation is that the car that the ketchup eaters rented was a dented Mitsubishi Lancer. From the comfort of our living room couch, Fadi ranted about how insulting he found it that people with such silver-spoon demands would not even pay for a decent car. Even though the job was below his level of experience, he would have been willing to chauffer the ketchup eaters if the wage and treatment had been suitable to the level of performance expected. Instead, he felt disrespected.

Given the effect that the political situation with Iraq and Israel has on the service industries, one of Jordan's main economic sectors, the gap between the ketchup eaters and bus riders is growing. Regional tensions have wiped out tourism and hurt spillover beneficiaries like restaurants and hotels. I actually did see a tourist the other day and am writing home about it. To be clear, the lot of the ketchup eaters isn't improving, but they don't live month-to-month like the bus riders. The ketchup family can still go to Safeway and shop to their heart's content, but Fadi is left eating a bowl of humus with a garnish of onions and pickles and trying to figure out how he is going to fulfill his dreams and get married. It's hard for me to attach a national demographic to this growing divide, because almost everyone I meet in Amman is either a Palestinian like Fadi or a Palestinian-Jordanian, meaning a Jordanian citizen of Palestinian descent. But I imagine that if there were a stark difference between Jordanian-Jordanians, i.e. Jordanians of Jordanian descent and from the East Bank of the Jordan River (also dubbed "East Bankers"), and Palestinian-Jordanians on the issue of who can afford life's luxuries, it would be a serious problem given the already existing tensions between the two groups.

The divide between the bus riders and the ketchup eaters is certainly on display for all to see. There are neighborhoods where every other car is a Mercedes or BMW, and rich Gulfies cruise around here in the summer. The other day, I had lunch with Tara. We ate on the enclosed rooftop of the high-rise Castle Hotel (home of a fine bathroom). The food was mediocre but expensive—about $18 for the two of us to have sandwiches and fresh juice. We must have paid for the view since you can see Amman in every direction.

Later in the day, we met up again for dinner at another relatively swanky place, this one downtown. Alcohol is easily available in Jordan, and there were several well-off and stylish locals around us drinking a beer and smoking a *hookah,* or water pipe. Tara and I sat on an outdoor patio that overlooked downtown and watched a striking sunset over the lower-income, square-block, cookie-cutter apartments built into the hills. There seems to be an appeal to checking out the poor from a distance. As we sipped our fresh mango juice and finished off a pizza, it struck me how strange it was to see different worlds living on top of each other, sharing space, and coexisting in a separate and unequal way.

I got a good look at the short distance between these two worlds on my way home from dinner. After Tara and I finished smoking our hookahs, she grabbed a cab back to the wealthy suburb of Abdoun, and I took a shared taxi to the Abdali bus station to catch a bus home to the "apartment across from the north gate of the university."

When I arrived at Abdali, however, it was deserted. The bus station is about a city block in size and caked black from the exhaust fumes that the buses spew out all day. Usually, the station is bustling with the roar of traffic, the honking chorus of taxis, the yells of peddlers trying to sell goods at impromptu markets, and the bark of food vendors that mingle between the station's lanes or have set up shop along the station's perimeter. At a little past 11:00 P.M., though, I found myself pretty much alone with the day's refuse. I looked for a place to sit and wait for a bus, but the bench under the six-lane metal shelter looked as if each piece of wood had been shoved up the exhaust pipe of a minibus. I considered the curb, but that was worse since the fuel and diesel leaks combined with deeply

Bus travel in Amman.

ingrained dirt. So I remained standing; waiting and wondering whether a bus would come so late at night. Twenty minutes earlier, I had been sipping mango juice on a patio overlooking poverty.

At around 11:30 P.M., a green-and-white minibus tore around the corner of the Abdali entrance. To my disappointment, the word *Baq'a* was painted on its front in green script. The Baq'a bus would drop me near my apartment, but its final destination was the Baq'a Palestinian refugee camp.

There is a system that goes along with bus-riding in Amman. All the minibuses here have a row of two-seaters, a row of singles, a four-person bench in the back, and room for three, including the driver, in the front seat. Many are decorated on the inside with fringe curtains, hearts, decals of the late King Hussein or the flag, and other elements of classic 1970s pimp-mobiles. *Al control*, the person who collects passengers' money and calls out the stops, stands in the doorway, with up to a maximum overflow of two people. He opens and shuts the door of the bus at each stop.

On the Baq'a bus, though, there is always an overflow of people. In fact, the bus is usually bursting at the seams. Whenever I've ridden the Baq'a bus, there are usually five or six people—looking as if they'd just come from manual labor jobs—hunched over in the aisle, a couple of riders standing with the control in the doorway, and three people squeezed into two-person seats. The driver and the control generally take care to keep the bus in good shape, sometimes barring riders from smoking. Though the Baq'a buses are usually decorated with the same amount of fringe and decals, the air is generally thick with cigarette smoke, as if every passenger is smoking two cigarettes.

Beggars, however, can't be choosers, so as the bus screeched to a stop, I jumped in and climbed into the second seat, a two-seater. It wasn't a comfortable ride. Maybe because of the time of night, the bus was only half full. The twelve other riders made a lot of noise, though, and they made me nervous. All were men, mostly my age or younger. Several around me yelled at each other and hit and squeezed each other in a way that under other circumstances might have seemed playful. To a paranoid gringo on the eve of war at a little before midnight on the Baq'a bus in Amman, it felt like a fight was about to break out. The riders weren't the kind of guys who asked for the Grey Poupon. Some were missing teeth, others had scars from burns and stitches on their arms and faces, and some seemed like they would just as happily smoke a butt as put it out on the back of the person's neck in front of them. Playing into my worst prearrival stereotypes and my abstract vision of life in a refugee camp, that ride was the most uncomfortable I've felt so far.

Watching those guys jockey with each other, I was struck by the feeling that they had nothing to lose. They seemed outside of the rules that I've learned here. There is a respectful discipline to public behavior in Amman, and they were in complete violation. Their loud and belligerent behavior toward each other conveyed a sense of destructive indifference and irreverence. With my paranoia surging—they had to know that not only was I an American living on the same USG tab that pays the bill for Israeli F-16s, but that I had just had a really nice dinner, smoked a water pipe, and looked out on their world from the balcony up above—I hopped off the bus several stops early. Justified or not, I wasn't interested in attracting their attention. I walked the rest of the way home.

When I got there, Fadi was lying on the couch, watching one of the *Look Who's Talking* movies. After the normal exchange of pleasantries, he told me that two tanks of our water had been stolen. Frustrated, I passed on John Travolta and Kirstie Alley and went to my room. Eating an $8 sandwich with a view overlooking a water-less Fadi and riding the late-night Baq'a bus was enough for one day.

The difference between the world of the haves and that of the have-nots is just so stark. Earlier this week, I went to a billiard club. Zeid, my conversation partner from Saudi Arabia, threw money around for a couple of hours while we played pool. An attendant in his early twenties stood by and watched us, racking the balls after each game. Zeid and his Saudi friends paid him no heed. I couldn't stop stealing glimpses at his stone face, looking for some indication of his feelings. What were his thoughts? What are the long-term repercussions of such an oil and vinegar mix of worlds? How long can one be expected to rack billiard balls for rich Saudis or drive the ketchup people around town for a pittance?

A month into my life in Jordan, it is clear to me that people talk about coming to the United States because they want to work and make money. I hear occasionally about the beauty of freedom of speech, but it is the upward mobility that we have between economic classes that is so attractive to people here. People gush about the minimum wage and the possibility of their twelve-hour workday adding up to more than a continued struggle within the confines of poverty. They want their work to add up to something that resembles dignity and the opportunity to realistically hope for more.

Well, that's all for now—

Love,
Ben

Letter 4

Life in the Seven-Layer Dip

August 27, 2002

Dear All,

I'm dipping deeper and deeper into the seven-layer dip. There is just so much going on here beneath the surface, and I'm coming face-to-face with social struggles that never came up in my grad school seminars. It is becoming evident to me that nationality and religion are in one sense the threads that bind Jordanian society; in another, they are jagged shards that cut divisions between people.

A routine trip to register at the U.S. embassy this past week offered a clear picture of the national fault lines that run through Jordan. I went to the Abdali bus station, but learned that there aren't any buses that pass by the U.S. embassy and that I would have to take a cab. So I hailed a taxi, and the salt-and-pepper haired cabbie and I went through the whole routine about where I'm from and where I learned to speak Arabic. He turned out to be of Palestinian descent. I've lately gotten tired of asking such Palestinian-Jordanians what part of "Palestine" they are from. About 35 percent of the time, the response is something like, "There is no Gaza, there is no

West Bank, it is all Palestine!" Those comments are usually followed by stinging criticism of American support for Israel.

After six weeks of hearing this reproach on a daily basis, I can regurgitate the arguments in my sleep. I am feeling less and less like I need recital practice. Even so, I responded to the cabbie's questions and asked him where he is from, out of politeness and a hope that he might be of Jordanian descent. I'm interested in learning more about the world as Jordanian-Jordanians see it. He wasn't though, and we lapsed into silence.

Breaking the quiet, the cabbie switched on the American radio station, Radio Sawa, which was playing, "Everybody Hurts" by R.E.M. Radio Sawa is an attempt by the U.S. government to build positive feelings in the Arab East toward America by capitalizing on the popularity of musicians like Mariah Carey and Montell Jordan. The USG-funded station has built a listenership by alternating popular American music and popular Arabic music every other song. During breaks, the station slips in news broadcasts that are intended to supply Arabs with "real news." As I've mentioned, there is a conviction in Washington D.C. that Arabs are inundated by slanted and false news. The thinking behind Radio Sawa is that balanced coverage, provided by the U.S. government, will make Arabs more sympathetic to, or at least understanding of, U.S. policy positions.

The cabbie really dug the R.E.M. song and understood the words even before I translated them for him. Actually, he sang along with the chorus.

"If you're on your own in this life, the days and nights are long,

when you think you've had too much of this life to hang on,

well, everybody hurts sometimes, everybody cries. . . ."

He remarked that the lyrics struck a chord and told me that all people could understand these feelings. Once the song was over, though, Sawa played a sound bite of President Bush calling for a "new Palestinian leadership not compromised by terror."

I gestured at the radio and asked Jordan's biggest R.E.M. fan, "What's your opinion of that?"

He turned the radio off and went ballistic. With a pulsing vein bisecting his forehead, the R.E.M. cabbie explained in Arabic, "I love the American people. They hurt. They suffer like the Palestinian people. You understand me?" He then raised his voice, "But I hate Bush, the American government, and the American policy! Sharon tells Bush what to do, and Bush repeats Sharon's words! Why? Why does America want to attack Iraq? Pakistan has weapons! India has weapons! Why does America want to attack the Arabs?"

He poured out the venom that I've become familiar with until we eventually arrived at the solitary and fortress-like embassy. As I opened the door to the cab, the cabbie reached his hand out, smiled, and said, *"Allah ma'ak,"* wishing that God be with me, another version of good-bye. The diatribe and rage had all been about governments; he didn't hold anything personal against me or the American people I represent.

I am departing for a four-week backpacking trip to Turkey and Syria in a few days and I wanted to register with the embassy before leaving Jordan. After an interlude of filling out forms, I exited the embassy and walked past the long visa line. I motioned to a gray-haired cabbie lingering in front of his car. The guy was older than my last driver and was fumbling around with half a loaf of bread and a cup of tea as he leaned against the side of his cab. He asked me to hold his bread while he put the tea in a cup holder and started the car. The cabbie insisted on sharing the bread and tea, but it was really hot and I didn't have much interest. We began the Arabic language tango, as he tried to downshift gears and hold his bread while we started up a hill. There was something awkward about the whole process, and then I noticed that his right thumb was a nub. He was missing the top joint.

We sped by the wealthy Martha Stewart homes of Abdoun, and as our conversation gained momentum beyond introductions, he launched into his own tirade. He was an East Banker from the south but was living in his car because he was separated from his wife and children. He hung around outside the embassy, hoping to pick up a U.S. diplomat or VIP who would help him obtain a visa to go to the United States. Poor him; instead, he got a sweaty unshaven grad student who asked a lot of questions. He told me that he wanted to go to the United States, where he could die in peace, far from all of the Palestinians who had come to Jordan and made money while he wallowed in misery. Because Palestinian-Jordanians are mostly shut out of high-ranking military and government positions, many of the Palestinian elites here are businessmen who, from the looks of their Abdoun homes and fancy cars parked out front, have done well.

The one-thumbed cabbie railed on about how much he hated the Palestinians and how they created problems everywhere: here, Lebanon, Israel, and the United States. In addition to Palestinian-Israeli strife, the Palestinian Liberation Organization and its leader, Yasser Arafat, played major roles in starting a civil war in Jordan in 1970, and also in Lebanon in 1975. As the result of a second major Palestinian immigration wave to Jordan, during and after the 1967 War, the PLO set up its leadership and base of operations in Jordan and launched repeated cross-border attacks against Israel from Jordan. This led to Israeli reprisals and put Jordanians in a catch-22 position.

On the one hand, Jordan's King Hussein felt pressure to stand behind the PLO attacks because of pan-Arab sentiment emanating throughout the region. Pan-Arabism remained a dominant political ideology of that time, a remnant of 1950s and 1960s discourse that asserted the concept of one Arab Nation unjustly divided by Western colonial powers and torn asunder by the artificial implant of Israel. If King Hussein didn't support the Palestinian cause and the Palestinian fighters, who alone actively fought Israel after the Egyptian-Syrian-Jordanian debacle of the 1967 War, then he risked breaking solidarity with the pan-Arab cause and being labeled a traitor. At the time, Jordan was surrounded by Arab leaders and revolutionaries who had few qualms about destabilizing the Jordanian monarchy and seeing the establishment of an Arab republic in the place of a kingdom. In the case of neighboring Syria, actual invasion and annexation under the guise of pan-Arabism was a real threat. To add further stress, the revolutionary and "anti-establishment" nature of 1960s and 1970s politics, and the boom of "freedom fighters" in the third world who sought to right the wrongs committed by imperial powers, placed the Jordanian monarchy—a no longer fashionable political system—in a precarious position.

On the other hand, if King Hussein supported the Palestinian attacks, Jordanians would continue to find themselves victims to Israeli reprisals that led to the loss of life as well as the destruction of villages and farmlands along the Israel-Jordan border. While Palestinians were already generally considered outsiders, the revolutionary PLO leadership was setting up a "state within a state" with armed Palestinian militias. The priority of these militias was to attack Israel, and they were popularly supported throughout the Arab world. The militias were effectively taking over parts of Jordan, setting up their own checkpoints, infringing upon King Hussein's sovereignty, and destabilizing the country. The damage caused by Israeli reprisals and the continued attacks pushed a difficult situation to a breaking point.

The breaking point came in September 1970, when members of another Palestinian militia, the Popular Front for the Liberation of Palestine, hijacked three airplanes, landed them in an airfield in Jordan, and blew them up. Embarrassed on the world stage and having survived a recent assassination attempt by Palestinian militants, King Hussein went to war with the PLO. The man who would become the great peacemaker of the 1990s sent Jordanian tanks into Palestinian parts of Amman and refugee camps throughout the country to destroy the Palestinian militias. Thousands of Palestinians were killed, and the PLO leadership was eventually expelled to Lebanon. PLO leader Yasser Arafat escaped death in Jordan when a delegation of Arab League leaders, who had come to arbitrate the conflict, smuggled him out of the country.

Arafat and the PLO moved on to Beirut and would eventually set up a similar "state within a state" in Lebanon. History repeated itself with cross-border raids into Israel—this time, though, along Israel's northern border, which it shares with Lebanon. Existing internal strife in Lebanon between Christians, Sunnis, and Shia was exacerbated by the PLO's actions, and civil war erupted. Coupled with an Israeli invasion, a siege of Beirut, and the ensuing Israeli occupation of a part of southern Lebanon, Lebanon's brutal civil war descended into another horrifying chapter of the Arab-Israeli conflict. The Lebanese civil war lasted from 1975 to 1991, and the PLO leadership was once again expelled. In 1982, they departed Lebanon and relocated across the Mediterranean, in Tunis.

Giving voice to one of the legacies of Palestinian-Jordanian strife, the one-thumbed cabbie asked me in Arabic, "Why do I like Sharon?"

"Why?"

"He kills Palestinians! Why do I like the United States?" It was part two of a macabre riddle.

"Why?"

"Because you help him! I hate the Palestinians! Expel the Palestinians from here! Expel them from Israel! Expel them from everywhere. I hate them!" He raised his right arm and shook his hand with the nub of a thumb in a fist. "I lost it in '70," he said, "when I was a soldier in the army and I fought the Palestinians."

On cue, we passed some Jordanian soldiers. "They get paid nothing! The Palestinians have all the money," the cabbie said, "and they buy up the land. Expel them!"

By this time we were passing through downtown, and I asked that he drop me at the nearby traffic circle, where I could catch a bus to the university. He told me not to get out; he would take me to the university. I replied that a cab was too expensive. (I would save $1.15 by taking a bus—I'm cheap, after all, and living on a fixed stipend!) So he then offered to give me the ride for free. Inside the cab, we argued about whether I would accept the free ride until he finally agreed to take my money and let me out. I left him and trudged off to look for a shared taxi that would cost about fifteen cents and that would take me to the right bus stop.

The Jordanian-Palestinian situation is complicated. People think that Israelis and Palestinians hate each other, but there is a pretty good case to make for Palestinians and Jordanians disliking each other more viscerally, if there was some way to measure stereotypes. Thirty years ago, Jordanians and Palestinians were shooting each other in the streets. For East Banker or Jordanian-Jordanians, there is deep resentment at what they perceive as Palestinian ingratitude. East Banker Jordanians took in Palestinian refugees, and in turn, many of them feel that Palestinians pulled them into a spiral of misfortune—namely, Israeli retribution and civil war. For the Palestinian-Jordanians, there is a feeling of never belonging. Given the depth and importance of roots here, even if Palestinian-Jordanian citizens serve in the army or government, their allegiance to Jordan is questioned despite building their homes, businesses, and lives in Jordan. Some Palestinian-Jordanians who see Jordan as home are never really able to feel "at home."

Issa, my friend from the Nef, is one of those guys. He is a Jordanian citizen but a descendant of 1948 Palestinians, meaning that his family members are refugees from the 1948 War. He is also good friends with Fayez the journalist, who's an East Banker. Issa's Palestinian-Jordanian friends question how he can trust Fayez and consider him a real friend. They are convinced that it is just a matter of time before Fayez betrays him.

In one late-night conversation that we had sitting in the hotel car, Issa explained to me the complications of being a Jordanian of Palestinian ancestry. While he faces this national divide here at home, the situation isn't necessarily better in the place that is supposed to be his real home. Issa has no family in "Palestine." He visited there once in 1996, during the heyday of the peace process, and in his words, he felt like a "foreigner." The Palestinians there did not see him as one of their own. He had not shared in their daily struggle, and he lives an alien life (of different struggles) in Amman. When asked about his nationality or where he is from, Issa will immediately and proudly tell you that he is a Palestinian from 1948, but a Jordanian citizen. Jordan is his home, but he is proud of his Palestinian roots. He is stuck in the middle, though, and limited by his national label—something that he personally will never be able to change.

This nationality issue dominates people's understanding of themselves and others, but there is also the issue of religion, which runs, neck and neck, as a strong contender for determining a person's identity. The fluorescent green lights of mosque minarets color the Amman skyline at night, but there are churches here, too. Roughly 95 percent of Jordanians are Muslims; the other 5 percent are Christians. This is without a doubt a Muslim majority culture.

Friday, the Muslim Sabbath, is shutdown day, with sparse traffic and stores closed at least until the completion of midday prayers, if not all day. The standard greeting when you enter a room is the Islamic greeting of *"Salaam Alaikum,"* or "Peace be upon you." When you hope something will happen you say, *"In sha'Allah,"* or "God willing," instead of "I hope." Five times a day, from around 4:00 in the morning to 9:00 or 10:00 o'clock at night, the call to prayer rings out over loudspeakers from mosques across the city.

In addition to everyone asking me about my nationality, they ask me about my religion. Before arriving, I had hoped to be honest, but it has turned out to be more difficult in practice. Israeli-Palestinian violence and a potential conflict with Iraq are sources of real tension that have spread from the political realm into the religious and personal world. It was my experience in Egypt a few years ago that people draw a line between Israel and the religion of Judaism. Egyptians I met at that time demonstrated little reaction when I told them that I am Jewish. This was before the second intifada, though, and in the midst of Camp David peace negotiations.

Also, prior to Israeli statehood in 1948, Egypt had large Jewish communities in Cairo and Alexandria. Older people still remember Jews as Egyptians, not just as the army next door. In Jordan, though, the Palestinian experience is the defining feature of opinions about Jews and Israel. Furthermore, it is widely believed here, on a popular level, that the Israel lobby in Washington, D.C., sometimes referred to as the "Jewish lobby" or "Zionist lobby," is driving the push for war with Iraq. So, it is only in abstract conversations that I've tested the waters on the distinction that Jordanians make between Judaism as a religion and Israel as a state.

I was at the Nef the other night, hoping to hang out with Issa and Fayez, but instead ran into one of their friends, Ghassan, who I had met once before. We sat on the outdoor patio, Ghassan insisted on buying me a tea, and we went through the usual Arabic conversational dance. Ghassan is thirty-five years old, but his thinning hair and brown teeth make him look older. He isn't married, lives in the southern port city of Aqaba, and is in Amman for work related to his advertising business.

Our conversation started off well, as we spoke about governance in Jordan and economic problems, but it took a different turn when we started talking about religion. Ghassan launched into a monologue from the *hadith*, which are a record about the practices, words, and traditions of the Prophet Muhammad. He repeated a particular hadith that Ali, my grammar teacher, has quoted in class, about how on the Day of Judgment, Muslims will kill Jews. The hadith specifies that stones and trees will call out to Muslims that there are Jews hiding behind them, so that they may find and kill them. Ghassan, an East Banker, explained that for this reason the Jews had to (eventually) be killed and that "Palestinians have to return to Palestine."

I asked, "What if the Palestinians and Israelis decided to agree on a peace treaty and to compromise on the land? Would this result be okay with you?"

"No." He wagged his finger, and his brow became creased. "I felt anger and great sadness when Jordan signed a peace treaty with Israel." He continued, "The Jews are very bad. You know, it was the Jews, the Mossad, who attacked the World Trade Center on September 11."

I responded, "How do you know that Jews are bad? Like all other people there are good ones and bad ones. Do you know any Jews? Have you ever eaten a meal together with a Jew?"

"No. Never in my life have I met a Jew," he proclaimed. "I would never want to sit together with one and eat a meal."

I wanted to lay my cards on the table for the shock value alone. I resisted out of fear of losing my access to the Nef, home to my longest-running relationships in Jordan.

This wasn't an isolated conversation; other people I've met in my social circles at the university or my wanderings on the street share these feelings. What's strange is the contrast between these individuals' hateful positions and their personal generosity. I wonder whether a comparison can be made to life in the American South before the Civil Rights movement. White people, in many circumstances, may have been friendly, kind, and hospitable, while at the same time holding positions of hate and ignorance toward blacks.

I'm not sure what would cause Ghassan and others to change their views. Seemingly, positive exposure to Jewish people that aren't the Israeli army would help. Maybe I should have outed myself to Ghassan and others. The whole situation poses an uncomfortable moral dilemma.

So, the other day, I did tell someone that I was Jewish. It was Kholood, my Arabic teacher from my dialect classes at the British Council. For the past four weeks, I've been taking an additional dialect class for two hours every night there. I study with a collection of eight expats ranging in age from eighteen to fifty. They vary from college students who are here for the summer to a Christian missionary couple. Our teacher, Kholood, is about thirty years old, wears her head covered, and is one of the sweetest and most sincere persons I've ever met. Perhaps more important, unlike my instructors at the university, Kholood is a very good teacher. She encourages her students to speak, exudes positive reinforcement by insisting how clever we all are, and shows visible pleasure in our achievements through her huge smiles and mother-hen-like demeanor.

I asked Kholood to give me private Arabic lessons starting in the fall, and we met to speak about the details further. For cultural reasons, Kholood cannot meet with me unchaperoned. So we met on the rooftop patio of a local hotel where we could speak in the presence of her uncle, who sat several tables away with a friend. After we went over the details of the tutoring, we started chatting about her uncle and the science and technology club that they run together with a few other people. The club is an assortment of professionals who educate each other about their different fields and provide each other with different kinds of professional support. Kholood explained to me that these meetings allow young club members to socialize with each other in a culturally safe environment, build their confidence, and develop professionally through activities like constructing robots, learning about nature, and performing laboratory experiments.

With Kholood now feeling more comfortable, she asked me the million-dollar question: Was I Jewish? She had guessed that I was Jewish from my first name and needed to know. When I told her that

I was indeed Jewish, she explained how she had not wanted to like me and to work with me, but after watching how I behaved in class with the other students and how I treated her with respect, she could see that I was a good person. She had never met a Jewish person before that was not an Israeli soldier, and she had a reservoir of stories of abuse at the hands of Israeli soldiers from her uncle and cousins who live in the West Bank from which to form her opinion. Because she thought well of me, she then asked me to study Islam with her and to convert. She wanted me to be able to go to heaven with her family and friends.

I could have gotten upset by Kholood's insinuation that if you aren't a good Muslim, then you are going to hell. She extended the religion, however, in such a forthright and sincere way that I couldn't be insulted. Instead, I was sad. Kholood was visibly disappointed, and for a moment I saw myself through her eyes—a misguided person on the express train to the eternal fire because I did not accept Muhammad as the final prophet and Islam as my path of life.

With my decision not to study Islam established, the conversation advanced to the difference between Judaism and Zionism. There were tears in Kholood's eyes as she described how land had been taken away from her family and how others had been killed. She told me how she text-messages her cousins in Jenin every night on her cell phone pretending just to say "hi," but really to see whether they would respond and were still alive. I tried to broach the topic of suffering on all sides, but Kholood wasn't ready to go there. She asked question after question about Judaism, from times of daily prayer to the Jewish position on the role of the Prophet Muhammad. In particular, Kholood wanted me to somehow get her a copy of the Torah so she could see for herself whether Jews were described as the chosen people and whether everyone else was considered to be animals, existing only to do their bidding, a tale that is urban legend here. At the end of our talk, Kholood implored me not to tell anyone else that I'm Jewish and expressed fear for my safety. She worried not about the people I meet and know, but the people that I don't know who would find out by word-of-mouth.

As I walked to my dinner date with Bashir, my new conversation partner, it struck me how difficult at times life must be here for religious miniorities. Islam is just such a prominent part of the everyday culture here. At a minimum, there must be situations that arise out of happenstance where Christian minorities end up feeling socially excluded, whether it is intentional or not. Other times, uglier and deliberate incidents can occur. I got a peek at one of these uglier and insulting incidents that night with Bashir.

I'd met Bashir twice before through a friend. He is a university student seeking to improve his English so that he can work overseas as an accountant after he graduates. I decided that he would make a good language partner because he corrects my mistakes and good naturedly tells me how bad my Arabic conversation skills are. It's a nice change of pace from the polite flattery that I usually receive from others.

Bashir and his teenage brother, Mohsen, picked me up and we drove to a private club on the way to Zarqa, a nearby city where they live. Bashir's father is a retired air force engineer, and this club, adorned with photos of the royal family, is a prestigious sort of place where current and former officers socialize and lounge about. The three of us drank Cokes outside, in a grassy area with other families, and watched a wedding procession. Mohsen stared at me the whole time and couldn't believe that a foreigner, much less an American, had come to Jordan to study Arabic.

Bashir told me about his eleven brothers and sisters, all of whom live in the same house or on the same street in Zarqa with his aunts, uncles, and cousins. He then invited me to come to his sister's home and eat dinner with the family that night. I gladly accepted the invitation, happy for the chance to have a family experience. In the car ride there, Bashir asked me about religion, and I told him that I didn't see much difference between the core values of different religions. Religion was a personal choice and one that didn't determine whether you were a good or evil person. There were good Muslims and bad ones, and good Christians and bad ones. He was thrilled with my answer and wholeheartedly agreed with me.

This was my first trip to Zarqa, a city of roughly a million people, a majority of whom are of Palestinian descent. Zarqa is visibly less developed than Amman, with both potholed and dirt streets and a dearth of streetlights. On the way to Bashir's sister's house, we drove past children riding bicycles in the dark and men sitting outside of bodega-like stores drinking tea. As we drove down Bashir's street, he pointed out house after house explaining that his aunt lived in one, his uncle another, his brother in a third . . . and on and on. His whole family lived on the same street together.

When we arrived at the sister's, Bashir led me into a bare, tiled room that connected into a sitting room with three couches. The sounds of children running around spilled out from a back room, but Bashir invited me to sit on one of the couches. Though we had called ahead, I was an unexpected guest. It didn't seem to me that Bashir's family was about to sit down to dinner. I could hear Bashir speaking with his older sister, and she went off to the kitchen and began to rattle and clank some pots and pans. Moments later, a pale 30-something man with blue eyes, a disheveled afro, and a beard that flamed down to his chest entered the room. He clearly had just woken up and was wearing a yellowish orange and white striped *galabaya*, a traditional robe. He looked like a character from a *Saturday Night Live* skit about the Taliban.

He asked Bashir, "Who is this?"

"He is a student from America."

"Is he Muslim?"

"No, Christian."

He was Bashir and Mohsen's older brother, and for the next hour and a half he tried to convince me to convert to Islam. Unlike my experience with Kholood earlier that evening, it was insulting.

No sooner had Bashir finished saying the word *masichi* or Christian than the brother's blue eyes sparkled. He smiled, gave me a big warm handshake, and said, "Peace be upon you and welcome. I welcome you to study Islam with us."

Hardly catching a breath, he launched into a stump speech with patronizing smiles and outrageous examples and stories of why I needed to convert. His pitch was 40 percent in English, 60 percent in Arabic. The English parts, meant to convince me of the main points, were especially annoying since his English was poor. He would ask his brothers for the translation of certain words, but to prove a point of subtle resistance, I would say the word before either of them could think of it. Bashir and Mohsen took delight in my behavior and their older brother's ineptness and took turns saying, "He's clever, I told you he's clever."

The zealot brother told me stories about there being no more prophets. He explained that converting someone was the best thing that you could do because you were spreading the message of the Prophet Muhammad. His eyes widened as he told me that "Americans give Jordan everything from big cars to planes"—he started extending his arms like wings so that I would understand—"to other technologies, and he could not deny America the most valuable product around, Islam."

He repeated over and over that I couldn't just be a Muslim, though; I had to be a good Muslim. People who beat their children and wives, use drugs, drink alcohol, and don't pray five times a day were not Muslims. I had to think about the afterlife and about going to heaven. As it stood now, I wouldn't be able to go to heaven because I was not a Muslim.

As his younger brothers looked on, with smiles of uncertainty, he told me that my family and I would be going to hell and joining all the other non-Muslims who had died before us and were already there. He told me that grandparents and other members of my family who had died were already there, and that he couldn't take responsibility for me going to hell, too. He implored me to come back on Thursday and to study Islam at the mosque with the rest of the foreigners. Thursday is salvation day in Zarqa.

He shared what he thought would be an inspirational story about another American, a heroin addict who was unable to sleep. The addict came to study Islam and in the middle of prayers, as he knelt with his forehead on the prayer rug, he fell immediately asleep. He had gained peace with himself.

The brother's agitated conversion speech went on and on, with me, my family, and other Christians repeatedly compared to drug addicts, thieves, and moral deviants. His eyes danced manically and I chose to focus instead on his untamed beard as I nodded my head periodically and wondered how I was going to get out of there. I looked occasionally at Mohsen and tried to decide if he was laughing at me or his brother. I looked at Bashir for help, but saw that there was none coming. At one point, I asked to use the bathroom. I called Tara and asked her to call me back in a half-hour so that I could use her call as an excuse to leave there gracefully.

When I came back, the zealot brother was sitting in the middle of the couch that we had been sharing, no longer at his end, and he launched into me anew from a closer range with the same arguments. I'm not sure if it was the substance of what he was saying, the insulting manner in which he spoke down to me in English and Arabic, or the fact that he was now repeating the same exact things to me as if I was a complete imbecile, but I became angry.

I was tempted to scream at him that you didn't have to be a Muslim not to eat your own children. I contemplated how I had ended up in this situation and my rage built up in my head against Bashir. Aside from my translation remarks, I had remained quiet for most of the brother's rant, waiting for him to finish or for Bashir to politely cut him off. I decided to switch gears and launched into a spirited defense of Christianity. My knowledge of New Testament theory is weak, though, so I had to focus my argument on loving thy neighbor and the Golden Rule. When that didn't stop the brother's barrage, I protested to Bashir and his zealot brother that I felt uncomfortable and that this was not appropriate. Bashir made an attempt at reining in his brother, but the zealot mistook my discomfort for weakness.

Looking to move in for the score, he asked about Muslim life in the United States. Incensed, I raised my voice and told him in Arabic not to make comparisons to the United States. In the United States, this sort of behavior was inappropriate. First, religion was a private issue, and second, we didn't invite people to our homes to insult them and their families. This struck a chord, since you don't do this in Jordan, either; people here take hospitality seriously.

With that, the conversion process ended awkwardly. Bashir began to fidget and Mohsen ran to check on dinner. It was ready, and the four of us adjourned to a set table outside and a dinner of sliced tomatoes, cucumbers, and onions; cold dips; bread; and oily scrambled eggs. A muhajiba middle-aged woman who was introduced as Bashir's sister brought each dish to the table in communal bowls and then departed.

After post-dinner tea and the requested phone call, I told Bashir that I had to get back to Amman to help my friend. Bashir offered to drive me home, and the zealot brother said good-bye with a big smile. He again invited me to come back on Thursday to study at the mosque. I could hardly maintain a facade of pleasantness in the car with Bashir. He repeatedly asked me why I was so quiet. I told him that I was tired, but I was furious. It's funny, Bashir and his brothers had no idea how offensive the whole experience was for me. Before I left their home, Mohsen even tried to lend me an *Ace Ventura: Pet Detective* DVD, thinking that I would be a new friend. If anything, maybe they thought that I had been rude for yelling at their brother.

This was an extreme situation. Insults of one's family and attempts such as this at conversion are not the norm here. People are incredibly hospitable in every way, really more than anything that we would ever expect at home. But people do constantly ask me what my religion is. On top of that, many of these same people, from the most sincere to the most insulting, are sure that they have answers that apply to everyone and that it is their obligation to share them.

At the same time, I have also encountered tolerance and coexistence. Many of my acquaintances have accepted me for the Christian that I'm not. Maybe this is in part due to my visitor status. I can't offer a concrete comment on what it's like to be a Christian day in and day out in Jordan, since I only pretend to be one. I can say, though, that my situation here, living as a minority with an asterisk, makes me feel isolated—whether or not people are trying to convert me. Islam is a critical part of the culture here, and if you aren't a part of the majority religion, I've personally found that it isn't something that you can culturally fake. There are walls and barriers. I would have to be a Jordanian (or Palestinian) Christian to really be able to speak to the social and cultural dimensions of these walls, but from my vantage point, it isn't difficult to assume their existence.

So while religion and nationality are the pillars of society here in Jordan, they are the criteria by which people create divisions between each other, too. The best way to understand this complexity is to consider the question of marriage, the most common social topic in my conversations. There is an obsession here with marriage. Young men are driven by the need to make enough money to buy an apartment so they can get married and move into their own home. Young women's primary role models are their mother, aunts, and grandmothers. In a family-centered society, the common goal is to have a family and children. Marriage is the cornerstone of a religious and moral life, while childbirth is the passing on or perpetuation of one's nationality.

I've seen Nadia on a semi-regular basis at the university over the last month. She is the muhajiba student who befriended me my first week there. She waits for me at my break, I share my oranges with her, and we talk about religion, the university, her family, my water problems, and Fadi. At first, I was wowed by her willingness to speak with me and I chalked it up to her desire to speak English. Last week, though, she asked me to meet her for coffee at a café near the university after school. I was blown away with surprise.

Over coffee, we sat in the View Café by the University's north gate and looked out at the evergreen trees and sprawling campus. After a little small talk, Nadia asked about Fadi. How often did he go to the mosque to pray? What was his citizenship? Where did he work? What was his level of education? Nadia is a twenty-nine-year-old Muslim Palestinian-Jordanian who will graduate from the university in the fall. She is very concerned about getting married and having a family.

From the order of her questions, the criteria are clear for the role of husband. Despite Fadi's personal attributes of kindness and his exemplary cooking and cleaning habits, he was not a contender. Even though Fadi goes to the mosque on Fridays, it isn't enough given the issues surrounding his nationality or really lack of citizenship. Nadia asked me whether there were any foreign Muslim students in my class or others that I knew of that she might be able to marry. The foundation for our friendship became clear.

I saw myself for a quick moment through her eyes and was conflicted. On the one hand, her plight was quite sad. Here was an educated, outgoing, and conservative woman who needed to find a husband who would meet all of the right cultural requirements. Nadia was driven to such a point of need as to seek *my* help. On the other hand, it was quite funny if you looked at it from the perspective of anyone who knows me as a middle-class American from Pittsburgh who won't answer the phone on Sunday afternoons because I'm watching the Steelers and yelling at the TV. I've come several thousand miles to live in Amman and play the role of foreign student matchmaker for Palestinian-Jordanian Muslim women? My, my, that masters degree is paying off.

Don't feel sorry for Fadi, though; he wasn't unfairly discriminated against. He has the same criteria for his own future wife, with a variation that he is afforded because he is a man. I had a similar experience with him last week, too. He, Marwan, and I went to Kalha, our local falafel joint for some humus, pita, falafel, pickles, hot peppers, and onions. Over our bowls of humus, the three of us had a serious discussion weighing the pros and cons of Fadi marrying Colette, his French friend who has lived in Jordan for a couple of years and teaches at the university.

Colette is nice and treats Fadi well, text-messaging him on a regular basis to say "hi," but there is no outward indication that she wants to marry him. Fadi says that a lot of foreign women come to Jordan to find Palestinian husbands and thinks that Colette is in love with him. Regardless, the key issue wasn't whether Fadi was in love with Colette or even attracted to her; instead, it was a question of her nationality. Since Colette is French, if Fadi married her, he'd have to move to France and wouldn't be able to fulfill his dream of speaking American slang. Since Colette isn't an Arab, Fadi would be forced to adjust to an extended family of foreigners, rather than slide into the bosom of a Palestinian diaspora community as he has planned. It did not matter that Colette isn't Muslim. In Islam, a child's religion is determined by the father. Fadi assumed that Colette would don the hijab once they were married.

Marwan advised Fadi to wait for a more appropriate match, and I agreed. Fadi's frustration was evident, though, when, as we chewed post-meal mint leaves, he slammed his fist down on the table and pronounced, "I have to get married!"

Marriage, Islam, and "Palestine" are the topics of conversation that dominate my everyday life. The more I see and learn here, the more it becomes clear how important matters of religion and nationality are within Jordan. There is a tension between East Banker Jordanians and Palestinian-Jordanians that can approach hatred. While Christians and Muslims certainly co-exist here, I believe that each have their own worlds too, worlds that are separate. It's startling how many differences there are beneath the surface and within everyday life among the people who we wholly refer to as the "Arabs" back home.

Well, Nadia and Fadi are going to have to live without my matchmaking and consulting services for a short while. I'm off to Turkey and Syria in a few days for four weeks of travel. I'll fly to Ankara, the Turkish capital, and spend two and a half weeks backpacking across Cappadocia and the Aegean and Mediterranean coasts, staying in Istanbul for a week in between. I'll cross into Syria from Antakya (the ancient city of Antioch) and spend ten days making my way from north to south through Syria, stopping in Aleppo, Hama, Palmyra, and Damascus before crossing the border and returning to Amman.

It is a trip that I've looked forward to for more than three years, from before I started studying Arabic. The chance to visit Syria as an Arabic speaker has motivated me through my language study. Syria is an entirely Arabic-speaking environment where the second language is French, not English. It will be a great language test, among all other things. I'll be in touch from the road.

Love,
Ben

Part Two

From American Superstar
to Baby Killer

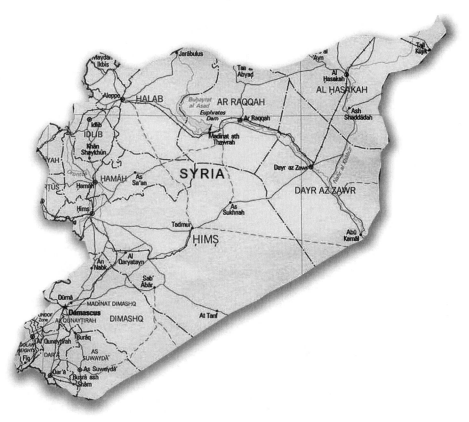

Letter

5

Istanbul to Antakya: From Europe's Back Porch to Syria's Doorstep

September 14, 2002

Dear All,

The sun set for me this evening over a backgammon board in a public park in Antakya—the Turkish border town that was once Antioch, where the apostles preached before embarking on missionary journeys. Tomorrow morning I will embark on my own journey, crossing into Syria. Since I touched down in the Ankara airport two weeks ago, I've visited a couple thousand years of history between Istanbul and Ephesus, hiked in the Goreme Valley in Cappadocia, and napped on the Mediterranean beach of Olympus. In Istanbul alone, my trip has been one of extremes: I prayed in a synagogue, was robbed in a brothel, and felt for a moment what it's like to be an American superstar.

Being a superstar is fun; perhaps that's why I've enjoyed Turkey a lot, especially Istanbul. There are other reasons, though, too. Coming from the desert of Jordan, Turkey's green countryside and the sight of water at every turn has been welcome. On the bus ride from Ankara to the moonscape rock formations of Goreme, I spent four hours looking out the window at farmers bent over lush green fields under an expansive blue sky. There is rain here; grass is a common sight, and water is plentiful. Turkey is a peninsula, and Istanbul, its largest city, is on the water, too. On the Golden Horn, the bend in Istanbul's old city where the Bosporus Straits and the Sea of Marmara meet, fishermen cast lines; ferries pick up and deposit commuters; and vendors sell nuts, newspapers, and grilled corn.

Beyond its natural beauty, there was something else, however, that I appreciated right away about Turkey. When I got off the plane, I met Western tourists, actually New Zealanders, wearing shorts. In Jordan, men and women don't wear shorts in public; shorts are for children. I was back in a cosmopolitan place, a crossroads of nations and people, and immediately felt the accompanying openness that

Istanbul's Golden Horn.

comes with the mixing of different cultures. With Turkey as a frame for comparison, I realized how isolated Jordan is right now, with a lack of diversity and few non-Arab international visitors coming to the country because of tensions surrounding a possible war with Iraq and the intifada next door. A weight lifted from my shoulders as the influence and proximity of Middle Eastern problems receded.

Feeling at ease is of course nice, but what I enjoyed the most about Turkey was exploring magnificent and sprawling Istanbul, Turkey's cultural heart and a city of 8 million people. Istanbul's depth of history ranks with heavyweights such as Jerusalem, Rome, and Cairo.

Once called Constantinople, Istanbul has been a cultural fault line between Europe and Asia, with the city literally stretched across the two continents. Emperor Constantine the Great made the city the eastern capital of the Roman Empire in the fourth century. The city was renamed and later became the capital of the Ottoman Empire after it fell to Sultan Mehmet II and the Turks in 1453. At the height of Ottoman power, under Suleyman the Magnificent, the Ottomans ruled from Hungary to Yemen and from the Persian Gulf to the Moroccan border. Rising European powers and nationalist and ethnic-based revolutions led the empire to crumble over the next couple of hundred years. Before its collapse at the end of World War I, the Ottoman Empire—still home to the caliph, the leader of the Muslim world—ruled the area that would become modern-day Turkey and the Arab Middle East, which the British and French eventually carved up.

Istanbul is a storybook with the Golden Horn glimmering under the sun, the minarets of domed mosques stretching to reach the sky, and uneven cobblestone streets angling through Sultanahmet, the old city. The grand Topkapi Palace sits on a hill overlooking the Golden Horn and the Sea of Marmara. A few streets away, Hagia Sophia and the Blue Mosque face each other across a set of gardens in a showdown of architectural greatness. Hagia Sophia is a microcosm of the city's history, reflecting both the Christian and Muslim periods. In the sixth century, Emperor Justinian I constructed the church's domed basilica of marble pillars and ornate mosaics. Sultan Mehmet II later converted the stunning church into the city's primary mosque. Crosses were covered, mosaics that portrayed Jesus and Mary were plastered over (human figures are forbidden in Islamic art), and four minarets were added over time.

Across the way from Hagia Sophia is the dreamlike Blue Mosque, with its six pencil-thin minarets and its smaller domes and minidomes that lead like steps up to the massive domed top. The Blue Mosque was the first mosque outside of Mecca to have six minarets. The sultan built the mosque across from Hagia Sofia to demonstrate the greatness of Ottoman and Islamic architecture and to eclipse the Byzantine basilica.

Istanbul's Blue Mosque is the face of Turkey on travel brochures and news broadcasts, with reporters shooting footage with it as background. It is ironic that a mosque is the image that represents Turkey. While 99 percent of the population is Muslim, and Turkey was the seat of the caliphate for hundreds of years, there is a separation here between religion and the state that is militant. Secularism was one of Mustafa Kemal Ataturk's primary tenets when he founded the modern Turkish Republic in 1923. He abolished the institutions of the caliphate and the ministry of religious affairs. Other Ataturk reforms included placing all schools under supervision of a government ministry; replacing Islamic courts governed by *sharia*, or Islamic law; outlawing traditional clothing, like the *fez* hat; and replacing the alphabet of Arabic script—the script of the Koran—with one that uses Latin letters instead. No Muslim majority country in the Arab East has taken such similar and radical steps to create a secular state. Yet it is a mosque (albeit, a stunning work of art) that is so often the chosen image to depict Turkey.

Eighty years after Ataturk's reforms, religion in Turkey remains a private issue. In cafés, carpet shops, and along the Golden Horn, people did ask me about my religion, but I didn't feel that my answer mattered. There is a Jewish community in Turkey that traces its roots to the expulsion of the Jews from Spain in 1492. There is also military cooperation between Turkey and Israel. Furthermore, there is no natural bond between Turks and Arabs. They have their own mutual ill-will built up over hundreds of years of Ottoman rule. Regardless of the reason, not once was there a follow-up question that reflected judgmental assessments on which religion holds the "correct" answers.

As in Jordan, there are mosques all over Istanbul and throughout Turkey, but the attitude concerning religion in the public domain seems different. On a Friday morning right before prayer and the weekly sermon, I visited the Suleymaniye Mosque, which sits atop one of Istanbul's seven hills. After touring the mosque and visiting the cemetery that houses the tomb of Suleyman the Magnificent, I watched men perform ablutions, washing their hands and feet in preparation for prayer. No one paid me or the other tourists milling about any attention. In Amman, I wouldn't visit the Husseini or King Abdullah mosques on a Friday. I would feel out of place, as if I was intruding.

It is very possible that a widespread presence of "the other" here in Turkey, or at least tourists, creates a moderating influence regarding religious views. Or perhaps the Turkish government's positions enforcing secularization have played a greater role in producing an environment where religion is a private subject. For one reason or another, religious practice in Turkey occurs within the mosque; it doesn't spill over into the street.

I've found the privacy associated with issues related to religion similar to the separation of church and state that we enjoy in America. Actually, I got the sense of a stark separation between public life and private life in general. The Turkish state sets the standards for public behavior—to include acute secularism—but people lead a different life behind their closed doors. In one carpet shop in Istanbul's old city, I met Ali, a dark-skinned fellow in his early forties with a heavy mustache and jet black hair. We drank some apple tea and played backgammon while I didn't buy a carpet. It turned out that his parents were Jewish and that his given name was Ehud. At some point, he had married and become Ali. As I asked him nosy questions about whether in a couple of days his family was going to celebrate Rosh Hashanah (the Jewish New Year), the shop's owner joined us. Ali dropped the religion subject and told me that I was a good backgammon player. He didn't want to talk about the Ehud part of his life in front of the owner.

I got a better sense for the private space and for religion when I celebrated Rosh Hashanah with a Jewish Turkish family. On Rosh Hashanah, Jews gather to pray and hear the blowing of the *shofar*, or ram's horn. The sound reminds Jews to "wake up" and to prepare to repent for their past year's sins ten days later, on Yom Kippur, the Day of Atonement and the holiest day of the year.

I planned my visit to Istanbul to overlap with Rosh Hashanah. I wanted to attend services and hear the shofar; it's probably one of the few chances that I will have this year to pray in a synagogue. I connected with a Jewish family, Sami and Suzette, who made me, a stranger, feel welcome. On Friday evening, we attended prayer services at the synagogue in the neighborhood where Sami grew up, and then we had Friday night dinner, which was also Rosh Hashanah Eve dinner, at his mother's home.

When Sami and I entered the synagogue, I was overwhelmed by the congregation's warmth. The sanctuary was packed, with men downstairs and women above in the balcony. At least twenty people welcomed Sami with kisses on each check when we entered. By association, they welcomed me with warm handshakes, and then each touched his right hand to his lips and then heart. Together we sang Friday night prayers, welcoming the Sabbath and the New Year. The tunes were different from what I was used to, but the prayers were of course the same, and I was reminded of childhood memories of going to synagogue on Friday nights with my father. Although I had never met anyone in the room before that night, I had a distinct feeling of being welcomed.

After prayers ended, there were more handshakes and kisses, and we proceeded to the home of Sami's mother, where my visit with what seemed like cousins I'd never met continued. Over dinner, I shared details of my life in Jordan. They found my efforts to learn Arabic admirable, but the decision itself to move to Jordan for the year very strange. Sami, a businessman, didn't quite see the opportunities or the reasoning behind developing a skill set geared toward the Arab East unless I was going to work in government. I told him a bit about the growth of Jordanian-American trade, but he explained that Turkey is more oriented to larger and more stable markets in Asia and Europe.

The family was very interested in the story of how my father's family fled Poland at the start of World War II and later came to the United States as illegal immigrants after stops in Siberia and Kyrgyzstan. In turn, Sami explained to me how after the Jews were expelled from Spain and Portugal in 1492, their families had immigrated to Salonica (Thessaloníki in modern-day Greece) and then Istanbul. When they would not convert to Roman Catholicism, large numbers of Sephardic Jews found new homes throughout the Ottoman Empire. The sultan welcomed Jewish immigration and is alleged to have criticized and thanked King Ferdinand for impoverishing Spain but enriching Turkey.

Sami spoke English well, but Suzette and his mother needed Sami to translate the conversation at times. All three spoke Turkish of course, and French too, but their first language is Ladino—a Jewish dialect of Spanish that their ancestors spoke in Spain and has been passed down for more than 500 years. Sami explained that many of the families in their community still speak Ladino, but that he and Suzette had a harder time teaching it to their children.

Sami and Suzette's use of Ladino at home with Sami's mother and Turkish in public underscored for me the separation between the public and private space, a separation that applies to both religious practice and ethnic traditions. The joy of prayer in the synagogue and the richness of Friday night dinner together were part of private life. Someone standing outside of the synagogue could have no idea what was occurring inside. When services were over, men removed their skullcaps and filed out of the synagogue in groups of ten to fifteen people spaced out over a few minutes. We waited our turn, along with everyone else, to leave and carried our prayer books, with covers facing inward, to the car.

In 1986, Palestinian terrorists from the Abu Nidal group killed more than twenty people at Istanbul's largest synagogue, Neve Shalom. The synagogue was attacked again in 1992 by a Turkish group called *Hezbollah*, but there were no casualties. Our exit procedures were a security precaution so that a large number of Jews could not be targeted exiting the synagogue at once. On the street, an outsider would be unable to discern any difference between the small groups of Turkish men and women leaving in different directions and any other Turks on the street.

I found a similar separation of public and private life in Antakya in the Hatay Peninsula, where there are a large number of ethnic Arab Turks. The Hatay Peninsula is the corner of land on the Mediterranean coast between Turkey and Syria. When it was part of Syria, it was called Alexandretta. In 1938, as French control in Syria dissipated, elections were held in Alexandretta to determine the province's fate. Violence and joint Turkish and French military control followed, and the next year, the elected assembly voted for unification with Turkey, which France did not oppose. While some Arabs and Armenians emigrated, a large number of ethnic Arabs remain in the Hatay Peninsula.

On the second leg of my ten-hour bus trip from the Mediterranean port city of Antalya to Antakya, my bus filled with dark-haired, sharp-featured men who looked like they could have been Jordanian or Palestinian. Many spoke in Arabic, and I listened in on families' conversations. A twenty-year-old sat next to me and tried to make conversation in Turkish. We ended up chatting for about thirty minutes in Arabic until he got off the bus. He was on leave from his military service. In Antakya, at my dive hotel, the clerk tried in Turkish to check me in, but it was in Arabic that we sorted out the details of my stay.

My Arabic experience in Turkey continued yesterday when I met Hathum, who turned out to be Hassan. Let me explain: I ate lunch at a restaurant after visiting the Grotto of St. Peter, home to the first Church and the place where the term *Christian* was first coined—as a reference to the converts of St. Paul. While paying my bill at the restaurant, I met one of the owners, a young guy only a couple of years older than me who spoke pigeon English and introduced himself as Hathum. After a few minutes of uneven conversation in English, I learned that he, too, spoke Arabic and was of Syrian descent.

Hathum was eager to show me around. Since I'd just come from the grotto (Antakya's main attraction), he drove me to a lookout overlooking the green countryside where we smoked a hookah and drank beer. We spoke some more about Antakya, Turkey in general, and Syria. Hathum's family owns a restaurant in the Emirates, too, and he has visited his uncle there. Hathum had no desire to live in Syria but did express an interest in better relations between Turkey and Syria (they nearly went to war in 1998) and a better life for Syrians. Hathum's family calls him Hassan, and they speak Arabic at home, the language his mother used with him when he was a child. So, in Antakya, they speak Turkish in the restaurant, but Arabic in the kitchen.

Throughout Turkey, from Istanbul's synagogues to Antakya's restaurants, I found a duality between public space behavior and private life. In the private space, people behave any way they want, whether it is praying or speaking Arabic or Spanish, depending on their ethnic roots. In public, though, secularism and nationalism seem to be paramount attributes of Turks. Stores, government buildings, and other public places are adorned with the Turkish flag and ubiquitous pictures of Ataturk. Turks express what seems like genuine admiration for Ataturk—the founder of the country—and his legacy. At the same time, secular does not mean liberal. In public places, I felt a certain traditional propriety about the behavior of the people around me that is hard to quantify. But perhaps my opinions were influenced by the shadows of 500 years of traditional norms and Ottoman history.

When I reflect on this duality, though, this split between public and private lives and behavior, beyond Ali, Sami, or Hathum, the image that comes to mind is of Layla, an outdoor dance club on the Bosporus in Istanbul. As an exclusive and private club, Layla is a palace of shared private life. Husa, a Turkish friend of a friend, took me to Layla for some nightlife. There was a Jack Daniels promotion that night, so we not only bypassed the throngs of young Turks waiting in line, but the doorman gave us a handful of coupons for free drinks. Within the gates of the outdoor club, under the Istanbul sky, a thousand young Turks, half of whom seemed to be beautiful blonde women in tight black clothes, drank Jack Daniels and raised their hands in the air to a thumping beat. Directly across from the club on the other side of the Bosporus, in plain view, was a brightly lit mosque. A striking scene, even if it was just a statement on cosmopolitan Istanbul and not all of Turkey.

Shortly after we arrived at Layla, a cameraman took my picture with Husa and his girlfriend Simla and asked for my name and profession, since the photo would run in a local entertainment magazine. I told him that I was Benja Orbach, IMF economist. The International Monetary Fund could use the positive press. The economic austerity measures imposed on Turkey as conditions for the enormous IMF loans intended to bail out the Turkish economy and stop inflation are highly criticized on the popular level.

It wasn't appearing in Turkey's paparazzi entertainment magazines, however, that made me feel like an American superstar. It felt to me like they love America here. These days I can't think of a better place for an embattled American to travel. A story of stardom to demonstrate my point:

One day in Istanbul, I took a ferry boat trip from the Golden Horn up the Bosporus to a place called Andalou Kavagi at the edge of the Black Sea. I sat on the deck for the one and a half hour trip as the boat made stops between the Asian and European sides of the city. We passed regal homes on the shores of the European side, where I imagined Gatsby-like parties taking place along the waterfront. Then we chugged by the Rumeli Fortress built by Mehmet in preparation for the attack on Constantinople. As we headed northeast along the Bosporus, the scenery changed to dilapidated wooden fishing shanties. Homes with docks and garages materialized again as we neared the last stop. At the end of the ferry ride, we were still in Istanbul.

At Andalou Kavagi, the last stop on the Asian side, I got off the boat and hiked to the top of a hill and walked around the Byzantine ruins of a castle that overlooks Istanbul on one side and the stretches of the Black Sea on the other. Looking out at the Black Sea and back at Istanbul, I couldn't help but smile. I was standing on a cliff, with Istanbul to the west and the Black Sea, the former Soviet Union, and beyond to my east. Looking out onto the vast horizon, I sensed that I had reached a great place. No one could have ever guessed that I would reach such a beautiful and faraway place, back when I was a short and skinny ninth grader forced to go swimming in a Pittsburgh public school pool in second period gym.

Perhaps my feelings of accomplishment were appropriate, because a few minutes later, I discovered what it was like to be an American superstar. As I spit sunflower seed shells over the cliff, a group of five cool-looking teenage Turks approached. They wore designer blue jeans and one of the two boys sported a FUBU football jersey. I thought that they might laugh at a scruffy looking tourist with a backpack. Instead, they asked in English where I was from, and when I told them, they responded with "oohs" and "aahs." Their faces were pictures of delight and astonishment; two of the girls blushed, and the boys acted as if I was Michael Jordan himself. The leader in the FUBU jersey stammered, "America, very very good."

Their reaction was an exaggerated version of the norm for how I've been greeted in Turkey. After two months of defending America in Jordan, Turks have welcomed my Yankee origins with superstar flourish, from Istanbul to Antakya. At first, I suspected that it had to do with Turkish shop owners trying to sell me something, but I think that this reaction runs deeper than being viewed as a great big dollar bill.

The Turks I've spoken with, from people on the street to a smattering of elites, value the pragmatism and efficiency that are so prominent in the United States. Beyond the convenience offered by quick-cash ATMs and drive-through service in the United States, our culture supports the promotion of people who think practically, who will make a deal and make decisions based on interests that seem rational rather than hold out for the impossible or inconceivable because of romantic ideals. As a stereotype, Turks share a similar view; it is part of Ataturk's legacy. Ataturk's reforms were practical measures to modernize Turkey and turn it into a twenty-first-century nation-state. There is an appreciation for Ataturk's vision and actions, which have set the country on a course for future success and achievement.

Like Americans, Turks have expectations for their government and they make practical choices. People I've met have expressed disappointment at the corruption of their government, *expecting* better and not resigning themselves to worse as their counterparts in Jordan do. This impatience with government shenanigans is a major issue in the upcoming Turkish elections in November and the primary reason for the widespread appeal of the religiously based AKP, or Justice and Development Party. Ordinarily, anything religious in the public domain would be abhorrent.

In addition to Turkish admiration for this practical approach to politics, Turks—especially young ones like these teenagers—are drawn to American cultural icons and output. American movies, music, and fashion are the standard bearer for cool. The teenagers that I met near the castle ruins were almost nervous to be in the presence of an American. One of the girls overcame her blushing to ask me if I would like to get married to her. Another nodded her head, and the look on her face made me think that I might have a choice between the two. I didn't know what to say, so I took their picture, gave them my sunflower seeds, smiled, and said thank you, I had to go.

I ran into this kind of American superstar status one night in Istanbul, too—after I was robbed at a brothel. I'd never been to a brothel before, but one night after several days of traveling by myself and not speaking the language, I was feeling lonely. As I sat across from the lit up Blue Mosque, a balding guy with a mustache started up a conversation with me. I was hoping to meet someone half his age, the opposite sex, and with less facial hair, but he seemed harmless. As it turned out, he was a Saudi visiting Istanbul for work. I welcomed the chance to speak Arabic, and he told me about his family in Jeddah and the Russian woman he had sex with the night before.

If it is in Arabic, I'll generally chat with anyone, no matter what the subject or the person's objectionable traits. So I asked him if he wanted to play backgammon. The prospect of returning to my hostel, where I was sharing a room with nine other backpackers in bunk beds, had far less allure. Abdullah, the Saudi, agreed and invited me for a drink. A cab ride later, we stood on the red carpet outside of a club in Taksim Square, the center of Istanbul's new city. Abdullah wanted to have a beer and to find the woman from the night before. He assured me that he would pay for my drink, and with nothing else to do, I agreed to stay for a short while.

I realized immediately that the club was not a typical club. Women in shiny tight clothes danced to a Euro disco beat on a little stage, but they swayed like robots, with bored, distant looks in their eyes. I thought it might be a strip club, but the women weren't taking their clothes off and no one was waving Lira notes. It was a brothel.

I should have left right away, but thinking I was going to have some fun at Abdullah's expense, I sat in a booth with him. Soon, a man with a bowtie came over and shook his hand. Abdullah ordered two beers, and shortly after our drinks arrived, two women squeezed into the booth with us, one next to him and the other, a petite blonde, next to me. Since I had no intention of buying the petite blonde's affection, I started asking her questions. Karina was a former professional skater from the Ukraine with a twelve-year-old daughter. As we talked, the man in the bowtie returned and asked whether we would like to buy champagne for the ladies. Abdullah was whispering furiously into his "date's" ear, but paused to motion "yes" with a big smile, so I said okay. The champagne arrived instantly, and we talked for another ten minutes until I told Karina that I had to leave.

She made a face, and the waiter returned and asked if we'd like more drinks. Abdullah again waved them on, so I said okay again, and two more beers arrived. Karina took a sip while I reiterated, this time to Abdullah, that I was leaving. He tried to convince me to stay, then called over the waiter, motioned to Karina's drinks, and said, "I pay for his beer and he pays the rest."

"What?" I was shocked. "You invited me. I am your guest!" The host-guest relationship is sacred in the Arab East and a measure of honor for the host.

"I invited *you* for a drink. I did not say I would pay for *her* drinks."

In Arabic, I yelled, "What? You invited me as your guest! *You* ordered the drinks!" By this time, Karina had slipped away and the waiter stood with five large men in tuxedos around our table. My fury grew to concern as I remembered Lonely Planet's warning about clubs that make foreign men pay huge tabs for drinks, whether they ordered them or not. I had chuckled after reading that warning and thought of a hapless tourist with a big fanny pack.

I reviewed my options, stuck in the booth in the corner of the club, with several gorillas flaring their nostrils at me, and asked, "How much?"

The waiter wrote "285,000,000 lira" on a scrap of white paper.

The dollar to lira exchange rate is 1:1,200,000 and with all the zeros on these notes and the common pictures of Ataturk on each bill, the issue of how much things cost was confusing. This was going to cost between $15 and $20. I pulled out 30 million lira.

The waiter looked puzzled. "No, 285,000,000."

There was another zero at the end. My color receded, and I became nauseous. I froze, unable to calculate the exchange rate. For a moment I thought it was $600. My mouth dried up, and I began to shake. "How much . . . dollars?"

The waiter pulled out a calculator, punched in some numbers, and turned the calculator toward me, having figured out the exchange rate. In little black crystal numbers, the display read "237.5." I had $30 and 40 million lira in my wallet. I wondered if they were going to beat me up and steal my clothes. I looked at Abdullah and thought about lunging for him—he'd set me up. Unfazed, he continued to whisper sweet nothings to the pale blonde woman next to him.

To make a long and humiliating story a little shorter, I pleaded for mercy from the waiter, who turned out to be the manager. The manager wanted to go to my hotel to get the money. When I told him that I was staying at the International Youth Hostel, I became even more worried that I was headed for the alley, pain, and shame. He realized there wasn't a bankroll stashed away somewhere, and I was skating on thin ice. I had no choice but to ask whether we could go to an ATM.

Twenty minutes later, after I withdrew 200 million lira from my account and handed it over to him, he said, "Maybe you think I am bad person. But I tell you something. This is not much money for lesson. It could be $1,000. Always ask how much something cost before you order. Come, I find you taxi."

A cab screamed by, and he hailed it. The driver was a young tough guy with slicked-back hair and a tight black shirt. He should have been at Layla, not driving around the city. My immediate thought was that he was going to screw me, too. Floundering in the nauseous world of my losses and shame, I flopped into the cab, at the mercy of what was to come. The cab driver said something in Turkish that I couldn't understand.

"I'm sorry, I don't speak Turkish."

"American?!"

I sighed, "Yes, I'm from America."

The driver flipped his arms into the air with excitement and surprise. His eyes opened wide, and his chin dropped as he gasped "America!?" while fighting off hyperventilation. I can't imagine what would have happened if Britney Spears had gotten into the cab instead of me.

He touched his cheeks with the palms of both his hands, like Macaulay Culkin in *Home Alone*, and looked at me like I was MTV personified. I couldn't help but smile.

"You speak Turkish?" he asked in English.

"No, I'm sorry. I only speak Arabic," I replied in English.

"Arabic?! You American, you speak Arabic? You Muslim?" He looked at me with utter disbelief and hero worship. "Me. Muslim. No, English, sorry. Very, very sorry."

He rummaged through some cassettes and slid one into the radio. The voice of Shakira blasted out of the car speakers as we pulled away. "Good?" he asked.

"Shakira? Yes, good," I answered.

He put his hand up so that we could high-five. We tore through Istanbul at breakneck speed, windows down with Shakira, who is of Lebanese descent, crooning that she would love us wherever we went. My nausea faded into the night as my smiling driver looked at me every three seconds in amazement. The next song on the tape was an Enigma remix.

"Enigma?" I asked.

He almost crashed the car. His chin dropped and his eyebrows shot up; he yelled "Yes!" and high-fived me again. "Very good!"

The driver looked at me the way a fifteen-year-old looks at an older brother who has come home from a college vacation with stories of grandeur. His positive emotions for things American, the wildcard that I could speak Arabic, and my appreciation of his music put me over the top. So the second lesson I learned that night is that even if you're an idiot tourist in Turkey, all is not lost if you are an American and know something about Top 40 music.

Tomorrow, however, my status as an American superstar comes to an end. At eight in the morning, I will get on a bus that will take me across the border and into Syria, high honorable mention in President Bush's axis of evil. I don't expect anyone in Syria is going to crash their car out of enthusiasm over my nationality.

Syria and the United States have a weak relationship, not just as measured by political cooperation or economic trade, but also in the breadth of contacts between Syrians and Americans. I know more Middle Easterners than the average Pittsburgher, but before arriving in Jordan two months ago, I'd met two Syrians—both were grad school teachers. Besides those two, I've never met anyone in America who has said good things about Syria. Hafez al-Assad, Syria's late president, was considered an obstacle to regional peace and a shrewd but brutal dictator who squashed dissent and killed thousands in the Syrian city of Hama in 1982. In many circles, Syria is considered Israel's greatest and most recalcitrant enemy. Henry Kissinger once observed that the Arabs cannot make war without Egypt and cannot make peace without Syria.

The sticking point over peace between Israel and Syria is sovereignty over the Golan Heights, a strategic plateau that overlooks northern Israel and the Sea of Galilee, Israel's main water source. Israel seized the Golan Heights from Syria in the 1967 War. The Golan Heights are a strategic buffer between the two nations that protect Israel's northern region and water supply. But unlike the West Bank, there are no religious or historical claims to the Golan as part of "Greater Israel" or biblical Israel. Rather, in New Jersey–sized Israel, the Golan is a green wonderland that Israelis have come to consider as part of their home. Throughout Israel, there are banners and bumper stickers that read *"Shalom eem haGolan,"* or Peace *with* the Golan, meaning make peace with Syria, but keep the Golan.

Given Syria's reputation in the United States as a repressive police state, there isn't the same kind of pressure put on Israel to return the Golan or to reach a peace agreement with Syria as there is for justice for the Palestinian cause and to make peace with the Palestinians. In a perverse way, it's this reputation as a bad guy and Syria's isolation from the West that, for me, is part of both its professional and personal attraction.

Professionally, it is important for me to see Syria in person and not to limit my opinions to popularly accepted clichés. As a Middle East expert, I would have a gap in my resume without gaining first-hand knowledge. Backpacking through Syria, meeting locals, and visiting historical sites is a way to form my own conclusions and to look at Syria as a country with its own distinct issues, beyond the conflict with Israel.

At the same time, visiting Syria is personally exciting, something beyond the mainstream of travel. Given the closed nature imposed by Syria's political system, a trip to Syria is a chance to travel to a different time. I've never been to a police state à la the Eastern bloc countries of the Cold War, or as described in George Orwell's *1984*. I'm fascinated by the concept of a cult of personality and the photos of the Assad family posted everywhere. As strange as it sounds, I want to experience an alternative reality, at least for a few days. In this way, I also think that I'll get a better sense for life inside the other police state next door, Iraq.

So, there are lots of reasons for going to Syria, and lots of reasons to be excited and nervous. Tomorrow it happens.

Love,
Ben

Letter 6

Adventures with St. Simon, Jackie Chan, and the Ghost of T. E. Lawrence

September 18, 2002

Dear All,

I've only been here three days, but I've already met the Syrian secret police twice and wandered through 1,500 years of history.

The first time I met the secret police was after my bus to Aleppo, Syria's second largest city, crossed the border at Bab al Hawa. A couple of plainclothes guys that seemed very gray, both in their clothes and their complexion, flagged down the bus, boarded, and checked everyone's passports. The Syrian and Turkish passengers seemed fidgety and nervous. As the only westerner on the bus, I shared their feelings.

Not only does the Syrian government deny a visa to any traveler with an Israeli stamp in their passport, but visas are denied to prospective visitors with entry or exit stamps from a Jordanian or Egyptian land border with Israel, too. This isn't just a superficial policy; the Syrian government wants tourists and businesspersons to make a choice between Syria and Israel. The visa application includes the question, "Have you ever visited occupied Palestine?" In this context, "occupied Palestine" includes Israel. Not only have I visited Israel, I've lived there. So, I lied. I earned my Syrian visa from the embassy in Amman by proving that I was the best kind of Lawrence—an Arabist, an aficionado for all things Arab. I conducted the interview with the Syrian consular officer in Arabic, produced a laminated and Arabic-printed Jordanian residency card, and most important, used my second passport, which is free of Israeli entry and exit stamps. Before leaving the United States, I requested a second passport with this trip in mind.

The first experience with the secret police was without incident: A heavyset man with a silver mustache flipped through my passport's pages with disinterest and handed it back to me. No one disappeared, and the bus rolled on to Aleppo.

The second time I met the secret police, though, was a bit more stressful. When I returned to my fleabag hotel from a rotisserie chicken and humus dinner that first night, a mustached man in his late thirties, wearing a short-sleeve, collared dark blue shirt and brown pants, sat at the lobby desk, waiting for me. When I checked in earlier and gave the hotel clerk my passport, he had looked at its blue cover and asked in Arabic, "What country is this?"

Not a lot of American tourists come to Aleppo these days.

The secret-police guy looked at me, pulled my passport from his shirt pocket, and asked me to sit down. In Arabic, he asked familiar questions, but with a Syrian twist.

"Where are you from?"

"America."

"Where is your father from?"

"Kyrgyzstan, in the former Soviet Union," I replied. Technically, this was not a lie, since my father, a World War II refugee, was born there.

"Where have you traveled to?"

"I just came from Turkey; I am living in Amman."

"Have you ever been to occupied Palestine?"

"No."

"What are you doing in Jordan?"

"I study Arabic and economics and am finishing my masters degree."

"Where are you going to?"

"I will stay in Aleppo and then travel to Palmyra and Damascus." I didn't mention that I was going to go to Hama, too, the city that Assad leveled in 1982, killing thousands. I thought it might be a sensitive subject.

"Have you ever been to occupied Palestine?" he asked again, studying my face.

"No, never. Maybe I'll go to Jerusalem later, but I wanted to visit Syria." I mentioned Jerusalem because it was just too impossible to believe that an American who spoke Arabic would have no interest in the historic and holy city.

He paused and looked me over some more. I was glad for all the Arabic practice that I've had at the Nef and my other Amman hangouts. I've also realized that it is more difficult to detect whether someone is lying if they are not speaking in their mother tongue. The rhythm of words isn't always fluid, and it can seem as if the person is struggling to find the right words rather than telling tales.

After about ten more minutes of questions about my family, America, and my life in Amman, my interrogator smiled at me, like I had passed some sort of test, and told me that I could go. I think he believed me and was pleased that I had chosen to go to Syria instead of Israel. He might even have seen it as a minor victory for Syria. The worm was turning: A white American guy who spoke Arabic was visiting Aleppo for tourism and not interested in going to Israel. I went up to my room, wrote exactly what happened into my journal for the record (I wasn't convinced that I was in the clear), stood my backpack in front of the door, hoping to buy a few seconds if someone kicked it in, and went to sleep.

Nothing happened that night, but the next morning, I checked out anyway and went to a "budget hotel," which is a rung up the ladder from "fleabag." Once again, my passport went unrecognized, and I had to explain where I was from. There were no more visits from the authorities, though, and the hotel staff left me alone. It was Yom Kippur—the Jewish Day of Atonement and the holiest day of the year. Even if I had broadcast to the hotel staff and the rest of Aleppo who I was, I don't think anyone could really have figured out the strangeness of my existence—a Jewish American who had lived in Israel, was living in Jordan, and was visiting Syria for tourism during the holiest day of the Jewish year. Maybe they should have arrested me. . . .

I spent part of the day walking around the shady Christian quarter of the Old City. I bonded with Syria's Christian minority and spent an hour with Tawfiq, a seventeen-year-old Syrian Catholic who plans to become a priest next year. He showed me the chapel, opening the locked door with a key straight out of a Camelot tale; it was brass and more than a foot long. Tawfiq proudly explained the history of the Syrian Catholic community, and then we reviewed his English homework together.

Not a bad day, but yesterday I wandered through 1,500 years of majestic history; it was the best day of this Turkey-Syria trip by far. I had arranged for a driver to take me on a morning trip to the Basilica of St. Simon and to some of the Dead Cities of northern Syria. St. Simon was a fifth-century shepherd turned ascetic monk who, according to my Syria *Rough Guide* would bury himself in the ground up to his chin and chain himself to rocks in the sun. As lore of his piety grew, pilgrims traveled great distances to request miracles. To avoid being touched, St. Simon stood atop a pillar for thirty-some years, preaching and offering advice. Originally, the pillar was three meters tall, but it was eventually replaced by one that was eighteen meters high (a meter is roughly a yard); I can only imagine that there must have been an incident.

Dead Cities are not something out of a Wes Craven film; they are the remains of Byzantine cities, sans their inhabitants. About 1,400 years ago, perhaps as the result of war or a change in trade routes, they were mysteriously deserted, but not destroyed. Some stand alone in the baking sun, while in others, local children play among 1,500-year-old tombs.

So, yesterday morning, I squeezed into a Mitsubishi Lancer with a vacationing French couple (she is a social worker for troubled youth, and he is a computer programmer) and our French-speaking driver and guide, an unshaven portly fellow with big gold glasses, and we were off. When we exited Aleppo, we passed the dominating statute of the late Basel al-Assad galloping into the distance on a stallion. Basel was President Bashar's older brother who died in a car accident in 1994. Bashar was in London at the time, studying to become an ophthalmologist. He was recalled to Syria by his father, President Hafez al-Assad, after the first choice for succession died. The father ruled for more than thirty years and spent his last years grooming the reluctant Bashar to take over the family business.

Once past Aleppo's city limits and the statue of Syria's fallen son, we drove through Kurdish and Arab villages, fields, and olive groves. In the tight village alleys, little children in brown school uniforms clamored amidst the oncoming traffic of goats, sheep, and chickens. Their uniform shirts were decaled with the crest of the Syrian republic.

As we neared our first stop, a place our guide called "Qarib al Shams," or close to the sun, my preconceived notion of a dead city was fulfilled. The city's remains, surrounded by waist-high stone walls, were both desolate and magnificent. Among the scattered ruins, a church and a tomb from the fifth century remained fully intact, preserved by the dry environment. The two-storied, roofless church towered over the landscape, with the keystone of the arch looking as if it would crash to earth at any moment. The wind whistled across the dry landscape, and the sun seared the scattered stones on the plain. With my back to the road and the Lancer, it was as if I had stepped back in time through a 500-year portal.

Back in the car, having bonded with my new French friends over this shared experience, we continued on to St. Simon's Basilica. Our

Qarib al Shams.

guide was now wearing a turquoise and orange Miami Dolphins hat to combat the beating sun. In Arabic, I eagerly asked him about Dan Marino, one of the NFL's greatest quarterbacks and a fellow Pittsburgher. Our guide wasn't familiar with Oakland Danny's heroic feats with the Dolphins or Pitt Panthers, nor did he know of other Dolphin greats, like running back Larry Csonka or former coach Don Shula. Worse, it turned out that he couldn't care less about them and didn't even know the Miami Dolphins' cheer, which has only two words. I tried to show him how it goes, but he was more interested in speaking French with the couple. It was a blow, and I mumbled in English that he wasn't a good fan and that he should give his hat to the next shepherd we passed. He was talking about soufflés and berets, though, and not listening. I let it go and focused on the passing scenery.

With the windows rolled all the way down and hot air blasting through the car, we sped along winding roads through more villages and rock quarries. The roads were no bigger than one lane and a shoulder, and there were several eye-shutting bends and crests in the face of oncoming, boulder-transporting, dump-truck traffic. Along the way, we drove through another village where the local children must like either visitors or racing, because several of them ran alongside our car and tried to catch us. One child rode a horse and was a contender for a while, but then our guide put the Lancer into gear and we pulled away. As we were racing the children, I noticed that the village dogs had ferocious spiked collars like Cerberus, the three-headed dog that guards the underworld. I asked our guide why the dogs were equipped with such armor, and he explained that they would be better protected when they fought the local jackals. Oh.

We triumphantly arrived at the Basilica of St. Simon shortly after the big race, and the site did not disappoint. The basilica's front is a stunning triple-arched entrance with chiseled leaves that appear to blow in the wind. Inside the arched entrance, there is a large courtyard with basilicas in all four directions. At their meeting point is St. Simon's pillar, which locals, pilgrims, and tourists have whittled to a stump in search of a miracle or at least a souvenir. The compound

Syria's future track and field stars.

was stunning for both its natural condition, the incredible detail of its original work, and the beautiful western view of the Turkish landscape. Like at the dead city, I again found myself at a portal to a different time. Usually throngs of tourists plague impressive ruins such as this, at least in countries that aren't on the State Department's list of state sponsors of terrorism. Here it was quiet—just me, the French couple, and a couple of locals. The only sound was a soft breeze stirring the parched September grass.

The return to Aleppo was uneventful, and after saying good-bye to the French couple and my guide, I faced the height of the 100-degree day alone. I wandered down Baron Street, the former stomping ground of T. E. Lawrence, in search of food and indoor entertainment. If I ever write a travel book about the Middle East, I'll call it *Chasing Lawrence*. Wherever I go in Jordan and now Syria, I cross the footsteps of Lawrence's ghost. After helping to lead the Great Arab Revolt in the deserts of Jordan and Saudi Arabia and the cross-desert attack of the Ottoman fortress in Aqaba, Lawrence moved on to Syria. Once Damascus was "liberated" from Ottoman rule by allied forces, Lawrence sought to fulfill the dream of Arab nationalism—the creation of an independent Arab state—under the rule of Prince Faisal, the great-uncle of Jordan's late King Hussein.

I put Lawrence out of my mind, though, because I was hungry, it was hot, and he's dead. At a bustling falafel restaurant, I indulged in some doughnut-shaped patties and a bowl of humus. The old man at the counter who took my money could have been the identical twin brother of Hamas leader Sheikh Yassin. I confirmed that he was not Sheikh Yassin, however, when Fake Yassin started yelling at the man in front of me in a deep voice and waving his cane at him like a sword. Sheikh Yassin is what Seinfeld would call a "high talker," someone who speaks in a very high pitched voice. He is also paralyzed, lives in Gaza, and is concerned with liberating "Palestine" and turning it into an Islamic state—not getting the right change from his customers. The resemblance, however, was uncanny.

After my meal, I continued along Baron Street and stumbled upon a couple of movie theaters, all of which were showing Jackie Chan films. From the sound level coming out of the theater, it

The Basilica of St. Simon.

seemed like Jackie Chan was actually fighting someone, live, inside. For a dollar, I bought a balcony seat, curious as to who watches a Jackie Chan movie on a Tuesday afternoon in Aleppo. The movie had already started, but thankfully the story wasn't too complex, and I could figure out the plot. It was actually a little more difficult to find a seat in the pitch-dark balcony. A bruised shin later, I became the most active viewer in the crowd, laughing out loud when Chan's costar, Chris Tucker, told a stewardess that he ordered kosher food and underscored his point by saying, "Shalom." It was a tough crowd.

When the lights came on, I looked around to see who else was there. Tuesday matinees in Aleppo are not a common dating activity; the crowd was a bunch of swarthy-looking single guys sitting by themselves. As I wiped some sweat from my two-day growth and noticed the desert dust and salt stains on my black shirt, I realized that I did not look so different from my fellow Roger Eberts.

A pistachio ice cream cone later, it was cool enough to be outside again, so I wandered over to Aleppo's Old City to explore and take pictures in the early evening light. After declining numerous requests to change money or to buy carpets, gold, or gum, I sat on a wall next to a boy selling nuts outside of the citadel. After a conversation about our families, the boy informed me that an American group would be playing "classical rock music" inside the amphitheater at 8:00 o'clock. Curious about what other Americans might be in Syria, I decided to clean up and return for the show.

At 7:30 P.M., I was back at the citadel, anticipating a big crowd and having to wait in line to get a ticket. As I approached, I saw that there was a crowd, so I went to the front of the line. Over the past two months, I've learned that there is never any reason to wait at the end of a line. You will never, ever be served. So, at the front, I asked a short man in Arabic, "If you please, do you have a ticket?"

No response. He looked at me like I was speaking Chinese.

"If you please, are you going to the concert?"

Again he made no response and just looked at me in disbelief. Feeling self-conscious, I fell back on a word common to Arabic and English: "Muzica?"

He grabbed a man behind him, a bit older and taller with a finely groomed goatee, and said something; his speech was rapid-fire. The man with the goatee looked at me and in English said, "We hate America and everything American. Don't bring your American music here. We want to send a message to American government and W. Bush. . . . We want nothing American in Syria! We hate America! You bomb Iraq and Palestine! You kill children! You want we kill your children?"

As he continued his rant, State Department travel warnings flashed across my mind, and I realized that I was in the middle of an anti-American protest. Though this group was relatively tame, I felt surrounded and wanted to move on. Before doing so, though, I felt obliged to defend the flag and the concept of cultural exchanges. Here, I'm the poster child for both.

In Arabic, I told him, "We are all people, and this is music. There are no politics here; this is music. This is culture, and it is important to have an exchange of cultures. I listen to Um Kalthoum because her songs are beautiful." Um Kalthoum is the greatest of Arab singers and a patriot who donated concert proceeds to the Egyptian government after the crushing defeat of the 1967 war. I continued, "it is not important that she is Egyptian. The songs are about love, not politics. Why can't they play American music here?"

After these opening arguments—where each of us did our best to use all of our big English and Arabic words, respectively—it became an argument in Arabic about U.S. government policies. The decibel tone lowered after the opening salvo, too. Ten minutes later, as we parted ways, my counterpart with the well-groomed goatee clarified that the American people were okay and could come, but that Syrians hated the American government.

Inside the amphitheater, there were a hundred other people, including roadies, TCBY vendors, and fifty teenage cadets "guarding" the premises. The show didn't start at eight, though, and as people trickled in, I became hungry. By 8:45 P.M., I was ready to leave, but I had no interest in walking through the protest again, so I continued to wait. If I had known what I was going to get, I might have joined the protest.

The band's performance was one of the most soulless outpourings of music that I've ever experienced. Four white guys, one of Arab descent, were touring the Middle East and putting on a display of "classic American rock and roll" as part of a cultural exchange. I'm not sure what we got in the exchange, but we came out on top. The group's grand appearance began at the top of the amphitheater as the foursome descended singing "We Will Rock You," a cappella style. They then launched into a few songs from the 1950s and 1960s with their guitars, fiddle, and drums.

The crowd's reaction was mixed. There were the cadets, families that included muhajiba women, young people who loved all things American, and then an assorted bunch that looked like they were asked to come in off the street to fill empty seats. One guy in front clearly loved the show; he did a jumping-jack-like dance throughout, pausing only to snap pictures. Some of the cadets danced a little, but when their headmaster entered the amphitheater, they quickly returned to standing straight and scowling. Others clapped along, too, but I don't think that people understood what was going on.

When the lead singer called out, "Do you want us to stop rocking?" The people around me yelled "Yes!" Though I would like to think that this was a sign of good taste, they most likely were just confused. The cultural gap was confirmed for me when the lead singer started talking about the band's website in English. I turned and looked at the stone-faced older woman in a head scarf behind me and shook my head, wondering whether this man knew that the Internet had only become legal in Syria a couple of years ago and that sites like Hotmail and Yahoo are still censored. As the band launched into a rendition of "Hound Dog" that would have made Elvis weep, I laughed, recalling the protest out front. If this was a threat, we are all in trouble.

Starving, I made my way back to Baron Street and enjoyed a feast of lentil soup, half a rotisserie chicken, humus (twice in one day!), and mineral water for $4 at the outdoor and leafy Shabab Restaurant. *Shabab* means "young persons"—specifically, "young men" in Arabic—and by coincidence or not, there were no women present. Groups of men of all ages sat around having a good time, drinking booze, chatting, and eating. The meal was enjoyable except for the stray cats that would hop down from the walls above and eat from discarded plates at empty tables. No one else seemed put out by it.

Looking to top the day off, and still hoping to find a fellow traveler with whom I could share all my deep thoughts about Syria, I headed over to the Baron Hotel for a beer. Instead of a beautiful backpacker with a love for majestic Syria, I had to settle once again for Lawrence's ghost. During Aleppo's golden age, the Baron Hotel was the city's most prestigious guesthouse, hosting the likes of Mustafa Kemal Ataturk, Teddy Roosevelt, Agatha Christie, and who else but T. E. Lawrence.

To my disappointment, there wasn't much going on, just some Germans talking about schnitzel and sauerkraut. As I sat on the patio speaking with a clerk who might have put the mint on T. E. Lawrence's pillow, a huge water truck with a hose coming out of the front grill made its way down the street. A man walked in front of the truck, holding the hose, spraying down the street and everything in front of him. A few hundred miles away in my neighborhood in Jordan, they are taking four-minute cold showers twice a week and not flushing the toilet. I smiled, shook my head, and finished my beer. It was a good way to end a great day in an amazing place.

Love,
Ben

Syria's Walls: Public Space and Private Worlds

September 24, 2002

Dear All,

The alternative reality of a police state is less glamorous than what I imagined. Tomorrow morning, I'll depart Damascus and return to Amman. As much as I've enjoyed the last few weeks of travel, I'll be happy when the shared taxi pulls into Abdali bus station and I return to my apartment. Syria is a culturally rich place where history lives on at naturally preserved ruins, and to categorize Syrians as "evildoers" is to misunderstand the situation on the ground. Still, I've found the atmosphere oppressive and am ready to leave.

The Assad cult of personality dominates the country's public spaces, and one could easily get the impression that this land is a family business rather than a nation-state. Public buildings and privately owned stores are plastered with pictures of the late father, the fallen son Basel, and the young president Bashar. Across the country, there are streetlamps, decorated with the likeness of the father, illuminating parks and squares. There are horizontal traffic lights that hang over major streets with the father's picture affixed next to the red or green light, too.

Pictures of Basel, the bearded and rugged fallen son, compete in number with the new president, his younger brother Bashar, in fatigues, with arms crossed, and forearms grotesquely exaggerated. Other images show Bashar with eyes focused on the horizon amid a montage of the father's face, the masses, and the flag. Billboards, constructed during the later years of the father's reign, depict the Assad threesome together: the leader, the hope, and the ideal. A pundit more irreverent than myself referred to the collection as "the father, the son, and the holy ghost." Across the country, by my informal count, the ratio of father to president to fallen son posters is roughly 5:3:2.

In addition to the pictures, there is a Big Brother presence that wafts through the air like the smell of fish. Since my meetings with

An Assad street light.

the secret police on my first day here, I haven't had a repeat incident. Yet I walk down the street with a story ready, waiting for someone to tap me on the shoulder and ask me what I'm doing here. This was especially the case in Hama, a quiet city along the Orontes River, which lies in the country's central corridor between Damascus and Aleppo.

Hama is the most picturesque city that I visited in Syria, as well as the place with the most oppressive environment—a bizarre combination that reminded me of Stephen King's fictional Castle Rock. Castle Rock is a sleepy hamlet in Maine that could be Anytown, USA, except for the various supernatural forms of evil that King conjures up to challenge and torment its inhabitants. Part of Hama's charm is the Orontes River, which snakes through the city. Along the river are enormous wooden waterwheels that were once used to lift water from the river but that still churn away and emit a heavy groan that could be mistaken for the sound of a giant pushing a boulder up a hill. Young men scale these waterwheels, ride about twenty meters (or yards) to the top, and then leap into the river below.

Given its central location, Hama is a good place to stage day trips to some of northern Syria's prominent historical sites, like the Assassins' Castle, the Roman ruins of Aphamea, and the Krak des Chevaliers fortress—another spot on the "Chasing Lawrence" tour. In addition, Hama has cheap but clean hotels and restaurants that serve delicious local food. At $9 a day, I was also able to hire Abdel Karim and his 1964 yellow Mercedes taxi cab. I spent Wednesday and Thursday visiting Hama's surrounding sites and then enjoyed a quiet Friday morning walking around town. In the cobblestone alleyways of Hama's old city, I inspected the bullet scars of the civil war that took place twenty years ago, when the Assad regime massacred an estimated 20,000 Syrians and plowed over part of the city.

For more than thirty years, political and military power in Syria has rested with the Alawites, a minority sect of Shia Islam. Alawites include some Christian religious practices in their traditions and trace their roots to the mountain regions of Syria and Lebanon. Though Sunni Arabs compose the majority in Syria and make up the Syrian merchant class, the Alawites, led by the Assad ruling clique,

Hama's waterwheels.

control the government and military. There are some similarities to the separation of political and economic spheres of power in Jordan—where East Banker Jordanians control the political system and the military and the Palestinian-Jordanian majority angle for power and wealth in the economic world. In Jordan, however, Jordanians and Palestinians argue about demographics, with East Bankers valiantly denying that they are a minority. In Syria, it is clear to all that the Alawite minority are a little more than 10 percent of the population.

The Alawites came from modest origins in Syria and gained power through the institutions of the army and the Baath Party. During the French mandate period in Syria, it was French strategy to weaken the majority Sunni Arabs, who opposed their presence, by empowering minorities such as the Christians and the previously victimized Alawites, considered backward by the Sunni upper class. In this way, the military served as a chief mechanism for Alawite political and social mobility.

A shining example of this "mobility" was Hafez al-Assad. Born to a peasant, Assad rose through the military ranks as an air force officer and became president. His rags-to-riches story differs slightly, though, from a fairy tale. He was a stalwart in the struggle against Israel, which served as a credential internationally within the Arab East and domestically, too. Assad became a leading member of the secular, socialist, and pan-Arab Baath Party, which sought to unite the Western-divided Arab states into one Arab Nation and emphasized the struggle against imperial powers and Israel. Assad's political choices were deft. Given his minority roots, he chose methods and mechanisms that portrayed him as the ultimate nationalist, always struggling against external threats for Arab causes.

His rise to power ended Syria's post-colonial period of instability. From the 1946 withdrawal of French armies to Assad's bloodless coup in 1970, Syria was a train wreck of a country, with coup after coup and a temporary unification with Egypt. In 1966, Assad, then an air force general, helped to lead a military coup that seized control of the government. As minister of defense, he took full control in 1970, ruling until his death in 2000. Despite the regime's totalitarian tactics, Assad continued to battle for control over the country, particularly with the religious Sunni Muslims who consider Alawites heretics. In particular, the Muslim Brotherhood challenged the Assad regime for policies that were not in line with *sharia* (Islamic law) and attacked Baath Party institutions.

An Islamic political organization founded in Egypt in the late 1920s, the Muslim Brotherhood seeks to apply Islam, in the form of sharia, as a full political and social system for Muslims throughout the Islamic world. For them, there is no power—secular or otherwise—higher than God; secular Arab regimes therefore rule unjustly. Historically, the Muslim Brotherhood gained popularity on the local level in different countries throughout the Arab East by filling the gaps of bad governance and providing social services—like health care, child care, and meals—with an accompanying religious message to the poor and educated non-elites alike. In some countries like Egypt, the Muslim Brotherhood has forsworn the use of violence as a means to achieve its objectives, although this was not the case in the 1940s and 1950s, when they assassinated gov-

ernment ministers and officials and organized riots and demonstrations. In other places, like the Palestinian territories, Hamas—a
Muslim Brotherhood offshoot—has fused religious doctrine with national liberation and actively uses terror and violence to try and
reach its objectives.

In February 1982, the Muslim Brotherhood in Hama revolted
against the Assad regime. It was a culmination of a back-and-forth
that included attempts by the Muslim Brotherhood to assassinate
Assad, as well as to attack other Alawite targets, and the regime's
arrest and execution of Muslim Brotherhood members. The revolt
was triggered when Assad decided to crush the Hama-led Muslim
Brotherhood once and for all. He sent his brother Rifaat, commander of the regime's Defense Companies—responsible for defending the regime against domestic threats—into Hama. In his
book, *From Beirut to Jerusalem,* Thomas Friedman (who was *The
New York Times* Beirut bureau chief at the time) explains that Rifaat intended to target Muslim Brotherhood leaders, make a public
example of them, and then kill them. Muslim Brotherhood leaders
and members fought back, however, and turned the operation into
a full revolt. Challenged, the Assad regime turned Hama into a
bloodbath. Over three weeks, the Assads sent in tanks and then bulldozers and literally plowed over and buried sections of the city, leaving bodies in their wake and making no distinction between
members of the Muslim Brotherhood and civilians.

Friedman describes visiting Hama a couple of months after the
massacre and walking over the bulldozed sections of the town, stepping on stray shoes, books, and clothing, and wondering what lay
beneath the gravel and smashed homes beneath his feet. It is esti-
mated that the Assads killed somewhere between 10,000 and
25,000 people in Hama. Officially, the death toll was claimed to be
1,200, though Friedman offers an account of Rifaat Assad privately
bragging about killing 38,000 people.

The Syrian government did rebuild Hama, although it left a vi-
sual reminder of the destruction, an indicator that the regime remains poised at all times to protect its hold on power. Twenty years
later, I walked to the top of a little hill near the center of town, once

the site of the city's citadel, which dates back to a few thousand years B.C. Listening to the groaning of the enormous waterwheels and looking past the meandering Orontes River, the squat apartment buildings, and a mosque, I saw the empty lot. It stuck out against the quaint beauty of the city like a mirror in the sun. The site of some of the heaviest fighting, it was Assad's reminder to Syrians that they lived according to the regime's discretion. I whipped out my camera, took a picture, and quickly looked around, expecting to feel someone's hand on my wrist.

While the massacre at Hama is one of the Arab East's noteworthy examples of brutality, such tactics are not unique to the Assad regime and to Syria. From Stalin to Saddam, the most important thing to every dictator is waking up in the morning. And, the first thing that the dictator confirms when he wakes up is that he will wake up again the next day. There are no sunset clauses, golden parachutes, or retired dictators. Authoritarian regimes turn their countries into personal realms, and the overriding goal is always to protect their rule. Any threat to the status quo is snuffed out

Hama, Assad's reminder.

immediately, and examples are set so as to deter thoughts of future challenges.

When Assad leveled Hama, he destroyed the existing opposition to his regime, and he sent a clear message to any future opposition. From 1987 to 1988 in Iraq, Saddam Hussein sent a similar message when he destroyed hundreds of Kurdish villages in northern Iraq and killed tens of thousands of Kurds, including by use of chemical weapons. At the time, Iraq was fighting a war with Iran, a country that had previously supported Kurdish fighters against the Iraqi regime. In 1991, Saddam once again showed the lengths he would go to in order to protect his rule when he massacred tens of thousands of Shia in southern Iraq. The Shia had risen up in response to the first President Bush's calls to overthrow the Iraqi government following the liberation of Kuwait. In both cases, with the Kurds and the Shia of Iraq, Saddam made clear to Iraqis that there would be no opportunity to capitalize on a perceived weakness of the regime as it fought an external enemy.

In democracies, the public domain i.e., the public space in the form of schools, parks, and institutions of government belongs to the people. Citizens elect representatives who are expected to secure the welfare of all citizens. Whether an American congressman is black or white, male or female, an elected member of Congress is expected to protect the rights of all Americans, regardless of their race or gender. In authoritarian-ruled countries like Syria or Iraq, however, the public domain belongs to the regime, not the citizens. The regime does not champion the rights of all its citizens equally; rather, it sets the rules for the public domain and enforces them in a way that promotes the regime's best interests and the interests of its power base.

For the sake of claiming a measure of credibility, the regime may cloak its control of the public domain in the facades of familiar and respected institutions. In some places, while cronyism and corruption are the norm, Islamic law is used as a key influencer in the judicial system. Questioning the implementation of justice therefore becomes a matter of questioning Islamic practice. Or, in countries where there is no freedom of the press or assembly, dictators may emulate other Western political practices and hold elections. Both

Saddam and Assad won several referendums where people had the opportunity to vote "yes" for them to remain president. By holding sham elections, dictators like Assad or Saddam are able to publicly paint their opposition as not only opposing the will of the people, but that of democratic practices, too. No matter whether the window dressing is religious or Western, though, the regime's actions are intended first and foremost to sustain its own rule and to build the personal security and wealth of its power base.

It is possible for a police state's citizens who are not a part of the regime's power base to achieve success and happiness. However, citizens' interests are only a priority for authoritarian regimes as they relate to maintaining stability and the status quo. Anything citizens earn in the public domain is at the discretion of the regime, not the fulfillment of a secured opportunity, an entitlement of citizenship, or a basic right.

Syrian citizens accept this relationship with the regime because of lessons like Hama. Should they decide to challenge the regime's ownership of the public domain, then the regime will come into the people's private worlds with crushing force and brutality to demonstrate its might. If citizens accept the regime's primacy, then, for the most part, they can hope to be left alone at home (there are, of course, brutal exceptions). In Syria, a clearly defined bargain has been struck between the people and the government. The people have ceded the public domain to the regime, and in return, they lead their true lives behind closed doors. Syrians have built castle walls around their homes.

On Friday morning, I walked through Hama's old city and considered the human implications of the city's scars. I walked past an old man who wore a matching white *galabaya* and knit skullcap. He sat on a step and dozed with his chin on his cane. I wondered where he had been twenty years ago and whether he had lost a son, a daughter, or maybe his wife in the massacre. Did the waterwheels groan those days as blood ran through the city's streets twenty years ago? Down by the river, a man zipped by on a moped, stopped in front of an iron door that was set into a tall stone wall, pushed open the door, and entered a courtyard. The door shut behind him as he entered his castle.

Of all the places in Syria that I visited, it was in Hama that I noticed the greatest density of Assad family pictures displayed in public. The city is a testimony to one man, his sons, and their country. On the outskirts of town, there is a creepy, giant silver statue of the late father towering above traffic. That statue is the image of Syria that Americans see on television and consider a menace. It is the face of a regime that has remained a fixture on the State Department's list of state sponsors of terror. It is a mistake, though, to assume that Syria is nothing more than the monolithic edifice presented in the public domain. While the air in the public domain may be pungent, it does not mean that a rich life does not go on inside of the castle walls.

Inside the walls, private life is indeed the same private life led by people all over the world. In Aleppo's Christian quarter, an open door to a walled schoolyard revealed little uniformed girls chasing each other and shrieking in happy voices. The sounds of families eating lunch together resonate in the centuries-old courtyards of Damascus's old city.

Earlier this evening, my last night in Damascus, I went to the top of Mount Qassioun, which overlooks the Syrian capital of 8 million people. I flagged a cab outside of the old city and negotiated with the driver to take me to the top of the mountain. Thousands and thousands of lights lit the night sky, with Damascus's green lit mosques shimmering against the black backdrop. Iyad, my driver, a short, unshaven, and friendly guy about my age, was welcome company. He offered to stay at the top of the mountain with me, explaining that I would never be able to find a ride back down to the city. We talked for twenty minutes in the dark open space lit only by the lights below. He told me about his family and a woman he had met a few weeks earlier and had fallen in love with. He had gone straight up to her, asked her for a pen, then a piece of paper, and then for her phone number. As we laughed, couples walked by holding hands and talking quietly. Though in a semi-public place, this was private life—life behind the walls.

Being an outsider in a secret-police environment of suspicion, I have found it difficult to taste private-world moments in Syria. On my Friday walk through Hama's old city and along the Orontes, I passed the graveyard lot, the site of Assad's reminder, on the other side of the river. On my side of the river, people darted in or out of beaten houses. Some waved and said "hello" or "welcome," but they carefully closed their doors behind them, keeping that private castle secret from prying foreign eyes and hurtful influences.

The night before, I did catch a little more than a glimpse of life behind the walls. After a sumptuous dinner of kebob, tabbouleh, and humus (I can't get enough!), I went for a leisurely stroll through town and stumbled upon an art gallery full of local artists' work. At a quarter past nine, I was the only gallery visitor. Two older men sat outside in white plastic chairs and wished me a courteous hello. Inside, as I wandered past the different paintings, I was approached by Rania, a muhajiba college student with shining blue-green eyes. She worked in the gallery and was the daughter of one of the men outside. She welcomed me with great pride and showed me the section of paintings that were the local students' work, including two paintings that she had done herself.

Rania asked me where I was from, and when I told her, there was a flinch of hesitancy in her eyes but also a spark of interest. She made tea, and we talked for a while about America's intentions in Iraq and about the relationship between our countries. She understood there were differences of opinion, such as with Israel, but she didn't like how the United States treated Syria as the recipient of dictates, rather than as an equal. We would have continued speaking, but Rania's father lingered in the doorway, and I took that to mean that it was time to go. As we said good-bye, Rania reached her hand out, looked me directly in the eye as we shook hands, and told me that she was glad to have met me and that we—meaning Syrians and Americans—needed to keep talking.

It's important to know that there are art galleries, students like Rania, and romantics like Iyad in Syria. The everyday people who live a full life within the private space of a police state should not be overlooked—here or as the pressure builds towards war, in Iraq. The normalcy of these people's lives, their hopes, and their aspirations may not be the most important factor in making decisions of war—but they should certainly be a consideration.

As Bush administration officials prepare for what seems like an imminent war with Iraq, we should all be aware that we are going to upset a delicate balancing act by which a lot of people already live full lives. Should we invade these castles and shake the lives within them so as to designate leaders and dictate terms, then we must offer something unambiguous in return. President Bush would do well to promise that the U.S. government will rebuild Iraq as it rebuilt Germany and Japan. It is significant that when the Assads destroyed Hama, they rebuilt the town afterward—that is the minimum that we must offer. I hope that if we choose war, we will stand for more than physical reconstruction.

This separation between the public domain and the private space is an important aspect of understanding life here. In Turkey, I noted the separation between the public and private world as related to religion and ethnicity. Turks keep their private lives—whether religious or ethnic—behind closed doors, but they share a common secular Turkish public identity and demand that their leaders do more with the public domain than hang pictures of themselves on buildings and parks. They want cleanliness, of the streets and such, but really of their government, which means transparent governance, a lack of corruption, and a business environment that offers opportunities for everyone, not just the regime's cronies.

In thinking about this separation and citizens' feelings of ownership of the public domain, I've developed a litter test. Turkish streets, bus stations, and other public places are pretty clean. Although there are street sweepers in every country, the cleanliness of the public space depends more on the volume of litter rather than the capabilities of a country's custodial force. In Jordan, so many times, I've seen people step out of shops or restaurants and throw their garbage onto the sidewalk or the street, with little regard for the cleanliness of public places. Jordanians would never do that in their homes, but the streets and parks don't belong to them. In Turkey, people generally take better care not to chuck their garbage out of their homes and shops to land wherever it may because they have a sense of ownership of the public domain.

In a dictatorship like Syria, the separation between the public and private space is even starker because Syrians have such meager expectations of the government to work for them. It would seem that Syrians have no compunction about stepping outside and throwing their trash three feet to the left. They have no ownership of the public domain. Syrians don't coalesce around certain issues like corruption because, for the most part, they seek only to have the government leave them to their own devices in their private worlds. For autonomy at home, they have given up the sidewalks and the street. That doesn't mean that they aren't nationalistic and proud to be Syrian, especially in the face of an external enemy, but they don't expect the public system to work for them. Their aspirations are simply that the government not actively work against them.

Traveling to Syria and Turkey has given me a new appreciation for my life back in Jordan. I felt relief upon landing in Turkey and leaving Jordan, and the opposite was true upon leaving Turkey and entering Syria. In Turkey, I felt as free as I do in the United States, but without the same sort of legal protections that prevent shakedowns (as I experienced in the brothel incident in Istanbul). In Syria, as I mentioned, I've constantly expected someone to tap me on the shoulder for questioning, and I have feared that if I were subjected to a justice system, it would not be an objective one. I have to admit, however, that the fear-based order created by the authoritarian nature of Syria's government has offered me some feeling of protection. I could walk the Damascus streets at 1:00 A.M. because even the thieves are too scared of the repercussions from the regime if they attacked a foreigner and caused public embarrassment for the government. Interestingly, litter bugs don't suffer from the same fear.

In Jordan, I don't enjoy the same level of freedom and comfort as I did in Turkey. I am careful about revealing my religious background and some of my political opinions. However, I don't worry about the Jordanian secret police coming to my door to interview me, perhaps because the Jordan-United States relationship is a good one and on principle, they won't harass Americans. In addition though, while the Jordanian secret police are a real concern for some Jordanians and Palestinians, they are definitely less intrusive than their counterparts in Syria. In Jordan, there is thus a more benevolent version of authoritarian rule than in Syria. Nevertheless, there is still order and a popular fear of chaos. Like in Syria, the trappings of the Jordanian system work to the advantage of foreigners in some cases; namely, by ensuring personal safety. The Jordanian economy relies on its reputation in the West for foreign aid, investments, and tourism; a public attack on a foreigner would generate great embarrassment and be quite costly for the Jordanian regime.

So, I'm happy to have traveled, and I'll be happy to return to my own castle in Amman. Hope everyone is doing well.

Love,
Ben

Part Three

Living the Life

"Fast Times" at Jordan University and Friday Lunch with Abu Alaa

October 27, 2002

Dear All,

University life is in full swing again, I've settled into a new one-bedroom apartment, and I'm following a routine that I hope will enable me to become an Arabic Jedi master. The apartment is located in Webdeh, a more residential neighborhood than the university area. It is fully furnished, has satellite TV, and lots of water—there is even a hot water switch that, if flicked a half-hour beforehand, delivers hot showers. I'm a ten-minute walk from the Abdali bus station, which means that getting to the university is just a twenty-minute bus ride. There are a bunch of stores a few blocks away, and I'm cultivating relationships with the supermarket owner, the water delivery man, the grocer, and the guys at two falafel stands, a block away from each other. There is also an empty lot at the end of my block, where I stop by almost every day to look out on an expansive view of the city.

Fadi was disappointed by my departure. He had started to think that we were going to live together for the whole year that I'm here. He didn't understand why I would want to live alone. The same has been true of others—they feel sorry for me when they hear that I live alone. They can't imagine how bored and lonely I must be. The truth, though, is that Syrians aren't the only ones who cherish their private space. I need it, too.

I enjoyed living with Fadi. He was incredibly generous, even renting a car one day and taking me, Marwan, and three other foreign students on a trip to the Dead Sea and then the northern border. The day-to-day aspects of my life with Fadi and Marwan made me feel part of a home, but at the same time, I found myself having very little of my own space and felt the very real drama of his problems related to marriage and work creeping onto my list of concerns. Combined with the reality of needing to start work on my research project, which will require Internet access, and the ability to shower regularly (so that I can present myself to interview people), I decided that it would be best to find a new place to live.

In addition to my having a more comfortable living situation, my university life has gotten better, too. It's not that my new teachers or classmates are special in any way; it's just that I'm more at home in the environment. I have class every morning, five days a week, and then a number of different options for the afternoon. Twice a week, I meet Kholood for one-on-one tutoring; I am trying to audit a masters-level international trade theory class; I have three conversation partners: Bahaa, Ibrahim, and "the Professor," who I meet on alternating days; and I read the paper and study in the university library.

I had high hopes for the trade class, but it looks like I'm going to drop it, by popular demand. I thought I would improve my professional Arabic vocabulary and meet economics graduate students who might be more interesting than the mix of princes, Lawrences, and true believers in my Arabic class. The economics professor agreed to let me sit in and was impressed by my "paper" credentials, a masters degree in international economics from Johns Hopkins.

On the first day of the class, the professor pointed me out and explained to the other students that I would be attending class. He neglected to explain, however, that I was not taking the class for a grade and that I just wanted to hang out in Arabic.

Thwarting my best-laid plans, the students voted to hold the class in English, so they could practice their professional English; they also made it clear that they wanted nothing to do with me. They regard me warily and cannot figure out my purpose for attending the class. The professor isn't helping my case. He asks the class softball questions, no one answers them, and then he calls on me as the last resort. Since they are basic questions, even I know the answers. So my choice is either to look stupid or to answer the questions in mistake-free English. Since I've decided to defend my Johns Hopkins education, I really can't blame the students for hating me. From their perspective, I'm this know-it-all American guy who already has a degree in economics, speaks English fluently, is fast becoming the professor's favorite student, and is going to bust the curve on the exam.

Leila, an attractive dark-haired student, talked with me after class the other day. She wanted to know where I am from, what I'm doing in Jordan, and . . . whether I could help her with her homework. I was thrilled with the 1980s movie sort of plot line that was developing, but it was a short-lived happy moment. One of Leila's equally attractive friends stormed up to her, demanded to know what she was doing, and pulled her away. Others have complained during class to the professor (in very fast Arabic) about me being there. Yesterday, two ladies took the direct approach; they came up to me after class and demanded to know what I was doing there. Between the students' angst and the fact that the class is being taught in broken English, I don't think I'm going to continue. I can't imagine any tears being shed.

I really like the library, though, and don't think that I'm going to be kicked out of there anytime soon—unless the librarian catches me speaking with people in the reading room. I spend a couple of hours in the main reading room three or four times a week, reading the newspaper with my dictionary or doing my homework for class. The reading room is furnished with several long tables that are surrounded by aisles of books. Students come and go. There are guys in sports coats and suits and others in jeans and collared shirts. Some women are completely covered, wearing the *niqab* over their face and gloves on their hands, and others wear tight T-shirts and jeans. Many of the students plop down all of their things on the tables and then go off to other places and hope that their books will take care of the studying on their own.

When the books aren't studying on their own and students are moving their pages, the atmosphere in the reading room is entertaining—well, at least for me. While some students are actually studying, the others are enjoying the university's status as an oasis from the conservative social pressures of Jordan. The university is a safe place where young men and women can chat with friends, see the opposite sex, and even engage them in conversation, in the library and on the rest of campus.

The freedom the students enjoy while at the university becomes even clearer later in the day, as it grows dark. In the fading light, groups of friends as well as couples sit together under trees or stroll back and forth across the emptying campus. Talking or sitting quietly, they enjoy moments of public privacy and the last gasps of their day together before going home to what are probably crowded homes and a full set of responsibilities. It's a romantic and bittersweet scene as the campus grows dark, the outdoor lights go on, and the security guards walk around, quietly telling groups of friends and couples that it is time to go home. In a way, it reminds me of playing basketball outside in the summer when I was in high school. At a certain point, we'd all realize that we could no longer see the ball and could hardly see each other. As the ball ricocheted off of our hands and passing became futile, it would become clear that, like it or not, it was time to head home.

The reading room won't bring back such misty water-colored memories of my adolescence, but it is still a scene. There is a middle-aged muhajiba librarian whose job is to walk around the room and "shush" people who are talking. She's a caricature out of a 1950s movie, only missing the wooden ruler. She stalks around the library, eyes blazing, just daring students to try and talk to each other. The click-clacks of her footfalls echo across the room as she pounces, tsk-tsking and protecting the library's solemnity. Repeat offenders, giggling girls, or chatty guys, she threatens to throw out into the cold linoleum hallway. I love it; it's a living cliché.

Truth be told, my favorite thing about the library is going outside, drinking a cup of coffee on the grass by the clock tower, and watching students wander by. The weather is like a clear blue Midwest fall day, and in a lot of ways it is like I'm back in college, except there is neither a football game on Saturday nor the encroaching doom of a freezing winter. My main people-watching activity is counting *hijabs*. I play this game where I count women by the tens. For each ten, I count how many are wearing the hijab. Generally, six or seven women out of ten are muhajiba; but most of the time, I cheat. Because of my own secularism and biases, I choose selectively when I start my count. If a flock of muhajiba women stroll by, I'll start counting after they pass. Sometimes, I'll scan the crowds and start my counting at a pack of T-shirt clad coeds, so I can reach a non-muhajiba majority. I'm a color commentator, not a stats-man.

One thing that has become painfully obvious to me is how beautiful the women are here. It's the "bizzaro" South Beach dress code, but leaving something to the imagination is very attractive. Other attributes of beauty and style become prominent and accentuated. Muhajiba women may cover their heads and wear a jilbab, but it doesn't mean that they aren't classy or taking care of their looks. I would actually wager that they are dressed to impress underneath the jilbab, but I have no way of confirming this hunch. I'd give a pinkie finger to enter the secret world of women here.

Each woman asserts her style to the outside world through her choice of shoes, handbag, and even head scarf. Calvin Klein head scarves are quite common. Also, hands become very attractive; so do lips, eyelashes, and definitely, eyes. I saw a woman yesterday who looked rather plain from afar in her jeans, gray jilbab, and navy hijab. But as she walked closer to my perch on the grassy knoll by the clock tower, I saw that she had the world's biggest and most beautiful green eyes. They had flecks of gray and blue that I could see from six feet away. I had no idea that eyes could be that size—she was one of the most gorgeous women I've ever seen.

My benefactors will be happy to know that I am doing something with my fellowship besides ogling women, drinking coffee, and making a nuisance of myself in econ class; there *is* some actual Arabic study taking place. Besides my private lessons with Kholood, I've found that the best way for me to learn has been to work with conversation partners, people with whom I trade English for Arabic conversation lessons. As I mentioned, I have three of them: "the Professor," Ibrahim, and Bahaa. I meet with each of them twice a week, the Professor and Ibrahim for about an hour and Bahaa for two to three hours.

The Professor teaches Arabic literature and speaks horrible English. He wants to know English because he's embarrassed at how bad his skills are, given his academic position. Also, the Professor's wife speaks fluently, and both of his daughters speak better than he does. But while the Professor wants to know English, he has shown no interest in actually learning. Our sessions in his office will start with me reading to him in Arabic for about thirty-five minutes, sometimes more. Then, when it's time to switch to English, we'll start talking, he'll butcher a few sentences, and then he'll give up. Someone will call, and he'll extend the conversation for ten minutes, or he'll ask his secretary to come in and they will speak for a while, or he'll tell me that he has an appointment. He is in denial regarding the dismal state of his English, something that he is reminded of whenever he tries to speak with me. He does love correcting my Arabic, though.

I really like both Ibrahim and Bahaa; they are both Palestinian-Jordanians but come from different parts of the Jordanian social spectrum. Ibrahim is a bus rider, part of the same demographic as Fadi, Na'el the barber, and Samer the Internet guy. He is twenty-two, has eight brothers and sisters, and lives in Zarqa. He studies elementary education and wants to speak English better so that he can impress his boss at his job selling sporting goods. He arrives five minutes early to our meetings, the equivalent of fifteen minutes early in America, and always greets me with a big smile. All of our sessions take place at the university, and we alternate turns buying each other coffee. We work exclusively on spoken language, and he is very eager to teach me slang and useful expressions. Like the Professor, Ibrahim's English is weak, and he has a hard time putting sentences together. Though Ibrahim tries much harder than the Professor, his response to his English shortcomings is to fall back on teaching me a new slang word or telling me a story about his bus ride that day from Zarqa.

During our meetings, Ibrahim's friends pass by in a constant stream, wishing him well. They enthusiastically kiss each other on the cheek a few times, as if they haven't seen each other in months. Ibrahim was quick to explain to me, with an earnest expression on his face, that men kiss each other by custom or tradition and that it doesn't mean he is gay. He wasn't sure how to convey homosexuality, though, and kind of wiggled his right hand up and down while lifting a knowing eyebrow. Ibrahim takes pride in introducing me to his friends and showing off what he has taught me. Even though he animatedly disagrees with American foreign policy, it's also clear that there is a certain amount of prestige to having an American language partner and friend, as opposed to a Russian or Turkish one.

As much as I like Ibrahim, Bahaa is my favorite conversation partner. He is a twenty-year-old who was born in Kuwait but is from the West Bank. He is a smiley, handsome, well-spoken, zealous, ambitious, and intelligent biomedicine major. If there were a middle class here, Bahaa would be in it. He has two brothers, and his parents are teachers. He graduated from the king's elite high school, where admission is determined by interviews and tests, and he seems headed toward a future leadership position of some sort. Kholood introduced us over dinner one night; he is a star member of her and her uncle's science and technology club.

Bahaa enjoys taking me to a new hangout in a different part of the city each time we meet. His English is terrific, and he is working with me to get from excellent to fluent. We usually eat and then read an article together in the other's language and discuss it. Our discussions tend to slip into debates about ongoing events in Jordan, American support for Israel, American intentions regarding Iraq, and the injustice faced by the Palestinian people. We also talk about love, a topic that is far more exhausting than our political discussions. We disagree on most issues, and I think that we each are trying to influence the other's point of view. Though we frequently raise our voices, everything is conducted in a respectful manner, and we always part amicably—probably because we are both convinced that eventually the other will see the light.

Two days ago, I went to Friday (the Islamic holy day) lunch at Bahaa's home. It was a very nice and hospitable gesture, even if his parents might have just wanted to check out the American who has been spending so much time with their son. I was excited to meet Bahaa's family and to enjoy some homemade food. When I arrived at the family's apartment with some sweets, Bahaa introduced me to his father and mother (Abu Alaa and Um Alaa), one of his two brothers, and four cousins who live with them, too. Two of the cousins are from the West Bank. One is in his final year of high school, and the other is in his first year at Jordan University. Due to the *intifada* and Israeli curfews and closures, it is better for them to go to school in Jordan. The other two cousins are younger and from the Gulf. They live with Bahaa's family because their parents consider the schools in the Gulf to be second-rate. I didn't see the whole apartment, but there could not have been more than three bedrooms, and there was only one bathroom.

After introductions, we gathered in the sitting room, furnished with wall-to-wall chairs and couches, where I talked with Abu Alaa, Bahaa, his brother, and a cousin about politics. Actually, it was mostly Abu Alaa asking questions about U.S. policy, Iraq, Israel, and September 11, with me trying to answer and the peanut gallery watching like line judges at a tennis match. Bahaa sat quietly and smiled. We go through the same routine every time we meet, and this was like my oral exam. It turned out to be really just a warm-up session—the main event was still to come. After the forty-five minute warm-up, lunch was served.

Um Alaa had prepared a Palestinian dish called *musakhan*, spiced chicken and chopped onions wrapped in thin, round flat-shaped bread soaked and covered in more spices and toasted pine nuts. She served it with broken-wheat soup and homemade *lebneh*, or yogurt. She was worried, though, that I would be a picky gringo and had also prepared chicken cacciatore in case I didn't like the musakhan.

We all gathered in the living room, where the long coffee table had been wrapped in plastic wrap. I was assigned a place of honor next to Abu Alaa, and we ate and ate; the food was delicious. Um Alaa, who wore her head covered since I was in the house, only joined us later. There wasn't a lot of talking, and I certainly didn't say much as I was busy trying to work my way through double portions. Everyone finished before me, including Bahaa's cousin, who I watched eat at least four pieces of musakhan and handful after handful of chicken cacciatore. Despite my best efforts, I was left with a pile of food and everyone watching me eat. At one point, I think that I fell asleep and awoke with more food on my plate.

Eventually I had to enter into a high-level negotiation with Um Alaa about what I would eat and what I could not. It was eerily similar to visiting my grandmother in Queens. Over the years, I've learned that an immediate and unwavering "No" to any offer of food that you don't actively want is critical to being able to walk away from the table. Any hesitation and that piece of meat ends up on your plate, and you aren't going anywhere until it is gone.

After lunch, I waddled back into the sitting room and engaged in the main event: a three-and-a-half-hour conversation with Abu Alaa over coffee and sweets. The topics: politics, the history of the region, and the meaning of life. We started out with everyone present for coffee and sweets. After an hour and a half, though, it was just me and Abu Alaa—two armchair quarterback warriors locked in a room indefinitely, with me not knowing when it would be polite to take my leave, and him, a generous host, accommodating me for as long as I could take it. After thirty minutes, the younger cousins had gone off to watch TV. Fifteen minutes later, the older ones and Bahaa's brother had gone to study and Um Alaa left to visit friends. She came back two hours later and was visibly surprised that I was still there. After an hour, Bahaa left—these topics were familiar turf for him. Between talking on the phone and studying, he darted in and out over the next two and a half hours to make sure his father and I were both still alive.

Most, if not all, of this conversation was in Arabic and was similar to my regular discourse with Bahaa. The apple doesn't fall far from the tree. The topics and arguments weren't that different, either, from what I get at the Nef, the university, or in my wanderings around Amman. Abu Alaa began with what is considered here the primary lesson of the Cold War: Military balance equals deterrence. If two sides are both armed to the teeth, they won't attack each other. In poli-sci classes, this is called mutual assured destruction.

Abu Alaa and others here are convinced that a "just peace" between Israelis and Palestinians is only possible when the Palestinians have an army and tanks. Only through military might will they be able to deter Israeli attacks. Until there is such a Palestinian army, suicide bombings are justified as the only Palestinian counter to Israeli aggression. From this perspective, Hamas suicide bombings are legitimate resistance. Abu Alaa asked rhetorically why Israel doesn't attack Iraq and Saddam, who, incidentally, is admired by many Palestinians as a genuine patron of the Palestinian people in comparison to other Arab leaders. He answered his own question by telling me that Iraqi weapons of mass destruction are a deterrent to Israeli weapons and attacks. Want further proof of this military lesson, he asked me, well, look no farther than the India-Pakistan standoff. What could be better than two nuclear states knowing that any attack assures its own destruction? What seemed to be omitted was another key lesson of the Cold War: The Soviets lost because they couldn't afford to spend all of their money on defense. Domestically, it wasn't sustainable. People had to eat; spending money on teaching kids to read is nice, too.

On the topic of lessons, Abu Alaa next repeated the often-heard argument that force works, citing Algeria and Vietnam as examples. According to conventional wisdom in this neck of the woods, the foreign occupier (the French in both cases, as well as the United States in Vietnam) was driven from the land by a weaker indigenous group through guerrilla warfare and terror. In the context of the

Middle East, such force, applied indefinitely, will eventually bring Israelis to their knees. I've heard many people here credit Hizballah's guerrilla war and terror campaign for Israel's decision to withdraw from southern Lebanon. The concept of what Israeli submission on Palestinian issues means, however, can differ. To some people it means a return to 1967 borders, to others the "full return" of Jews to Europe, Yemen, North Africa, and other sources of immigration. This would match a "full return" for all Palestinian refugees to mandatory Palestine. Of course, this lesson doesn't take into account that Israelis have nowhere to go "home" to, and unlike the French or Americans, they live on the same land as those they fight.

In an argument related to Israeli origins and places to go, Abu Alaa gave voice to the contention—espoused by Yasser Arafat during the Camp David II negotiations in 2000—that Jewish or Israeli ties to Palestinian land are contrived. There is a widespread lack of recognition for Jewish ties to the land, Israel's accomplishments as a state, and Israelis' accomplishments as individuals. Archaeological remains pointing to the existence of Jewish civilization are dismissed as having been planted by the Israeli government. Israeli homes and farms are Palestinian homes and farms that were stolen. Today, if you don't answer your door in three seconds, the Israel Defense Forces (IDF) will shoot it open. The legitimacy and recognition that Israel receives as a state are a result of creating facts on the ground with military force; they are not due to a historic Jewish place or presence in the Holy Land.

At one point in the conversation, Abu Alaa explained to me that politics in the Middle East are like shifting sands in the desert. He gave voice to a feeling of powerlessness when he told me that "you can wake up one day and everything has changed." At the end of World War I, the French and British redrew the region's boundaries, ignoring ethnic and religious differences and setting up their own spheres of influence. After World War II, the United Nations redrew the lines of Palestine and recognized Israel as a state. In 1967, Egyptians, Jordanians, and Syrians found that war with Israel had dramatically shifted the boundaries of their states. And in 1990, Abu Alaa awoke one morning in Kuwait and the Iraqis told him that he now lived in the nineteenth province of Iraq and that he should put an Iraqi license plate on his car, so he did.

Foreign powers and authoritarian regimes dictate the terms of life in the region. Abu Alaa believes that the best one can do is to adjust to the pressure and carve out personal space at home. A belief in God and acceptance of fate becomes much more relevant when one has the perception of going through life as the pawn of powerful forces that don't necessarily act justly.

It's also easy to understand why no one here supports confrontation with Iraq. What positive benefits will someone like Abu Alaa and his family gain from military adventurism? On a personal level, lives may be thrown into shambles, if not destroyed, and on a collective level, land is lost and innocents will be subjected to death and destruction for the sake of grandiose ideas that in the end have little meaning in relation to the ebbs and flows of daily life.

Abu Alaa's sense of powerlessness was matched by his penchant for conspiracy theories. Not just in this conversation, but in many other discussions, I've come to understand that there is a passion for and an adherence to conspiracy theories here. Circumstantial evidence, rumors, and doubts are given almost equal credence to fact. A jury would never be able to convict because there is always reasonable doubt. If I were inundated with the front-page whitewash that passes for news in most Arab newspapers—detailing the minutia of the doings of the royal family or the president's family, depending upon the country—maybe I, too, would become extremely skeptical of everything.

The problem that I face, though, in my marathon discussions with the conspiracy theorists, is that it is very difficult to come to agreement on anything when there isn't common ground in the form of a basic set of facts that serves as a point of mutual departure. Abu Alaa gave voice to the most galling conspiracy theory, which is repeated often: that the Arab brain is not capable of executing something like the September 11 attacks. They were perpetrated by the Israeli Mossad. If this is the starting point of a discussion, how can one ever intelligently discuss the U.S. rationale for the war in Afghanistan?

One of the threads of many of the conspiracy theories here is that everything returns to "Palestine." For Abu Alaa, like so many others who I've debated, the problems of the world all stem from the Palestinian issue. Injustice in "Palestine" is a cancer that affects everyone. Particularly in the Arab East, the Palestinian issue serves as an excuse, and Israel is used as a scapegoat for all problems. Dictators remain in power and use Israel and the Palestinian struggle as reasons for the necessity of military states and emergency laws. The West created Israel, and the resulting Palestinian problem, to divide the Arabs and the contiguity of the Arab Nation.

When I asked Abu Alaa what word he thought of when I said "America," his answer was Palestinian. He said, "Israel, Sharon."

There is a lot of hot air blown around related to the Palestinian struggle in the Arab East. However, here in Amman and in Abu Alaa's salon, due to geography and demography, where something like 60 percent of the people in Jordan are either Palestinian or of Palestinian descent, there is a genuine popular sentiment regarding this issue. This sentiment doesn't translate into anything more than angry and victimized talk, but still, people here have an emotional connection to Palestinian issues that I found lacking in both Syria and Egypt.

As late-afternoon shadows streamed into the windows of the salon, our conversation reached a "moment." We had passed the three-hour marker. The coffee was finished and the sweets had been eaten. Um Alaa had left and come back. Bahaa wore a confused and concerned look on his face as he poked his head into the room intermittently. The opposite of the four-minute mile, I was going to break the four-hour conversation mark. We'd covered contemporary Middle Eastern politics and the last hundred years, too. We were either going to go back to biblical times or to a higher and holier level. Abu Alaa tilted his head back, as if to get a better, more complete look at me. He lifted an eyebrow and asked, "Why are you here?"

It's very possible that he was really asking me, "Why are you here in Jordan?" or even "Why are you still here in my home?" Remember that I'm not yet an Arabic Jedi master, really much more like Luke when he gets beaten up by the sand people in *Star Wars* and Obi-Wan saves him. So, I might not have understood the context, but I'm pretty sure that he meant, "Why are you here on earth; what is your purpose?"

I thought about it for a minute and said, "To make the world a better place."

He paused, looked at me again in an appraising way, and asked, "What gives you the right to decide what 'better' is? How will you make that judgment?"

Given Abu Alaa's perception of powerlessness and the shifting sands of the Middle East, this response was humbling but not surprising. Sometimes I forget how activist we are by nature in America. Our ancestors were doers, not observers. At some point in time, they demanded some kind of life improvement, undertook hardship, and made the choice for change based on the belief that they could create something better. They left their home country and came to America to start anew. This may be one of the biggest cultural differences between Americans and others. Here, for instance, change is not perceived with the same kind of optimism or in such positive light. Further, due to the nature of the history of foreign interventions in the Middle East, change that is brought about by outsiders is perceived even more negatively.

Kholood, Ammo, and Bahaa.

Here, any change, not just those induced from the outside, upsets the order and can easily be a gateway to new problems and instability. Tradition is so important here; people don't like to leave things to chance or the unknown. Jordanians and Palestinians marry into families; marriage isn't just between two individuals. Extensive relationships of trust are built upon foundations of a long-running history together. There is something very comforting about knowing exactly where someone is from and that they won't deviate from the accepted course, ruin things, or perhaps bring shame.

Stumped, all I could do was turn the question around on Abu Alaa and ask him why he was here. He told me that he was needed by his wife and his family. When he was no longer needed on this earth by anyone, he would die.

Our time was up. All that needed to be said had been said, and I was no longer needed there. The next time Bahaa poked his head into the room, I excused myself and said that I really ought to be going.

Between the food, the Arabic, and the welcoming people, it was a wonderful experience. With the exception of the 9/11 conspiracies, I'm no longer shocked by the discourse. I hear the same points over and over and Bahaa, in fact, actually expresses many of these opinions on a regular basis. For that reason, I do wonder sometimes about helping him with his English. If some of his opinions remain the same, what kind of positions will he take when he is a leader and he can articulately express himself in different languages?

I always come back to the same thing on this question, though. First, I would guess that many of my friends and acquaintances here—especially Kholood, who surely must have some suspicions about me—ask themselves the same thing as they teach me Arabic. Yet they continue to do so and to expect the best. Second, I hope and believe that I am teaching Bahaa more than just how to communicate better in English. Every now and again, I win a point or a semi-concession in one of our political discussions, and I feel like it is a point with one of Jordan's future leaders.

Love,
Ben

Letter 9

Anti-Americanism: America Haters and the Assassination of Laurence Foley*

November 3, 2002

Dear All,

During my cab ride home Monday, my driver expressed to me how sick he was over the murder of Laurence Foley. He told me in Arabic that "no religion—Islam, Christianity, or Judaism—permitted such actions" and that a Jordanian could not have done this act. Laurence Foley was the U.S. Agency for International Development diplomat who was murdered here, outside of his home, on the morning of October 28. He was sixty years old and on his way to work.

---

*A version of this letter appeared as "The Assassination of Laurence Foley" in the October 30, 2002 edition of the *Pittsburgh Post-Gazette*. Other parts draw from my masters thesis, "Usama bin Ladin and al-Qa'ida: Origins and Doctrines," published in the *Middle East Review of International Affairs (MERIA) Journal*, Vol. 5, No. 4 (December 2001), pp. 54–68, and available at http://meria.idc.ac.il/journal/2001/issue4/orbach.pdf.

I was taking the cab home from a visit to the grade school for foreign students where Kholood teaches Arabic. Kholood had asked me to meet her students and to talk to them about the importance of learning Arabic. I had focused our discussion on the importance of language as a mechanism in bridging the gap of understanding between the Arab East and America. Whether or not a Jordanian is responsible for killing Laurence Foley, his tragic murder is a poignant reminder that this gap is growing at an increasingly dangerous rate for Americans and American interests.

Watching and reading the news, it is clear that "anti-Americanism" is a growing concern for Americans. No one wants to be hated, and I certainly understand the difficulty in coming to terms with what would drive people to attack us. Some U.S. leaders and government spokespersons say that we are hated because of our freedom, but the picture is really much more complicated. Anti-American sentiment is rampant from France to South Korea—where the people are also free—and has proven to be deadly in the Middle East, most recently here in Jordan.

Over the past few months, and especially in the past few days following Laurence Foley's murder, I've been thinking a lot about anti-Americanism and its roots. Since Monday, I've asked myself, how it can be that in Jordan—our closest Arab ally and the beneficiary of debt relief, a free trade agreement, and U.S. aid—an American diplomat was stalked and murdered outside his home? If it could happen here, then what can be expected in Afghanistan, Iraq, or other hostile countries of this region that attract or will attract American officials and civilians?

The answer is complicated, of course, but I've reached the conclusion that there are two main strands of anti-Americanism: There are *American policy critics* and *America haters*. It is important to make a distinction between them. Many people in Jordan fall into the first category; they like Americans but do not like the U.S. government's policies. Perfect examples are the REM cabbie I met on the way to the embassy in August, Fadi, and the university students who wear Duke T-shirts or USC sweatshirts beneath their silver map-of-Palestine necklaces which include all of Israel. These policy critics appreciate American culture, music, and entertainment, yet when the subject of the American government and U.S. foreign policy in the Middle East is discussed, they express only resentment and anger at America's policy choices.

When it comes to foreign policy, America is dismissed as a self-interested power. In addition to what is considered overly-biased support for Israel, many criticize present and past U.S. support for the Saudi royal family; Egypt's strongman, President Hosni Mubarak; Saddam Hussein; Osama bin Laden; Iran's former ruler, the Shah; and even the Jordanian king. At the same time, there is a wistful hope for an American intervention, but only on behalf of pan-Arab and/or Palestinian interests.

Though there might be an admiration for Saddam Hussein's support of the Palestinian people among Palestinians here, there is also a widespread recognition of his brutality and an accompanying sympathy for the suffering Iraqi people. However, people react incredulously when President Bush explains, as he did in his October 7 speech in Ohio, that action against Iraq was necessary because weapons of mass destruction are held by a "murderous tyrant" who "has tried to dominate the Middle East, has invaded and brutally occupied a small neighbor, [and] has struck other nations without warning. . . ." To the locals, such words do not bring to mind Saddam Hussein, but rather Ariel Sharon and Israel. People here are very sympathetic toward the suffering that family members face in the West Bank and Gaza and are angry with the U.S. government for the support provided to Israel.

Policy critics who fault the United States for our Iraq and Israel policies live under the same authoritarian rule and in close proximity to the America haters, the Islamist militants like bin Laden who make up the other strand of anti-American sentiment. Despite this geographic closeness between the two groups, the policy critics of the Arab East should not be confused with the America haters. The policy critics here are more similar to the policy critics that have sprung up all over the world today. Whether as related to Iraq or the Kyoto Agreement, some of our policy choices have raised "anti-American" sentiment in places such as Mexico and Turkey that historically have had close relationships with the United States. Mexicans and Turks, like the policy critics in the Arab East, don't hate our freedom. Vice President Cheney raised eyebrows all over the world when he said that conservation may be a sign of "personal virtue, but it is not a sufficient basis for a sound, comprehensive energy policy." The governments of Mexico, Turkey, South Korea, and other countries have real foreign policy interests—whether related to the environment or their national security—that our government's actions are not helping them to achieve.

Compounding the real policy differences that feed this stream of anti-Americanism is the patronizing tone that sometimes marks the words of the Bush administration's major figures. While tone may not be as important as the substance of these disagreements, it does matter, especially in the Arab East, where the United States is unlikely to make policy adjustments on the big issues in the region. Tone, in contrast to policy, is something that we can improve rather easily. Publicly explaining and debating our positions, in detail, is worth the effort. Engaging in discussions and listening are universal signs of respect.

It is important to demonstrate that we respect the concerns of our traditional allies and our friends of convenience, who have become American policy critics, for a number of reasons. At a very minimum, our world is connected economically. We can't continue to live at such a high standard without international trade—the export of manufactured, technology, and farm products and the import of so many goods, not the least of which is oil. We are also increasingly connected socially to the rest of the world, not just because we are an immigrant-rooted society, but because of the cultural impact of globalization, and in particular the boom in the importance of the Internet. Our worlds are more connected than ever before, and our fates are intertwined, regardless of how we'd have it. Most important, though, is that our personal security is linked, too, and we need the American policy critics as allies to defeat that other branch of anti-Americanism: the America haters.

America haters murdered Laurence Foley. Foley wasn't personally targeted because of our position on the International Criminal

Court or the Kyoto Agreement, or the more local issues of disagreement on whether the United States should go to war with Iraq or sell arms to Israel—though some of those positions likely contributed to the reasons Foley's murderers decided to join a terrorist organization. The people who murdered Foley are of the same ilk as the people who planned and attacked the World Trade Center, viciously killed journalist Daniel Pearl in Pakistan, and bombed the U.S. embassies in Kenya and Tanzania.

At their core, America haters, such as the people who committed these crimes, are nihilists. They gain status and self-worth from the destruction of others. Disagreements over policy have contributed to their disaffection and hatred, but these are men who have chosen this path in life for more complicated reasons. Mainly, their honor has been permanently insulted as a result of some real or perceived injustice. With feelings of frustrated shame, they became zealous militants and crossed the line from engaging in debate over policy grievances to using violent terror to try and achieve their objectives as well as to gain retribution for their suffering state of injustice.

Since the September 11 attacks, Osama bin Laden has become the face of the America haters. Bin Laden, Al Qaeda, and the other Islamist *jihadis* (holy warriors) claim to struggle for a monolithic Islamic state that will stretch across the Muslim world and be ruled by a caliph under sharia. They seek to overthrow the region's regimes, which they consider heretic, corrupt, and thieving. Of particular ire to bin Laden and his kind are the Saudi royal family, who claim to be the guardians of the Islamic holy places, Mecca and Medina. Because many of Al Qaeda's leaders also come from Egypt and were brutally suppressed by a regime they consider to be an American lackey, Egyptian President Mubarak and his government are high on the list of targets as well.

The United States, in turn, is reviled by these terrorists as the supporter and backer of these and other regimes, the power that keeps them afloat. America is further hated for waging war worldwide against Muslims, murdering and humiliating them. Most offensive to bin Laden and his followers, though, is the U.S. military presence in Saudi Arabia, which they consider a foreign occupation of the two holy places of Islam. The haters seek a U.S. withdrawal from the region; they offer no possible compromises. To them, their struggle is clear—they have divided the world into two: the abode of Islam and the abode of War.

On paper, the idea of overthrowing oppressive regimes is nothing new. It is a concept that has always been a part of politics and government. What is different about bin Laden and the flock of America-hating jihadis is the combination of their extreme demands with their organized destructiveness and their proven capacity to employ modern technology—which grants them disproportionate influence and power. In addition, they don't just attack the specific target of their rage, but they are content to destroy innocents and bystanders as well. In a February 1998 *fatwa*, or religious decree, bin Laden declared that any Muslim wishing the rewards of God must "kill the Americans and plunder their money wherever and whenever they find it." Later that year, he reiterated the inclusion of American civilians as targets for jihad. He stated that, if the American "people do not wish to be harmed inside their very own countries, they should seek to elect governments that are truly representative of them that can protect their interests." He continued, "Any American who pays taxes to his government is our target because he is helping the American war machine against the Muslim nation."

As I mentioned, a certain type of individual is drawn to such an ideology. Political psychologist Dr. Jerrold Post, an international expert on the psychology of terrorists (with whom I took a class when I was in graduate school), argues convincingly that people are drawn to political violence not purely as a way of expressing their ideology, but also as an end in itself—owing to certain personal and psychological characteristics that they possess. Post's contention is that "individuals become terrorists in order to join terrorist groups and commit acts of terrorism." Post's theory is that the "cause is not the cause." Rather, fighting provides these individuals with an identity, a group that functions as a community, perhaps a respected leadership position within that group, and a set of ideas that gives them a purpose in life.

This view could easily apply to bin Laden and other haters. Common trends become clear whether you're looking at bin Laden's background, that of the 9/11 killers, or some of the others who have undertaken or attempted attacks over the last few years. Many of the haters who have come to infamous prominence over the last few years are a combination of disgruntled drifters, culturally insulted young men, and societal failures unable to carve out places of honor and success for themselves. Bin Laden himself was one of many children; his wealthy father died when he was young, and he was reportedly a Beirut playboy in the early 1970s, drinking and getting into bar fights. His life lacked purpose until he went to Afghanistan to join the *mujahideen,* the Muslim holy warriors fighting the Soviet superpower. Not only could he define himself against a great enemy and gain a sense of importance, but he did constructive things: raising money, visiting wounded mujahideen, and building Afghan roads. For him and others, the Soviet-Afghan war and the triumph over a superpower was a watershed moment in Islamic solidarity and a personal turning point. Bin Laden may have left home a spoiled playboy, but he returned to Saudi Arabia as a self-perceived conquering hero because of his deeds and accomplishments in Afghanistan.

In the 1980s, thousands of militants traveled to Afghanistan to fight the Soviet superpower, the communist heretic that occupied an Islamic land. Many did not even know where Afghanistan was on a map, but they were galvanized by a chance to find an outlet for their anger at the conditions they faced at home and the possibility of an honorable escape from their empty and routine existence. They could become heroes: fighting and dying as martyrs, a fate that brings honor to one's family, forgiveness for one's sins, and an afterlife in paradise. As I wrote in my masters thesis, one young fighter, who came from a poor family of ten children in Yemen, described the training and fighting this way: "When you have a gun, you're free. You feel as if you can do anything."

Other haters we know of that have joined Al Qaeda fit similar profiles of lost souls looking for meaning in empty lives. There is Ahmed Ressam, the Algerian who attempted to cross the U.S.-Canadian border before New Year's 2000 in order to commit an attack. He was unable to hold a job, had attempted to join the Algerian military and police, and allegedly spent a lot of his free time watching Clint Eastwood movies. Nizar Trabelsi is another drifter turned America hater. He is a divorced, failed professional soccer player who became a petty criminal, cocaine addict, and heavy drinker before finding religion. He was caught planning to blow up the U.S. embassy in Paris.

Then there is Mohamed Atta, the Egyptian leader of the 9/11 attacks. He became a radical while living and studying in Germany. There are accounts of other 9/11 hijackers drinking alcohol, going to strip clubs, and playing video games in the days before the attack. Perhaps for Atta in Germany and for others in this group, the availability of opportunities to indulge in Western vices—activities that were both highly attractive and forbidden by their cultural background—led to a state of conflicted discomfort: a rejection of Western values but a simultaneous questioning of their own "home" values. After indulgence in what Iranian militants have called "Westoxification," these men may have engaged in self-loathing. And they may have grown determined to punish the system that lured them from the proper path and led them to face questions they were ill-prepared to answer. Professor Fouad Ajami (the department head of Middle East Studies at my graduate school), eloquently argues that Atta and others "were placed perilously close to modernity, but they could not partake of it."

Following this line of thinking, these haters become anti-modernization. They've realized that they can't compete in today's world, or they've decided that they won't compete. One way or another, they've been insulted and shamed—by the social conditions they grew up under, by ever-present feelings of subjugation from both foreign and domestic powers, by their lack of political rights and economic opportunities, or by exposure to the Western world, where a different set of opportunities is easily accessible for all. Ajami calls them "Nowhere Men." There is nowhere for them to go.

Rami Khouri, the leading English-language columnist in the Arab East, has written that these are men who go down into the basement. They descend from the quiet discontent of the "Arab

Street" to a place he has dubbed the "Arab Basement," where they make bombs and plot to attack the forces, near and far, that have driven them into the dark. In the context of today's ongoing discussion about anti-Americanism, these "Arab Basement" bomb-makers and "Nowhere Men" are America haters.

They harbor ill will toward Americans and view the U.S. government as the power that maintains the unsatisfactory status quo in which they, their families, and communities live. Haters only find meaning in their lives from attacking and killing their enemy, in what they believe is the path of God. Like bin Laden in Afghanistan, they perceive themselves as overcoming incredible odds to triumphantly change history.

On a practical level, they have tried but cannot defeat their regimes at home. So, they have taken to attacking the faraway enemy, the United States, the one that they have convinced themselves is the root of all their problems. In some ways, it is an easier path to take, especially if the scope of targets is broadened to include an unarmed older man outside of his home in the early morning—as they did with Laurence Foley.

Our policy options concerning the America haters are limited. We are at war with bin Laden and the haters, and we have to deal with them accordingly. At the same time, military options alone won't protect Americans and U.S. interests. There is no substitute for waging a complementary war against the root causes and conditions that transformed these disaffected drifters into basement bomb-makers. In particular, we need to address the lack of political and economic opportunities that characterize life in the Arab East for young people and for women. And this is where we need the American policy critics on our side.

There are a lot of development and assistance costs involved in combating the root causes of terror, and we need the the Arab East's American policy critics not only to share in this major endeavor, but really to lead or guide our efforts. We also need to cooperate with the policy critics on some very specific issues, like tracking terrorist financing and tightening border checks. It is impossible to succeed at doing these sorts of things alone. Yet, beyond these nuts-and-bolts sort of details, it is the American policy critics who have to affect the norms of their own societies and specifically make the act of joining a terrorist organization and seeking out opportunities to kill for God unacceptable. We can try to influence and offer support, but it is the leadership within the communities, villages, cities, and countries of the Arab East and the rest of the Muslim world who must convince potential haters that taking those fatal steps down into the "Arab Basement" is morally, socially, and even economically a mistake.

President Bush said, "You're either with us or against us in the fight against terror." We might feel that way, but such a public statement isn't helpful. Ironically, that is just how bin Laden has divided the world—into two. Not allowing for ambiguities, bin Laden defines Al Qaeda as the representative of Islam and America as crusaders bent on a religious war. For obvious reasons, the American policy critics here don't necessarily want to be *with* us. But they don't want to be with the terrorists, either. I'm sure the American policy critics recognize the haters for the damage that they are doing to their communities at a whole different level than we ever will. The haters would love for us to lump the Muslim world's American policy critics in with them, for the policy critics to have nowhere to turn, and for us to see the haters as representative of the masses. Our goal must be to isolate the haters, not to allow them to isolate us from our allies in this part of the world and in Western countries with similar security and economic concerns.

In the short term, we need to figure out what it will take to convince American policy critics that we are in this struggle together against the haters. Dignity and honor are so important in the Middle East, as they are, in truth, everywhere. We really need to do a better job of emphatically treating the American policy critics here with respect. If they see us as only insulting them, rather than consulting with them, we'll receive their cooperation only when it is convenient to their immediate concerns. U.S. citizens' safety at home and abroad is best served by maintaining alliances and relationships around the world. That means working toward including some of our allies' interests in our own goals and making an effort to explain all of our policy choices with greater nuance and respect to dissenting critics. Along these lines, improving our tone alone and engaging in public dialogue and debates, even if we consider them unnecessary or a waste of time, would appease some policy critics. It might also keep some drifters from taking that last step into the basement and becoming haters.

In contrast, shortchanging the concerns of allies, forgoing the diplomatic process, and not communicating with the world will lead to a situation of exacerbating anti-American tensions while overextending and isolating the U.S. military and diplomatic corps. If we don't show greater respect for our allies, we will likely fail to prevent further attacks on American citizens like those suffered by Laurence Foley, Daniel Pearl, and the victims of 9/11. Our actions and behavior will increase the number of American policy critics who remain silent in the safety of their homes, rather than increase the number of religious and secular leaders and citizens who, though they may still disagree with U.S. policies, may at least feel compelled to step out into their streets and foster an environment that rejects the haters. These leaders can't and won't come forward if they are going to be publicly labeled as being politically associated with America, and that tag carries connotations that are only negative.

So where does that leave me, a Pittsburgher alone in Amman? To be honest, I'm not very comfortable with the new, paranoid feeling that I have a bull's-eye on my back. For the past week, I've left my apartment at a different time each morning and have found three different ways to walk to Abdali station to catch the bus. I no longer take cabs to my apartment, instead hopping out a couple of blocks early. Worst of all, I've started lying about my nationality, telling random strangers that I'm Canadian, when they ask where I'm from.

The killing of Laurence Foley has reminded me of how I felt in Jerusalem in the winter of 1996, after the third suicide bombing in two weeks. Two of those bombs were a week apart and on the bus that I rode to downtown Jerusalem every day. I remember sitting in my kitchen, listening to the news on the radio, and trying to figure out why someone would blow up themselves and a bus full people. I worried about leaving the apartment and felt as if I was looking at everything outside my door for the first time, and with a lot of caution. I was terrorized.

There are similarities to how I feel now, but differences too. It scares me that Laurence Foley was targeted outside of his home and that he was stalked. All the people milling around here, the cabs that drive by my apartment and the workers down the street—how can I know whether someone is out there watching for me? In Jerusalem, everyone in Israel was in it together. The target was indiscriminate—on one of those buses, foreign workers from Eastern Europe were killed. Hamas suicide bombers couldn't care less about them. Here, though, I feel alone, and as if I am the target.

At the university this past week, I looked at people in a different way. I wondered how they felt down deep about what happened to Laurence Foley. I've noticed a cycle where there is initial sympathy for the victims of attacks such as this, and then the denials and the conspiracy theories come later. Frequently, in my never-ending string of conversations about international affairs, people will express regret over the September 11 attacks and disgust for the killing of innocent civilians. Later in the conversation, though, they mention that Americans should expect that sort of thing, given our policies and our attacks on Iraqi civilians and the Palestinian people.

The day after Foley's assassination, the *Jordan Times*, the semi-official daily newspaper, ran an editorial condemning the attack, and King Abdullah called the assassination an attack on Jordan itself. This kind of incident is a nightmare for Jordan, a real international embarrassment. The kingdom's dirty laundry was hung out for everyone to see. Jordan lives off of foreign aid, its reputation in the West, and the security it guarantees within its borders, whether as an investment environment or as a tourist destination. So at least I know that the Jordanian government will do anything, absolutely anything, to prevent something like this from happening again.

And how do I feel living abroad at a time when anti-Americanism is in vogue? Because almost everyone I know is an American policy critic, it does hurt to see that we've gone from hero to villain in the world's eyes. Sixty years ago, my mom's father and uncles fought in

Europe and the Pacific to save the world from fascism. The United States rebuilt Europe; we offered powerful ideas, innovation, and hope. Today, we come across as a bully.

All along, I've hated lying about my religion, and it's become worse now that I lie about my nationality to the random person in the street. Yesterday, I was watching an al Jazeera program that showed dramatic American moments from the 1960s onward. From my perspective, the show was a highlight reel of American culture. Images of Muhammad Ali streamed across the screen: There was Ali, the conscientious objector, at a press conference, and Ali, the champion, winning his title back from George Foreman. In a lot of ways, Ali is everything that is great about America—a powerful champion with principles. The clips rolled on: the American hostages coming home from Iran, and Martin Luther King Jr. on the steps of the Lincoln Memorial, shaking his head and declaring, "Free at last, free at last."

I got choked up. I couldn't help it. Maybe it's related to my recent feeling of being under siege, but the swirl of emotions came from a sense of patriotism and an equal sense that things aren't right. Ali, MLK, and the perseverance of those poor hostages—each sent a rush of pride through me. But I also felt like I was watching clips of history—it felt far away. Given the day-to-day resentment that I sense from American policy critics, and these sudden violent flashes of hatred from the America haters, I worry about how many great moments we have left as a world leader. It is a frustrating and empty feeling.

That's probably enough for now. Thanks for the e-mails of concern. I'm okay, just shaken a bit. I'm doing my best to stay safe.

Love,
Ben

Letter

10

Fasting Without Feasting*

December 7, 2002

Dear All,

Two nights ago, I stood on my roof at dusk, looked out onto the city and the scattered and blinking decorations that stood out against the purples of the sky, and listened to the call to prayer. The month of Ramadan was over, and the celebrations of Eid al-Fitr could begin.

Muslims believe that it was during the month of Ramadan that God first revealed the religion of Islam to Muhammad. This was the first of a series of revelations that were later recorded in the Koran, Islam's holy book. Observing Ramadan is one of the five pillars of Islam. The other pillars are confession of faith, that there is no God but God and that Muhammad is God's messenger; prayer five times a day; charity to the poor; and completing the *hajj*, or pilgrimage to Mecca, once in a lifetime.

---

*A version of this letter appeared as an essay in the *San Francisco Examiner* on December 27, 2002.

147

As I listened to the overlapping calls to prayer from mosques that were further away, interrupted by an occasional cheap fire-cracker, I felt part of a moment. A whole city, a whole country, and more or less a whole region were celebrating their faith together at the end of a month of heightened religious observance and daylong fasting, from predawn darkness to sunset. It was heartwarming. Had I observed Ramadan like the unknown majority here, perhaps I would have felt a similar feeling of ownership from the inside, rather than relief that the month-long observance was over.

In the days leading up to Ramadan, I was excited about the forthcoming holiday. In fact, Ramadan was one of the things that I had most looked forward to in my year here. In my Arabic classes in the United States, we read texts and watched videos about how Ramadan is celebrated around the Middle East—visits to family and friends, late nights at coffee shops, and feasting on special sweets and inordinate amounts of other foods. It seemed great: not quite Mardi Gras, but really cool. And for me, it was cool, for about a week.

Before the start of the holiday, I thought that I wanted to partici-pate in the full—well, almost full—Ramadan experience. I wasn't going to wake up at 4:00 A.M. for breakfast, but after a big meal at the more reasonable hour of 7:00 A.M., I fasted all day like everyone around me. I left my water bottle at home, skipped lunch and my afternoon coffee, and did my best impersonation of whatever every-one else was doing. I was excited, like the freshmen from Florida who I met my first year at Michigan, who were thrilled by their first winter, before they realized how cold it got. The Ramadan mood was fresh around me; everyone wished each other well, at the university and in my neighborhood. Except for the fact that I was always thirsty, it was great. By observing Ramadan, I was part of something that everyone else was doing—a feeling that hasn't come so easily for me thus far. My teachers, cabbies, and neighbors would ask me if I was fasting, and I would delight them with my affirmative answer.

Slowly, though, I began to realize that I was not truly a part of what was going on and that Ramadan was taking a toll on my every-day life. Bahaa couldn't meet anymore because he was too busy at night eating with his family. The professor completely abandoned me. I'd show up at his office at one o'clock, as planned, to dish out some English punishment, and he wouldn't be there. I'd call his cell and he'd explain that he was at home, offer a dramatic pause, and say that it was "Ramadan." After he missed three appointments in a row, I stopped bothering him.

The reading room in the library turned into a morgue in the afternoon. I started going home from school earlier so that I could be poised to break the fast as well. But I realized that I was spending an extra half-hour to hour in traffic jams every day between 1:15 and 4:00 P.M. Everyone else in Amman was on their way home for *iftar* (breaking the fast), too, and they were honking their horns along the way. At the same time, people were constantly yelling at each other and me. They missed their cigarettes and coffee. Traffic would just stop in places, and people would yell and yell at each other, sometimes getting out of their cars, which caused even more horn honking. The horn honking would go on and on, a deafening expression of a frustrated rage. Everyone was hungry. Then, after four o'clock, it was like someone hit the mute button: People disappeared, and it became impossible to get anywhere.

To demonstrate, a Ramadan tale:

At the end of the first week of Ramadan, I was heading home from Kholood's house at about 4:10 P.M. My private lessons with her remain a constant in my schedule. Generally, we read the paper together and talk about the articles. I also practice interviewing her on different subjects, and sometimes we do translation, too. Anyway, the usual process of getting home is a five-minute walk to the shared cab station, a ten-minute shared cab to the Ghagadan bus station, a ten-minute walk through downtown to another shared cab station, another ten-minute ride to my neighborhood, and a final five-minute walk home.

This night, though, five shared cabs flew by me without stopping, their drivers in a hungered frenzy to go somewhere else. When one finally did stop, I asked the driver if he was going to the bus station, and he unloaded on me for asking stupid questions. A shared cab's destination is written on the side of its front doors, but

I like to ask. In addition to the Arabic practice, it is good to confirm the destination. This is not a habit developed out of paranoia, but rather experience. Too many times, I've just jumped in, hoped for the best, and fifteen minutes later been told to get out in a place I'd never seen before because it was the end of the line. When I got into this shared cab and closed the door, the driver yelled at me again, this time for slamming the door. I told myself that it wasn't personal; he was hungry.

The driver flew through narrow alleys, and I gripped my seat, thanking God that everyone else was already at home waiting to eat, rather than out on the street. Six minutes later, the runaway train deposited me at Ghagadan, and I stood alone at the deserted bus station. Ghagadan is at least three times the size of the Abdali station. It was eerie to be there with a couple of cars, a handful of people, and no buses. I hurried through downtown, my stomach growling, passing shops that were either shuttered or abandoned. I imagined that I was a character in Stephen King's *The Stand* after a super virus kills 99.4 percent of the population. An iron sat out in a tailor's window and clothes swung on hangers in a soft wind. The one exception to this apocalyptic scene were the humus and falafel joints where single men, some pretty poor looking, sat hunched over dishes of food, waiting for the call to prayer so that they could eat.

I made it to the shared taxi stop, fully aware that I too was really hungry. The way the shared taxis work is that four to five people pile into a taxi at a designated starting point and get off at different spots along the route. As people get out, others waiting along the way can get in. Some of these shared taxis are bigger sedans with bench seating that can reasonably accommodate so many people. Many of the taxis, though, have bucket seats, meaning that two people have to share the passenger seat in an awkward manner. A lot of the time, it is two women scrunched together in front so they won't have to sit in the back with men. Several times, though, I've had to squeeze my six-foot-two frame into the passenger's seat with another man. It's a far cry from the thrill of riding "shotgun" in high school. Instead, it is an experience of sitting partially on the gear knob while the driver shifts up and down, navigating Amman's hilly landscape.

To get out of the shared cab, it is customary to say to the driver, *"Allah ya'atik al-afya,"* or "May God give you strength." I only learned this expression a couple of weeks ago from Bahaa. Until then, I'd been saying *"Bidee anzil,"* which literally means "I'd like to get out or descend." Bahaa explained to me, between gales of laughter and snorting Pepsi out of his nose, that I was basically demanding from the driver to be let out of the cab *now*! Well, at least they think I'm Canadian and not American.

Back to my Ramadan tale, I arrived at the shared taxi stand at two minutes to iftar. As a result, everyone with a family was already at home and poised over their food, waiting for the call to prayer to ring out so that they could chow down. This left me alone with the driver of the first taxi in line. As the call to prayer blasted through downtown, he started yelling at me to buy the whole cab and to pay the fare for five spots so that we could go. The shared taxis will only depart if they are full. I refused on principle to be extorted, grew more annoyed and hungry, and stalked off to find a regular cab—

Downtown Amman.

which would be about twenty cents cheaper than paying the fare for the full shared cab.

Finding a cab was no simple task since downtown Amman was a ghost town short of the tumbleweeds blowing past the saloon doors. Well, in this case, I really do have a friend in Jesus, because I found a Christian cabbie. He dropped me at home, famished. I went up the steps and found an empty apartment with no iftar. This was disappointing, but not really a surprise since I live alone and did not marry either of the Turkish girls that I met in Istanbul—a questionable decision in retrospect.

I'm not sure that I'm the only one feeling like an outsider these days. Hazim is another friend of mine here, a Palestinian-Jordanian who went to Johns Hopkins for his undergraduate degree and moved back home after graduation to work in his father's construction business. He is the friend of a friend from graduate school, and he has greatly improved my quality of life in Amman over the past two months. Hazim has some sort of hospitality gene running through his body. He's gone out of his way to introduce me to a number of his friends, taken me out to different clubs on Thursday nights, and invited me to play basketball at the American high school with other friends and a handful of expats for a twice-a-week hoops game that is by invitation only.

It's been great to play ball again, and there are usually pretty decent games, except they play zone defense here as the rule, a departure from the man-to-man we play at home. With the start of Ramadan, though, the games have gone from five-on-five with anywhere from two to seven people waiting to play next, to a handful of Christians struggling for enough people to play three-on-three. All the Muslim players are at home with their families breaking their fast. Once they've eaten so much, they don't feel like coming out to play. Instead, they go out with friends or family to restaurants or coffee shops to eat some sweets, smoke a hookah, and play cards.

So, as quickly as it came, basketball has now slipped away. Hazim has taken me out a few times with his friends Ramis, Rasha, Kindi, and Bouran to play cards and to smoke a hookah. Kindi went to Purdue as an undergraduate and Bouran studied at Georgetown.

Hazim, who is Greek Orthodox, just seems miserable, though. All the clubs have closed because of Ramadan, restaurants only open at night, basketball is a no-go, and to top it off, he hates playing cards—the Ramadan evening pastime. Although I've speculated about the feelings of Christians here in the past, I can only guess what it must be like for him and others. For me, Ramadan is a novelty event, a change in the usual schedule. For Arab Christians, this is a yearly event that turns their worlds upside down. All of society is observing the holiday, and everyone, regardless of faith, is expected to respect the revised social norms. Even the worst sport can grin and bear it for a week, but for a month? It can become tiresome.

So, after a few more days of coming home hungry to no hot dinner, being stuck in traffic jams, and getting yelled at, I decided that Ramadan was not for me. I went to *Ras al Shaytan*, or Devil's Head, a primitive beach in the Sinai Peninsula in Egypt where Ramadan is not in effect. I stayed in a bamboo hut, listened to some locals play the drums, and swam in the Red Sea. I found some Israeli tourists to play backgammon with, and I celebrated my own favorite holiday, Thanksgiving.

If I were living with a family, or if I were Muslim, I think I would really like Ramadan. The whole work schedule changes, Muslims go home for a siesta in the middle of the day, eat a delicious meal with their family every evening, and at night hang out with friends, smoke a hookah, and play cards. And in the morning, there is no expectation of any work getting done. What's better than that? There is a feeling of communal participation in something together. And it's not just here, but across the whole region. There is a steady stream of Ramadan programming on TV, with the details of how Ramadan is celebrated in neighboring countries like Syria and Lebanon. For me, though, fasting with everyone, coming home to prepare my own iftar, and then breaking the fast alone was a letdown. Despite best efforts, I felt like an outsider.

There are a lot of good things that I did get to experience piecemeal, though. For example, I went to Kholood's house for iftar one night, which was super. We broke the fast with dates, a traditional practice; had huge portions of *maqlubeh*, a Palestinian chicken, rice, raisin, sumac, and almond dish; ate fantastic homemade sweets like *qatayaf*, stuffed pancakes with cheese or nuts; and watched people pray on TV in Mecca. As funny as that might sound, it was a beautiful sight: people from every country and of every skin color lining up in endless rows and praying together.

The times I was invited to share in a family's iftar, it felt wonderful, like I was a part of a community. But these were just a handful of incidents in a month of tiptoeing around other people's revised schedules, making early trips home from the university to eat lunch behind curtains pulled tight, sitting in frustrating traffic jams, and dealing with the rampant bad breath that results from fasting all day. I had more in common with the Christians and Ramadan cheaters smoking in the bathroom than I did with the majority at large.

I don't want to discount the sense of sharing that Muslim Jordanians extended to me and to others, including the poor. But I was mostly left feeling the limitations of the holiday as an outsider. I wonder what Thanksgiving in America is like for new immigrants. As the end of the month neared, I picked up random comments from friends and teachers that led me to believe that Ramadan fatigue sets in for others, too. I am guessing that many others are happy to return to their routines, cigarettes, and coffee.

More to come soon. Hope everyone is well.

Love,
Ben

Letter 11

Anti-Americanism:
American Policy Critics and
a Night at the Club

December 27, 2002

Dear All,

Dressed in a navy turtleneck, my brown faux-suede Syrian coat, and a pair of Old Navy jeans, I exited the cab and approached the crowd. It was 11:30 on a Thursday night—the big weekend night in Amman since everyone has Friday off—and the sign in front of the velvet ropes read, "Couples Only." A line of twenty Jordanians wearing New York clubbing clothes stood before me. The men wore leather coats, dark pants, and dark shirts, while their lady friends were dressed in colorful tight outfits. Purple-jacketed attendants zipped about, parking BMWs and Lexus Jeeps.

Nai (rhymes with "fly") is the place to be for Amman's young and well-off elites. Unlike Amman's few expat bars that are frequented by foreign students, peace corps volunteers, and Western professionals, Nai is all about status. If Nai were located in New York, it would be one of those places where the doorman doesn't look at you unless you are with a lady. Despite being American, the equivalent of a gold card in five-star Jordan, I would have had no chance of getting into Nai at this time of night if I wasn't meeting Ramis, a Jordanian friend and a club regular.

That night, I noticed that something was amiss since the maître d' was not outside and the heavy wooden door, which looked to be lifted from the Giant's castle in *Jack and the Beanstalk*, was shut. The line was pushing forward, and two people at the front pounded furiously against the massive door, demanding to be let in so that they could start having fun. My superpowers of American citizenship were going to be useless under such circumstances. With my cell phone, I called up Ramis, who was already inside, to see what he could do.

I might be one of the last anti-cell-phone Americans around. I don't really like talking on the phone to begin with, so I find the idea of being accessible all the time unsettling. I reluctantly bought a used cell phone in Jordan only because the apartment that I shared with Fadi did not have a phone line. Beyond this sort of necessity, cell phones are an important accessory in Jordan. At restaurants, people park their cell phones in front of them on the table and wait for text messages and phone calls. Rarely is there a sense of frustrated interruption when it chimes or rings. For many, such an "interruption" is more like a welcome invitation to a new social opportunity. Grudgingly, I admit that this night at Nai was one of the times that a cell phone came in handy. In fact, I can see the commercial now: "Fastlink: Never wait in line at Nai again! Call your *wasta* right now!" "Wasta" is the term for a go-between or connection. Usually a wasta is someone with authority who you bribe for a favor or for access.

After exchanging pleasantries with Ramis, I told him that I was waiting outside. Within three minutes, the big wooden door opened up and a doorman, a guy built like a stuntman from a documentary about fraternity life at Ohio State, pushed the angry couple back. Ramis stepped forward with the black-suited maître d' whose gelled hair is a carbon copy of former Lakers coach Pat Riley's slicked-back style. Searching through the crowd, Ramis pointed me out, and the maitre d' —whom Ramis tips handsomely—beckoned me forward.

Like the Red Sea, the line parted down the middle. Young Jordanians whose shoes cost more than everything I wore and who had arrived in Beemers and SUVs stepped aside so that the American from Pittsburgh could enter the club. They weren't angry, though, because those are the rules here. The rules aren't "first come, first served," not everyone is equal. Seeing the doors open for a VIP was just more evidence that the destination was worth the wait. It even seemed as if some of them hoped that I might take them with me. For all they knew, I was Ben Affleck. Now, if they had known that I was really Ben Orbach, a falafel-eating, bus-riding graduate student who listened to Steelers' games on the Internet, then they might have been upset. Such knowledge would have muddled their assessment of how the "meritocracy" works.

Ignoring the surging line behind me, Ramis and I greeted each other at the doorway. Keeping the outside world beyond the giant door, we descended the steps into the den of Amman's ketchup eaters. Ramis told me that the door was shut because there had been a fight earlier—a rare and exciting event. Due to the fight, the club was less crowded than usual, but still full. We made our way over to a long coffee table surrounded by couches and chairs, where Ramis's wife, brother, and some other friends sat. I exchanged kisses with everyone and settled into a cushy sofa next to Ramis.

Nai's two-tiered main room lay before me. In the club's upper level, decorated in an exotic Eastern style with gold-trimmed chairs and couches covered in maroon velvet, groups sat, ate, and danced around similar tables. In the lower level, just a few steps away, more of the young and the beautiful danced, drank, and worked the room between the wooden and brass bar, the small dance floor, and a thumping deejay booth shielded by transparent flowing white curtains. Despite the fact that at least 80 percent of the clientele were Arab, it was Arabic-peppered English that resonated throughout the room. There was added excitement because of the time of year (Christmas vacation) and the night's "homecoming" feel. Almost everyone there had some connection to the West, and many of the night's clubbers were home on vacation and catching up with friends.

Ensconced in that maroon couch and facing the crowded room, I got a better sense for how Amman's young and wealthy dressed. Some men looked as if they had just come from work, wearing suits and ties. Others, like the stocky twenty-year-old kid in front of me, looked like they had just come from spending *baba's* money. With his hair gelled into place, he wore faded jeans and a cutoff black tank top, like what we used to lift weights in when I was in college. A snake tattoo slithered around his upper right bicep. It wavered between a relaxed state and a predator's pose as he flexed his arm at his side.

As for the ladies, they weren't wearing much, and the clothes they did wear were very tight. By my informal calculations, 83 percent of the women were showing midriff, and 64 percent wore black boots with three-inch heels. Pants ranged in style from tight jeans with no back pockets to leather pants, most accompanied by dangling belts. As for shirts, 91 percent wore revealing tight shirts (no matter what their body type, though at least 62 percent pulled it off well), most of which were tank tops. Since I could see almost everyone's midriff, I took special note of the large number of tattoos located partially above the ladies' waistlines. Jihan, a very cute, friendly, and dark-haired Palestinian-Jordanian friend, later told me that a lot of these tattoos weren't real. Still, image is image.

Jihan studied as an undergraduate in London and only recently returned home to Amman to work. She was drinking a rum and coke so that others in the club would not know that she was boozing. Another male friend at the table ordered her drinks for her so that there would be even less of a chance that someone there would get the wrong idea and say things that would tarnish her reputation. In an amazing clash of worlds, Jihan was making the transition from running free as a college girl in London to living under curfew in her parents' house in Amman and having friends order her drinks. Throughout the night, between dancing and talking with guys, she would text-message her mother from her cell phone, repeatedly asking permission to extend her curfew.

As I recounted the week's misadventures for Ramis and his wife Rasha, the deejay played the hit song *"Feino"* ("Where is s/he?"), and there was an explosion of energy throughout Nai. People were already dancing at their tables, but many of them now jumped on top of the tables. Each in their own cluster, women took turns shaking their hips and snaking their arms while others clapped around them. In some groups, men jumped on the tables and did the same, their hip-shaking cheered on. The electricity of the scene was contagious.

Even so, I couldn't shake the questions: What did these bold and beautiful dancers do during the day, and how did this club scene coexist with life upstairs, outside, and on the bus? For someone like Jihan, what did a night like this mean? Was it an escape, a chance to pull those sexy club clothes out of the back of the closet? Was it a reminder of how independent she was just a few months ago, and how she longed for similar circumstances here in her home? Or was it just plain fun?

I wondered what sort of nonalcoholically induced hangover Jihan would face in the morning when she met outside conservative, bus-riding Amman by the light of day. Perhaps when your family has enough money, someone like Jihan can avoid such a reckoning indefinitely. She can buy her way into a stratospheric existence of working in a Western-style company, exercising at an exclusive gym, driving from place to place in her own car, and partying on Thursday nights at Nai. Still, I'd imagine that there are some things that money cannot buy.

"Feino" ended, but we continued to have a good time chatting and dancing to a mix of Arabic and American music. My friends relished that they would not have to go to work in the morning. Ramis runs his family's ceramics factory and recounted the week's factory bloopers. The food arrived as he finished a story about the factory's rodent problem and his foreman's decision to publicly hang an already-dead rat as a warning to all other vermin.

Reserving a table entails spending a minimum amount of money. To make sure that that minimum is spent, waiters serve an obscene amount of appetizers as part of a set menu. Despite animated protests that the food would not be eaten, the waiters—"bus riders" from upstairs and outside Amman—robotically brought out enough dishes to cover the entire table. Ramis offered to pay for the appetizer bonanza even if it was not served, but the waves of grape leaves, meat on a stick, and humus continued. In a part of the world where you can almost always get around the rules, cut corners, and slip through with a joke, a wink, or a tip, it is fascinating to see where firm stands are taken. The delivery of appetizers at Nai is apparently a redline that cannot be crossed.

As I bit into an unappreciated grape leaf, I looked past a guy in an L. L. Bean button-down shirt to my left and saw a group of fellas that had just stepped out of an NSYNC commercial for McDonald's. One "bad boy" was wearing a black thermal hat and wraparound sunglasses with gold lenses. Unconsciously, I asked out loud, "Who do these guys think they are?" But the music was loud, and no one answered. I got my answer, however, when I saw that one of his wannabe homies, wearing a similar black hat and a tight black T-shirt, had a gun strapped to his lower back; he was a royal prince.

I lost interest in that sideshow when the deejay put on a James Brown remix, and the club went nuts again. Everyone started singing in English, and people climbed up on all of the club's chairs and tables to shake their hips. Three beautiful women slipped behind the deejay's curtain and danced with him in a way that made me reconsider career choices. My grape leaves forgotten, I jumped up as well, smiled broadly (I felt good), and shook my head internally in disbelief.

On my way home at 4:00 A.M. (the club was still hopping when I left), I couldn't stop thinking about all of these wealthy Jordanians and Palestinians, dressed in American and European labels, dancing and singing to American music with such sheer joy. I tried to reconcile that image with the anti-Americanism that is so prevalent here, but I couldn't help but feel as if these people loved America. In their most valued downtime of the week, they spoke our language with each other and lived our popular culture. *Haneen* is an Arabic word that means "longing" or "nostalgia." It is frequently used in the context of longing for one's homeland and is a popular Palestinian name. As far as I know, there isn't an Arabic word for "longing for America," but that is what this night, this scene, and this club seemed to be about. These Jordanians' feelings surpassed admiration for American culture. Their feelings were ones of radiant ownership; my music was their music, too.

With that cultural connection established, I questioned what it must be like to feel so strongly positive about one part of a culture and then so hurt, rejected, and targeted by another of its components, its politics. This crowd and the larger majority in Amman are highly critical of U.S. support for Israel and the potential invasion of Iraq. At the same time, as was clear this night, America is a second home and a cultural standard for many young elites who either worked or studied in the United States, or became enamored with American culture by a less direct route.

Tired, but not ready for bed, I made myself some tea and went up to my roof. Sitting on a cinder block next to my landlord's satellite dish, I looked out at the neon green mosque lights of a sleeping Amman and grappled with three ideas and their intersection: American magnetism, American cultural power, and anti-Americanism. After nearly six months of relationships, interactions, and conversations, I have come to believe that there is a certain magnetic draw to things American here. Beyond tastes in clothes and music, for many in Amman—not just Nai's patrons—America is an idea, a wonderful escape, and a land where anything goes, relatively.

From a personal standpoint, I benefit greatly from the perception of America as a concept akin to hope. When I meet new people —from the relatively exclusive university setting to downtown's Hashemite Square—I immediately receive the benefit of the doubt as being knowledgeable, worthy, or cool when I tell people that I am American. Once a real creature like me emerges from the dream of what America is, there is a certain draw to gaining the approval of that person. Or, as also can be the case, it can be appealing to reject Americans and things American in order to assert your own independence—though I have only rarely experienced such behavior first-hand.

To employ a sports analogy, America is like Michael Jordan. Many people who did not live near Chicago cheered for Michael

Jordan because he was the greatest and most talented player and they wanted to share in that greatness and success. At the same time, others across the country cheered against Jordan because they did not want anyone to dominate in such a way. In either case, there is an attraction to America because America is the yardstick by which to judge one's own accomplishments and perhaps subsequent self-worth.

Such American magnetism emphasizes the startling power of culture. Back home, when we consider power, we think of military force, technological innovation, and economic might. While there are people here who fear the display of American force in Afghanistan or who seek to tap into American consumer markets, America's power is most greatly demonstrated through the export of the ideas, possibilities, and entertainment generated by our universities, books, music, television shows, movies, and rags to riches immigrant stories. This same cultural power is America's most successful means to gain favor among the people of the Arab East and beyond. It is through Mark Twain stories, Martin Luther King Jr.'s March on Washington, and movies like the *Matrix* that America has created attractive American magnetism, American dreams, and the personal stories of hope that seem otherworldly.

When people who have never traveled to the United States say that they hate America but love the American people, it is because of our cultural output. They don't personally know us. Cabbies sing along with Mariah Carey, I watched the *Fugitive* with a spellbound Fadi, and there is a guy at the university with a Nike Swoosh shaved into the back of his head. These are all symbols, and people take their symbols of America from the entertainment and creative ideas we provide.

Recently, I was arguing about the future of Chinese power with a Turkish graduate student named Ahmet, who studies at the university with me. In Arabic, I explained to him that because of China's economic potential, future generations will learn Chinese the way the rest of the world learns English today. Ahmet dismissed my argument and told me that China would never be a powerful empire because no one would watch their movies. By way of background,

Ahmet's wife wears a head scarf, and he has complained in the past about how she can't study at Istanbul University because it is illegal for Turkish students to wear head scarves. I laughed at Ahmet's movie argument, but after the other night at Nih, I might have to reconsider.

People all over the world might buy Chinese VCRs, and *Crouching Tiger, Hidden Dragon* was a good movie, but they are mostly going to play American movies on those VCRs. VCR power, or the power of culture, will remain an area where America maintains a comparative advantage and exercises a great amount of influence. To be sure, VCR power feeds the repulsive side of American magnetism as well. Just as there are Mariah Carey lovers, there are Britney Spears haters. They seethe in anger and discomfort when she dances half-naked across their screens with a can of Pepsi. But when the commercials are over, attractive magnetism that has been created over years would seem to eclipse the repulsive magnetism that is decried by a vocal minority seeking a target for their frustrations. Overall, VCR power serves as a positive counterbalance toward politically rooted anti-Americanism. For all of Fadi's policy complaints, he still dreams of marrying a Palestinian-American and working in a place where he can speak American slang.

Without VCR power and the attractive American magnetism that it stimulates, would Americans, like me, receive the privileges and attention that I have enjoyed these past six months? It is true that my wealth (relative to my Arab peers) has taken me places. It is also true that warm gestures of hospitality are the norm and not the exception in the Arab East, especially in Jordan. So, there are other factors at play, but given the mounting tension and anger resulting from American foreign policies connected to Iraq and Israel, I am grateful for the positive impact that VCR power has on my life here.

On a global level, the issue of VCR power and the impact of attractive and repulsive American magnetism are integral to understanding anti-Americanism in Jordan. The term "anti-Americanism" has been thrown around gratuitously since the 9/11 attacks, but as I wrote in my earlier letter, after the assassination of Laurence Foley, there are two different streams of anti-American thought that should not be lumped together into one generalization. A more nuanced approach reveals two generalizations instead: America haters and American policy critics.

America haters are the "Arab Basement" drifters, the Osama bin Laden nihilists. They are the people who murdered Laurence Foley and who U.S. soldiers hunt across Afghanistan and Pakistan. They seek the overthrow of regional governments that they consider heretical and are outraged by many of the aspects of VCR power (see Spears, Britney and the Pepsi can). Yet, some of these haters have studied at American universities and appreciated aspects of American culture while living in American communities. In such cases, it is possible that their hatred extends to their own weaknesses and indulgences, or their inability to reconcile a new world's norms with the standards of their familiar and traditional culture.

In the end, however, America haters are repulsed by American magnetism and simultaneously degraded by their lack of autonomy and opportunities at home. They respond to American power with violence and destruction in the name of God. America haters are a small minority in Jordan, though. It is policy criticism, not hatred, which characterizes the majority of anti-Americanism witnessed in Jordan, by the rich and poor, the educated and uneducated.

American policy critics have a different agenda and, to a varying degree, a different source of displeasure than bin Laden nihilists or haters. Policy critics oppose the substance of American foreign policies rather than America's character as an immoral and aggressive power. For them, it is more the unjust nature of American policies that deserves criticism and not the actual act of "interfering" that is so loathed by America haters. American policy critics—bus riders and ketchup eaters alike—are attracted to things American, yet they struggle to come to terms with the disappointing choices of the U.S. government. *Their* America wouldn't fingerprint Muslim visitors, sell F-16 jets to Israel, and reject entry visa applications. It is difficult for Jordanian and Palestinian policy critics to accept our home as an actual place, with its own people, interests, and inconsistencies.

With American policy changes since the 9/11 attacks, American policy critics have grown vocally upset because their interaction with American political power has become the equivalent of receiving a body blow followed by a punch to the face. In some ways, for Nai's patrons, attractive American magnetism casts America as a big brother to look up to and follow, but not to emulate exactly. The urban elites of Amman seek to apply the best American ideas offered, from music and television to business models, but in their own fashion. In turn, they covet recognition, respect, and approval.

While they may succeed at home, sadly, they do not receive the recognition that they long for, nor do they gain the input they feel they deserve in the halls of American power because, in the end, they are not relevant constituents. It would be nice to please everyone, but American foreign policy is dictated by America's strategic interests, its special interests, and its citizens' interests. The interests of Jordanians and Palestinians, no matter what their sentimental ties of affection, are of secondary importance, at best, to American foreign policymakers. When the Arab East's policy critics make such an emotional investment, however, and the returns are a stereotypical blame for the 9/11 attacks, rejection, and policies considered unjust, it makes sense that they would express resentment and criticism. This is the body blow.

The punch to the face comes with the actual impact of what they see as America's unjust policies. The United States is the most powerful country in the world and therefore is perceived by policy critics to be responsible for securing world justice. With each unpopular and "unjust" American foreign policy decision, Jordanians and Palestinians not only feel disrespected, but their world is physically shaken. Israeli-flown American F-16 fighter jets have bombed the homes of Jordanian-Palestinian's families in Gaza and the West Bank. Factory owners, exporters, and laborers have lost their jobs because trade with Iraq is now difficult to impossible. From the perspective here in Jordan, men and women are continually victimized by U.S. policies that intentionally maintain Arab political "weakness," the occupation of Palestinian lands, and the exploitation of Arab oil.

To an outsider like me, who has entered this fray with logic influenced by a Western graduate school, such an argument seems conspiratorial, but here it is the bedrock of political discourse. Educated elites and "street" pundits alike have built their own world of rights and wrongs, crafting their own concept of justice that fits their worldview and their place in that world. While American policy critics only passively seek the realization of justice, they still look to the United States to guarantee such "justice."

Even though VCR power leads policy critics to favor the American people (*and* not the American government!) in a general sense, it has a negative consequence on questions of justice and common interests. Jordanians and Palestinians might conclude that because they share the same preferences as Americans for movies and music, they also share policy interests and views on what is just. While Americans and Arabs might be able to agree on the abstract meaning of justice, its application is subject to one's interests. We certainly have our own relativism in the United States. A Pittsburgh steelworker would consider steel subsidies that support his factory's output and protect his job from unfair competition a just policy. However, that same policy is unjust to a Detroit autoworker who just lost his job because those same subsidies increased the price of steel, cut his factory's profit margin, and forced management to make cost-reducing layoffs.

Because justice differs by values, interests, and perspective, it would be impossible for the U.S. government to satisfy American policy critics. The Bush administration would have to become the henchman of a perspective that is not their own, that strays from historic policy choices, and that consists of some norms that many Americans might not feel comfortable supporting. Historically, U.S. foreign policy has been based on strategic goals, like protecting oil resources, which tend to lead to shifting positions and foreign accusations of hypocrisy (like calling for the protection of human rights while supporting the Saudi regime). There is room to bring policies closer to *our* ideals, but it would be a colossal mistake to make decisions based on others' concept of justice and honor.

Washington D.C. policymakers and Amman's policy critics have different perspectives on what is just and America's role in dispensing such justice. The frustration of this reality—the one-two punch of attractive American magnetism and rejection, and then the impact of America's "unjust" policies—is what makes up the bulk of anti-Americanism in Jordan. They hate American foreign policy, not America.

While the administration should by no means pander to the Arab East's American policy critics, it is certainly a mistake to treat such critics as if they belong to the same flock as the America haters. Instead, the administration should show American policy critics a measure of respect by better explaining the rationale behind policy choices. While there will still be disagreement, such choices would be more easily understood and adapted to in the future. I don't think the Bulls and Michael Jordan would have been so popular around the world if he and the Jordanaires would have talked trash to the crowd while beating their opponents.

Building upon areas where American and Arab interests and perceptions of justice overlap would also serve to decrease the tension among American policy critics. VCR power could be employed effectively to create new and shared bonds between different peoples. Were I giving advice from my rooftop perch, I would recommend policies that establish and support fora like American-Arab publishing houses, recording companies, and studios which take advantage of local creativity and allow young people to earn the recognition and prestige that they covet, both at home and internationally. I would also put an emphasis on expediting student and exchange visitor visas (while maintaining security standards, of course); encouraging more American scholars, professionals, and students to travel to the Arab East; and creating more American studies programs at Middle Eastern universities. America's unofficial ambassadors are a great asset in building better relations with the people of Jordan and the other countries of the Arab East where American policy criticism is the vogue. And to kick off this campaign, I would also launch a Mariah Carey friendship tour to five Arab capital cities. In this case, the pen may be mightier than the sword.

Happy New Year to all of you!

Love,
Ben

Letter 12

A Woman's World

January 12, 2003

Dear All,

Since my mother's visit last month and having had the opportunity to see things a bit through her eyes, I've been thinking more about the life of women here in Jordan. Before her visit, I was aware of foreign women's harassment issues, but I hadn't paid much attention to local gender issues. Given that I mostly interact with men, I'd unconsciously come to terms with the fact that the world of Jordanian women was one that would remain secret to me.

My mom visited for a week, and I planned out her trip so that it would be part "Jordan's Greatest Hits" and part "A Day in the Life." We hiked through the ancient pinkish-red city of Petra, stayed at the Movenpick resort at the Dead Sea, and spent a day at the Roman ruins of Jerash. We also rode the bus, sat in the library reading room, hung out at Hashemite Square, and visited my neighborhood supermarket and grocer. Throughout it all, I did my best to demonstrate to my mother that Jordan is the wonderful and safe place that I've come to appreciate. At the same time, I spent the seven days walking around like a giant guard dog, ready to pounce on anyone who looked at my mother funny, said something vulgar, or might dare to brush up against her in a nonaccidental way.

Two female classmates have clued me into the issue of harassment in Jordan. Both are tall blondes; one is from Germany and the other from Wisconsin. Each has several stories of being stopped by strange men offering unattractive invitations. The German woman has been confronted and inappropriately touched several times—usually by boys or teenagers—and has taken to yelling back insults, following catcallers, and even attacking those who have offered unwelcome advances. She told me that she once followed home a high school student who had vulgarly propositioned her, kicking him in the rear along the way and yelling at him. The story was hard to believe until I ran into her one time at Abdali, pointing a finger in the faces of three sneering teenagers and threatening them.

Despite all this, I consider Jordan much better than Egypt on this issue of harassment. When I lived in Cairo a few summers ago, I literally heard men shouting to Western women in the street, "I want to fuck you!" or asking whether their cousin could have the chance. It also seemed as if a disproportionate number of female tourists had horror stories of creeping hands on long bus trips. Given the emphasis on respect and shame in the traditional culture here, such behavior directed toward Jordanian women would never fly. For some reason, though, perhaps as the result of American movies and TV shows, there is a popular perception that most Western women are waiting for the chance to drop their pants.

A couple of years ago, when I spent that summer in Cairo, I escaped the noise and pollution of the city for a long weekend and traveled by bus for nine hours to Farafra, an oasis in the desert. I spent a couple of days wandering around the groves and took a jeep into the desert, but the highlight of the weekend was eating fresh mangos with Mohammed. Mohammed was an engineer from Alexandria, in his late twenties, and had been working in Farafra for a few months. He took me to restaurants, and we paid the Egyptian rate rather than the tourist price. Over that weekend, we spent a lot of time talking, drinking tea, and eating those mouth-watering fresh mangos right off the cart.

The night before I returned to Cairo, Mohammed and I sat at an outdoor ahwa drinking tea, and a beautiful strawberry-blonde Danish woman who was staying at my hostel walked by and waved to me innocently. Mohammed turned to me and said, "Tell me something, Mr. Benyamin."

"Yes, Mohammed?"

"How can I make foreign women love me? What do I say so they will have sex with me?"

I laughed. "Well, Mohammed, men have been trying to figure that out for years."

"When Mr. John was here, he told me that I need to bend with one knee on the ground"—with this, Mohammed knelt before me— "raise my left arm, reach my hand to the sky, put my right hand on my heart, look her in the eye, and say, 'I want . . . no, I need . . . to make love to you!'"

As Mohammed knelt earnestly before me, with one hand over his heart and the other outstretched to the sky, I wondered whether Mr. John, a British guy I had heard a lot about and who had visited the oasis a few weeks earlier, was either a jerk with an odd sense of humor or a great protector of foreign women's rights. If every Egyptian man who wanted to sleep with a foreign woman used the Mr. John formula for pitching woo, at least foreign women could laugh and see the harassment coming.

Beyond the issue of harassment for foreign women, traveling around Amman and Jordan with my mom led me to take greater notice of some of the difficulties that Jordanian women face. Jordanian women and their male caretakers must contend daily with the concept of what is culturally appropriate within their social system. The question of honor is always dwelling beneath the surface, and threats to a woman's honor or reputation lurk in what are seemingly the most commonplace and innocuous situations—from riding the bus to walking on the street after the sun has gone down.

On the issue of transportation, getting around isn't the easiest thing to do if you don't have a car or cannot afford to take cabs—whether you are a man or woman. The main options are buses and shared taxis. There is etiquette, though, to bus riding that makes the experience a culturally safe one for women. Typically, women sit alone in a single seat or next to another woman in a two-seater. If there is not enough room for a woman to sit once she has gotten on to the bus, then a man gets up so that a woman will not have to stand. If a woman sits next to a man, it is her choice, which isn't altogether rare, but it is rare to see a man sit down in an empty aisle seat next to a woman. If a man and woman who aren't together do sit in the same seat, there is a clear gap between the two of them so that they won't touch.

Similar rules apply for riding in cars. In a private cab, if the woman is alone, she always sits in the back. If it is a shared cab, the woman never sits in the middle. If she is part of a couple, then the man sits in the middle and the woman sits next to the window so that she only has physical contact with the man she came with. If she is alone, the other riders will reposition themselves so that she is either sitting next to a door in the back, or in the passenger's seat up front by herself.

As my mom and I rushed to Abdali to catch the bus to the ancient Roman ruins of Jerash, I worried that we would not be able to find two places next to each other. Although I wanted to sit next to my mother so we could chat, it was the cultural impropriety of my mother sitting without me that concerned me. When we arrived, there were only three open seats left on the bus, but none together. I looked around for a woman for my mom to sit next to, but there were only two women on a bus of about fifty people and they sat with their husbands, each next to the window. So, I politely asked a man sitting next to one of the three empty seats to leave his seat so that I could sit with my mother. He, of course, obliged.

We were the only tourists in Jerash that afternoon, one of Jordan's main attractions. It was similar in Petra, a place that should rank among the world's greatest tourist attractions. Petra dates from the Nabatean and Roman periods. The ancient city's heyday was in the period before the death of Christ; Rome took control of the city in the second century. Petra is known for its beauty, though, not its historical relevance. The city is a collection of red, pink, purple, and blue buildings whose edifices are carved out of the fronts of sheer rock facades. Part of the final scene of *Indiana Jones and the Last Crusade* was filmed at the Treasury, Petra's main building. Magically, the colors of Petra change according to the time of day and the position of the sun. Morning pinks turn ruby red in the evening. If foreigners weren't scared to travel to the Middle East, tourists would flood Petra as they do the Great Wall of China or the Colosseum in Rome. My mom and I were in Petra for two days, and we saw less than twenty other visitors.

Jerash also would be a major tourist attraction under other circumstances. While Jerash is not on the same level of grandeur as Petra, it is home to some of the most complete Roman ruins in the region, and from A.D. 129–130, the city was the center of the Roman

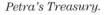
Petra's Treasury.

Empire. The highlights of the ruins are an incredible sprawling oval plaza and a theater originally built in the first century and still used for concerts. Also, there is the Temple of Artemis, where you can feel the fourth column sway in the wind if you place your finger or a key in the crack between its bottom and the ground. *The Rough Guide to Jordan* explains that this was by design, in order to absorb the shocks of powerful winds and minor earthquakes.

With Jerash to ourselves, we had a great afternoon wandering around and reading about the city's history until I noticed that it was already four o'clock. It would be dark within an hour and the last bus left for Amman at dusk. Were I alone, I wouldn't have really cared and could have hitched a ride with someone or found a shared minivan. With my mom as company, though, I had to find a means of transportation that would be culturally acceptable and would fulfill all of Jordan's social norms. Here, one doesn't hitch a ride with one's mother. Doing so would send one of two unattractive signals: an outward message of disrespect for my mother or the alternative message of stupidity and helplessness.

As we stood outside of Jerash's ancient city and I tried to make arrangements to return to Amman, my mom pointed out that there were no other women out at all. I looked around and realized dumbly that she was right. There wasn't one single woman on the street, waiting for the bus or just passing by on her way somewhere. There were, however, a lot of men hanging around. Going to the university every day, which is packed with women circulating in groups or walking alone, I never fully realized that there aren't a lot of women out and about in public. Of course, there are couples and families, but at night, the absence of unaccompanied women is glaring. As it got darker in Jerash and I realized that we'd missed the last bus, I grew worried for my mother's comfort and tried to surround her as much as possible, a difficult task for one person to accomplish. Eventually, I found a middle-aged tour guide with a car who was returning to Amman. I paid him for a ride to Abdali, and my mom and I sat in the back seat of his car.

The practicalities of this constant effort to protect a woman's honor and reputation obviously impact a woman's independence.

Jordan, Jerash's oval forum.

My mom is also Dr. Orbach, an English writing instructor at the University of Pittsburgh and one of two undergraduate advisers for hundreds of English majors. She is a personable and accomplished individual, but for seven days, I wouldn't let her walk out of my sight, pay for anything, ask for directions, or really do anything without me. She became my responsibility. Even though we used her credit card at restaurants and hotels, I was the one who gave it to the clerk or waiter, and I signed her name. At Petra, when I went to the bathroom, I asked my mother to sit by the bathrooms rather than a few hundred feet away. When she went to the bathroom, I waited outside. The parent-child relationship was reversed.

This wasn't overboard behavior or paranoia. And it wasn't the case that there are violent marauders here that I was worried would do harm to my mother or commit some sort of terrible social injustice. I've been Jordanized, and I was adhering to societal norms. I was showing respect for my mother and sending an outward message that this was a woman whose honor was cherished by her family. As a loving son, I didn't want anyone to view my mother in a way not considered respectable. Furthermore, it would have been a blight on my performance as a dutiful son had people thought that she was there alone. People may have surmised that she did not have sons or a husband who loved her and that protected her from the dangers of the outside world; they might have even thought that she was a person of ill repute. I would consider such conclusions a total personal failure on my part.

A responsible Jordanian son or brother would never leave his mother or sister to face the outside world alone. It is the man's responsibility to provide in every way, whether that means paying a bill or instructing a driver of a destination. In a couple, whether husband and wife or parent and adult child, the man is the conduit to the outside world. It would have been socially weird and sent an ambiguous message had I allowed my mother to sit next to a stranger on a bus or to negotiate room rates with the clerk at a hotel.

While I fulfilled my responsibilities as a son and as a man, my issues of honor and respect curtailed my mother's ability to be an independent person. After reflection, I wonder how this type of protective behavior makes women here feel. On the one hand, such attentive behavior is the ultimate expression of affection and devotion. On the other hand, it may feel overly protective and limiting. The experience led me to realize that women become restricted by the norms of a society where men need to protect the honor of reputations. Still, I can only speculate about how a woman must feel in such a male-dominated public space. What if she does not have a responsible son or husband escorting her around and handling logistics?

Kholood, my closest female friend in Jordan, doesn't seem to go anywhere without her maternal uncle dropping her off. He is almost a full-time chauffer and chaperone. Kholood gets picked up and dropped off, whether it's at the British Council or the school for foreigners where she teaches. Her other option, an expensive one, is to take a cab. When she conducts private lessons with someone like me, there is a chaperone present in the house—either her mom or her uncle. Kholood is smart, educated, and makes a lot of money (relatively) to help support her family. Her life is full of success, and she appears to be happy. Still, I wonder whether on some level, deep down, she feels limited or frustrated. I truly don't know the answer. I would guess, though, that Kholood only experiences the protective gestures of her family as symbols of their love and concern. She knows her family cares about her because they do all these amazing and time-consuming things to support her and that enable her to work.

Given the complexities and social rules that women live by in public, women must gain a lot of comfort from being in situations where there aren't any men around. Here's an irony: Even though I took my mom to Jerash, Petra, the Dead Sea, and Amman's best restaurants, and even though I introduced her to my friends and neighbors, her richest experience probably came at the university library's reading room. The reading room was the only place on her trip where my mom got to conduct herself in public as an independent individual rather than conforming to the role of a mother being looked out for by her son. I had to go to class for two hours, so I deposited my mom at a table under the watchful eye of the librarian and guiltily promised to return soon. She planned to do some journal writing and reading. When I rushed back a few hours later, she was bubbling over with excitement.

Soon after I'd left, she was approached by several female English-language students, all of whom wore the hijab, and some the niqab, the Islamic face covering. They surrounded her and peppered her with a million questions in English, seeking to practice and of course to find out what this curly-haired American woman was doing at their university. They couldn't believe that they had found a university-level English teacher from America, there in their library among the dictionaries and reference books, just hanging out and waiting for her son. What were the odds? They talked the whole time that I was gone and even exchanged e-mail addresses.

While I'm thrilled that my mom could have her own experience, and I am not surprised at all by the way the students welcomed her, I can't begin to express how jealous I am. She's here six days and she entered the secret world of women! I've been here six months and don't get further than sitting behind them on the bus!

Given all the social rules that dictate a woman's behavior in public and around men, women here in Jordan must truly enjoy the freedom they experience in "women only" environments. I imagine that such situations offer a chance for them to more fully be themselves since they are free of the burden of managing social perceptions and threats to their reputation and honor. My mom actually told me that her time in the library with the female students was the most physically safe that she felt during the whole visit—despite my best efforts. The various comforts offered by such female-only environments are certainly a positive within this social system. Looking at the flip side, however, I actually think that the social system affords men in an all-male environment, such as at an ahwa, an element of comfort, too. Perhaps such comfort comes from a sense of being free of certain caretaking responsibilities and social pressures that involve the opposite sex.

Yet, there are negative aspects to such a traditional social system too. One of them is certainly the dependence created by having a male caretaker always present or at least nearby. In October, when Kholood took me to the international school to speak to her class about the importance of learning Arabic, her uncle drove us. We were late and Kholood assured me that we would be there soon, but from the context of her subsequent conversation with her uncle, it became clear that she didn't know how to get to the school from her home and didn't know exactly how much longer it would be. Her uncle drove her every day; there was no reason for her to worry about such things.

In American cities, women live in a system that emphasizes choice and independence. Rites of passage in the United States are about gaining independence from home. Going to school for the first time as a child, going out on dates, going to college, renting an apartment, finding a job, and choosing someone to marry—these are all experiences marked by making choices and establishing one's own self, based on individual interests. If a Western woman were put into a situation where she had to deal with the expectations and norms of the traditional system, I can only picture her feeling voiceless and without power. For Jordanian women, I think that the ladder of accomplishments is different. Of course, I'm generalizing, but the most honorable thing that a woman in Jordan can do is to grow up well as a good and honorable daughter and make the transition from her father's house to her husband's home, becoming a good wife and mother.

How can a Western woman who made the choice to come to Jordan to advance her career by taking a job in a foreign country, or to enhance her professional marketability by studying Arabic, or who decided to travel here independently out of a sense of curiosity, feel comfortable within the parameters of such a system? Combined with the verbal harassment that at least some Western women face here, it amounts to a difficult situation.

For Jordanian women, whether or not they are religious, wearing the hijab makes a lot of sense. Covering one's hair offers a woman protection and a respite from unwanted attention. The hijab sends a clear message that a woman is a respected member of society and not liberal in her morals. Harassing a muhajiba woman would lead to a visit from brothers and cousins; honor killings of women are regular occurrences in Jordan. To the uninformed Jordanian, though, a woman walking around in Western clothes with hair exposed communicates an alternative message that has been fed by our entertainment industry (through VCR power) and perpetuated by local rumors. It is a popular perception among students at the university that in America, a woman has to live with her boyfriend before he'll agree to marry her. For the average bus rider here, who doesn't go to business meetings with elites or who isn't privy to life at the university, the only women he sees not wearing the hijab are foreign women in the streets, women in the movies and on TV, and his family members at home.

I was worried about some teenager harassing my mom as we walked through crowded downtown Amman. While trying to point out sights to my mother, I watched every man that passed and every stray hand; I was ready to explode in a protective fury. Thankfully, nothing happened—but had there been an incident, and I reacted violently, I would have been entirely justified. Whether part of the legal code or not, the rights of a male family member protecting the honor of a female relation are sacrosanct. As it so happens, though, the rights of foreign women are protected pretty well, too, if you prosecute a case to its fullest. I know of a situation where a taxi driver lost his driver's license and is facing jail time for grabbing a Canadian woman exiting his cab.

So, with this new awareness for gender issues in Jordan, I traveled to another part of the Arab East, Morocco, to meet a friend from graduate school for a ten-day backpacking trip. When I arrived, I couldn't believe what I saw. First, the Moroccan-style jilbab is much different than the jilbab in Jordan, Syria, or Egypt. Not only do a lot of men also wear them as an outer-layer over their clothes, but instead of a gray or navy coverall-type smock, the jilbab is a colorful long pullover shirt with a hood, and many women don't wear the hoods. The result is a lot of beautiful women in turquoise, peach, and magenta jilbabs walking around smiling. In the sunset pink-colored old city of Marrakech, I freely exchanged smiles and hellos with local women. In Amman, even at the university, this doesn't happen. It is possible that nervousness about Iraq has added tension to everyone's demeanor in Jordan, but I think that the openness in Morocco represented a cultural difference.

One morning in Mekenes, another of Morocco's five Imperial Cities, I was looking for the train station and approached an older man to ask for directions; he couldn't help me. The woman in a black jilbab sitting a few feet away looked at me expectantly. I was befuddled, but out of some lost instinct, I asked her for directions. I would never speak with a strange woman in Jordan, much less one covered to some degree. She told me where to find the station, or actually she gave me directions to where she thought it was.

This was all topped by the train ride from Fes to Casablanca. At a local station just past Rabat, a female Moroccan college student got into our carriage by herself and sat down next to my friend. We were speaking in English and she interrupted to ask us where we were from. We spent the next forty-five minutes talking, and she decided to skip her stop so that she could spend the afternoon showing us around Casablanca. My friend was sick and stayed in the hotel, so that left just the two of us. As we walked through the old city and she told me that her father had two wives—you are permitted four in Islam—she linked her arm through mine. I almost had a coronary, so great was my disbelief.

Later in the evening, as we strolled through the streets of Casablanca with our arms still linked, she sang to me. When I took her to the train station to say good-bye, she gave me kisses on both cheeks, a French good-bye. I was stunned and wondered when and how my trip had gotten rerouted to Europe. There are definite cultural residuals from the period when Morocco was a French protectorate, from such behavior to the local dialect of Arabic, which is heavily littered with French words.

The trip to Morocco was a good reminder that every place is different. Stereotypes that include generalizations about "the Arabs" or "the Muslims" have limited use. There are undoubtedly commonalities between people and shared aspects of culture, like religion, language, and history. Yet the intricacies of gender issues differ greatly between parts of Morocco and parts of Jordan. I'm not sure how useful it is to speak about the problems of "Arab women" or "Muslim women" or to speak generally about Jordanian women and Moroccan women together. Many rural Moroccan women face the same issues as their Jordanian counterparts, but there is also a fine line between a useful generalization and an exaggerated stereotype. That line is not always easy to see.

I also realize that it is a mistake to conclude that Islam is the root for such conservatism on gender issues. Despite the stereotypes and the extremist behavior of the Taliban, there is nothing inherent in Islam that dictates these social norms. All the women I met at that club on the Bosporus in Istanbul were Muslim. Furthermore, I know both Jewish and Christian communities that would have no problem with the social structures that govern conservative Jordan. Instead, in Jordan, the social framework that guides the behavior of women and the men who love them can likely be attributed to a tribal culture and its strict traditions regarding interactions between men and women. Religion is a solid pillar of Jordanian culture, but it is tribal traditions that really are a guiding force in social behavior.

These traditions are reinforced by a dearth of exposure to positive Western ideals and strengthened by the widespread presence of negative Western stereotypes. A couple of weeks ago, I caught an episode of *Friends* on TV. Given the context in which I live, I was suddenly appalled by the show's content. I loved *Friends* when I was in college, perhaps for these very same reasons, but the show is entirely about beautiful women talking about casual sex while three good-looking guys try to sleep with half of New York. In the episode that I saw, Lisa Kudrow's character had a new boyfriend who had a hard time keeping his unit from flopping out of his boxers and gym shorts when he was sitting in the group's coffee shop hangout. Last month, I also saw a B movie on TV about an American high school student who slept with his teacher's wife. If these are the images of America and Western morals, in the context of where I live in Amman, it would seem pretty easy to decide to protect from outside influence the honor and reputation of your daughter, sister, and wife like your life depended on it. I can also understand, in the context of these images, stories, and shows, why the morals of foreign women are considered questionable, at best.

To alter the negative perception here of Western women, we might put greater effort into delivering more substantial messages about the various and important roles that women play in the United States via speaker programs at U.S. embassies and the broadcast of documentaries and movies that highlight the roles played by female leaders of the civil rights, labor, and feminist movements. We don't want to censor shows like *Friends*, but at the same time, we might be able to promote a more wholesome image of women—especially Generation Xers—without resorting to the distribution of *Little House on the Prairie* episodes. I admit that this is a more difficult nut to crack, and perhaps less profitable than trying to figure out how to increase the Arab East distribution of *Maxim* magazine, where beautiful big-breasted women fall out of their shirts on the cover. It would certainly be worthwhile, though, and could have a spillover influence on culture here.

The tribal culture influences everything, not just the role and perception of women. Part of seeing the world through a tribal lens is being hyperprotective of private space. In Morocco, I went to two synagogues, where to my disappointment, I was basically ignored by *my* tribe because I was still an outsider and a potential threat. I have no idea what kind of discrimination those Moroccan Jews have faced in their lives, but an outsider isn't going to come in and just be accepted as part of their community. As I mentioned in my description of Bashir's street in Zarqa, families comprise an entire city block in some places here. At the university, the students who study education spend all day hanging around the education building; it is their area. Among those students, there are further subgroupings by nationality, religion, city, and neighborhood.

Tribal structures are the basis for political rule in many places in the Middle East, such as Syria, Iraq, and Jordan. Israel has a democratic version of a tribal system, with voting blocs divided between Ashkenazi and Sephardic Jews and a further divide with Russians and Ethiopians, not to mention Arab citizens of Israel. Going back to the point made repeatedly by Abu Alaa—my conversation partner Bahaa's father—there are a lot of shifting sands here in the Middle East. Boundaries of nations have changed several times over the past 100 years, and the results have yielded states that aren't really states. Tahseen Basheer, a former high-level Egyptian diplomat who was a guest lecturer for a couple of classes in my Arab Political Thought seminar in graduate school, offered the following insight: "Egypt is the only nation-state in the Middle East. The rest are tribes with flags."

Even as boundaries have changed over the past 100 years, tribal allegiances and relations have remained constant. And history and culture (to include religion and national traditions) in Jordan are rooted in tribes and community. To understand the people and the politics here, not just the role of women, you must understand tribal structures and traditions. People don't act for the benefit of the state. They act for the benefit and honor of their family and tribe. There is a missing component of public trust and little stake in the public good.

From a Washington, D.C. policy perspective, it's easy to say that women should be treated in a manner consistent with the universal standard for decency and equality. Bridging the gap, however, between such rhetoric and the tribally influenced realities on the ground is more difficult. It will take careful study and a lot of meaningful little steps. It seems that in the post-9/11 environment, some policymakers have a strong interest in remaking the Middle East. Perhaps there is a notion that there are more Ataturks out there, and we just need to find them and support them. As a reminder, Kemal Ataturk was the founder of the modern Turkish Republic. Overnight, he instituted social and political reforms creating a secular governing system, changed the Turkish language and dress customs, and transformed Turkey after World War I from a crumbled empire to a modern state with defined borders. Despite Western yearnings, an Arab Ataturk has yet to emerge.

Notwithstanding the amazing transformation that has taken place in Turkey, I'm not sure that the Ataturk model is a blueprint that can be replicated. Radical changes in the social and political fabrics of tribal societies cannot take hold through force alone. With the separation between public and private worlds, tribal cultures will hold fast to their private world and continue their disinterest in participating in the public domain and the doings of the state. Washington, D.C. policymakers might consider how in other places such as Scotland, Japan, and most recently, Eastern Europe, people transitioned from their previous social structures, took ownership over their public domain, and developed public trust. To me, it seems worthwhile to pursue answers to questions like: What makes people return books to public libraries? And what will enable a woman to sit next to a man on a bus and avoid the stigma of damaging her honor?

My sense is that sometimes a shock to the system can be useful, but that trust and a shared life are built over a long time period, not through coercion and fear, but through the delivery of benefits that reinforce difficult changes. Along these lines, there are no quick fixes here in Jordan or in Syria, either. I would guess that the same is true in Iraq, too.

Perhaps lost in my thoughts about tribalism and gender is how wonderful it was to see my mom. We had a great time at Petra and at the Dead Sea, but the best part was really just having a visitor, my first since arriving here in July. Hope you all are well.

Love,
Ben

Letter 13

Crossing Palestine

February 2, 2003

Dear All,

I walked Amman's empty streets, past dark homes and shuttered stores and toward the bus station and a bus that would take me to the King Hussein Bridge. At a few minutes to 6:00 A.M. last Friday, I was headed to Haifa. To get there I would cross Palestine, a place I never knew existed.

Amman and Haifa are about eighty miles apart on a map, but it's a distance divided by border crossings, bypass roads, and checkpoints. To traverse those eighty miles, I planned to take a bus from Amman to the border, cross the border at the King Hussein Bridge, share a taxi to Jerusalem, and then take another bus from Jerusalem's central bus station two hours north—all before sundown and the start of *Shabbat*, the Jewish Sabbath.

Crossing the Jordan River was to be a watershed event for me. I've lived in Amman for more than six months, and I've traveled to neighboring Syria and Egypt, but not to Israel. It wasn't the daily violence of the *intifada* that kept me away, but rather a sense that I had already come to know Israel. Seven years ago, in 1996, I studied at Hebrew University in Jerusalem for half a year. I was a history student, and Jerusalem was my Mecca. The Western Wall, the Church of the Holy Sepulchre, the Dome of the Rock, and the Al-Aqsa Mosque—the physical foundations of Judaism, Christianity, and Islam—are all located within a few minutes walk of each other. I visited each of them regularly and spent hundreds of hours exploring the Old City's crowded markets and quiet rooftops. Every alleyway, conversation, and moment was a lesson in history and culture.

In 1996, I was a witness to historically important events. Following the Israeli assassination of Yahya Ayash, a chief Hamas bombmaker, there was a Hamas terror campaign in February and March that derailed a then-vibrant peace process. The No. 18 bus that I rode downtown every day was attacked twice in eight days by suicide bombers. Forty-five people were murdered. In April, when I was on a hiking trip with friends in northern Israel, the Israeli army evacuated us from our campsite. War had started between Israel and Lebanon, and we woke up later that night to the lights of Katyusha rockets in the sky, shot by Hizballah into northern Israel. A couple of months later, hard liner Benjamin Netanyahu edged into office by less than 30,000 votes, defeating Nobel Peace Prize winner Shimon Peres. I was so distraught for what I thought were the dwindling prospects for peace that I retreated to the Sinai Peninsula to check out and escape reality for a few days. I sat on the beach, played backgammon, and smoked a hookah. Living amid all this history and through the day-to-day turmoil of the Arab-Israeli conflict, I gained an understanding and appreciation for Israelis, and an admiration for their resilience in the face of what seemed like an endless siege of hatred.

At the same time, life in Jerusalem raised so many questions. I developed an interest in Arab history and the people who exerted such influence on my life. It was this interest that led me down a path lined with a few thousand Arabic flashcards to the decision to make my graduate studies a full-time endeavor and to live in Jordan for a year. To fully appreciate the experience of living in Jordan, I've tried to separate myself from parts of my background. I've fought natural comparisons between life in Jordan and life in Israel and chose not to visit Israeli cousins and friends.

One of the reasons that I decided to spend the year in Jordan, rather than Egypt or Morocco, was my interest in the Palestinian world. As I've detailed in these letters, living in Amman has not disappointed on this front; I've been regaled with 1,001 Palestinian narratives in the form of logical arguments, angry diatribes, and soft pleas for justice. One of the most poignant moments of my experience came at the end of August when Kholood partnered me for a conversation exercise with her cousin Jamil, who was visiting for the summer from the West Bank city of Jenin.

A shy seventeen-year-old, Jamil munched on a bag of chips and told me about his life in Jenin, the city that saw major fighting between Israeli soldiers and Palestinian fighters in the spring of 2002. The Israeli army forcefully entered the Jenin refugee camp after a suicide bomber from there killed thirty Israelis at a Passover Seder. Since the incursion, Jenin has become a part of Palestinian lore. Palestinians accuse Israelis of massacring hundreds while Israelis contend that they used utmost caution and killed fifty-two Palestinians, most of whom, they claim, were militants. A U.N. investigation confirmed the Israeli account. Public opinion in the Arab East reached a different conclusion, however, as massive demonstrations raged across major Arab cities protesting the Israeli military action in Jenin.

While Jamil explained how he avoided Israeli patrols on the way to school, I had difficulty grasping the reality of a life built around avoiding the pressures of checkpoints, curfews, and a siege. I wondered whether any of Jamil's classmates had become suicide bombers. In Amman, Jamil was my teacher's cousin and a kid, but if I were an Israeli in Jenin, I doubt that I could have viewed Jamil in the same way so easily. I would probably be scared of him.

As I chastised myself for viewing Jamil as a potential suicide bomber and unfairly projected my own thoughts on to Israeli soldiers, I couldn't help but think of my Israeli cousin Elad. A thirty-year-old father of three, Elad takes care of the baby chickens on a cooperative farm and leads youth camping trips. Whenever I visit, we go on hikes and he'll walk me through the remains of 3,000 years of history, from the period of the first Jewish temple to the Arab-Israeli wars of the last fifty-five years. The beauty and the history of the land, and Elad's enthusiasm for sharing that history, make these hikes a lot of fun.

Many modern Orthodox Israelis like Elad develop a love and appreciation for the physical land of Israel from their youth. They believe it is their birthright and consider the land a gift from God, given to them as part of a holy covenant with Abraham, Isaac, and Jacob. For many of these modern Orthodox who wear knit *kipot* or skullcaps, childhood entertainment and fun center on the overlapping spheres of active Jewish religious practice and total commitment to the land. There is nothing better than going on a *te-ul*, or trip. Interestingly, there is a commonality here with the diaspora Palestinians I've met. Ali, my grammar teacher from the summer used to speak with awe about the bread of his village, and Ibrahim, my language partner at the university, has told me about his village's orange groves. Many diaspora Palestinians share a deep respect and appreciation for the land.

Elad, too, knows the history of every stone in the Galilee, yet despite the fact that he is a loving father and a good family man, many of the diaspora Palestinians I've met in Amman would see him as nothing more than a former paratrooper and an imperialist occupier. As I've detailed in past letters, there are a lot of people in Amman who reject Israel's right to exist and who speak of returning to lands now known by Hebrew names.

Jamil and Elad . . . "Palestine" and Israel. On my way to the bus station, I was filled with concern that my immersion in Amman would lead me to discover that the understanding and appreciation that I had developed while in Jerusalem was nothing but superficial bliss. At the same time, I feared that my return to Israel would trigger a flood of colorful, warm memories that would cast a shadow over my life in Jordan. The two worlds have a hard time coexisting in reality. Deep down, I've been scared that I can't even manage the process in my head, so I've avoided Israel.

Yet, the point of choosing to live in Amman was to learn things that aren't available in a seminar. Every day, I hear about Palestinian suffering at the hands of Israelis. While I will never understand what it really means to be a Palestinian at the mercy of Israeli rules, I wanted to gain a semblance for what it was like to be a Palestinian at an Israeli checkpoint. The process of crossing an Israeli border into the West Bank offered at least a closer vantage point.

By 7:45 A.M., I was walking across an asphalt parking lot at the Jordanian border and toward three officials in crisp blue uniforms, navy sweaters, and sparkling shoes. They smoked cigarettes on a bench and watched a young worker with sleep-starched hair throw water from a barrel across the parking lot in an attempt to clean the ground. I greeted the officials and asked one with a finely trimmed goatee if it was possible to enter "Palestine."

My use of "Palestine" was significant. As a Jewish American who grew up during the heyday of PLO terrorism, "Palestine" had once been a dirty word. At that time, the existence of "Palestine" implied the destruction of Israel. At that point in the morning and in my life, I considered "Palestine" an idea, a historical term, and a dream. Although there are Palestinian people and Palestinian lands, there is no functioning Palestinian state. Rather than engage anyone in Jordan on these semantics, though, I conformed to local norms and simply said "Palestine," leaving terms like the "West Bank" or the "Palestinian Authority" for nightly news broadcasters.

Sighing, the official stood, took my passport, and motioned me inside the small building. As he flipped through my passport, I asked him not to stamp it. Evidence that I had exited Jordan and traveled to Israel would prohibit me from returning to Syria. He nodded, and another official collected my departure tax. It turns out that my worry was unnecessary: Jordanians do not stamp passports at the King Hussein Bridge because they unofficially still consider the West Bank part of Jordan. Jordan maintained sovereignty over the West Bank between the 1948 and 1967 wars.

When I asked to actually cross the border, I was politely told to wait. So I sat on a bench and watched the water boy flick water across the lot. While I thought about the luxury of garden hoses, four muhajiba women and a middle-aged man joined me. At eight-thirty, the six of us climbed aboard a bus to cross the river.

As we rolled over a white steel bridge that seemed more for show than necessity, I was nervous about little details, like not having my passport stamped by the Israelis. Yet, I could take for granted that as an American, and as a Jew, I was going to enter Israel that day. To me, the Jordan River was just a creek in the reeds below, but for the five Palestinians on the bus, the giant white bridge was likely appropriate for the journey and their feelings. They didn't know Israeli soldiers as sons and daughters. In minutes, for all they knew, they would render themselves vulnerable to disrespect, disappointment, and abuse. For them, crossing the Jordan was not akin to stepping across a creek.

The driver stopped twenty feet past the bridge's guard house and in front of two Israeli soldiers with bulletproof vests and M-16s that seemed a yard long. A redheaded soldier with a goatee, a couple days of growth, and a gold stud in his left ear motioned us off the bus. A red T-shirt peeked through his uniform, which was unbuttoned on top and untucked below. He looked over our group while his dark-skinned and also unshaven partner checked the bus for anything suspicious. I imagined the thoughts of the immaculately put together older lady next to me: "These are the Israeli Occupation Forces [as they are referred to on the news] . . . thieves, killers, and occupiers . . . and they can't tuck in their shirts?"

Once at the terminal, where a line of a few people mysteriously already waited ahead of us, workers sent travelers' luggage through metal detectors under the watchful gaze of soldiers. A khaki-vest-clad man with eyes hidden behind dark sunglasses leaned against an outer wall, stared in my direction, and spoke into his walkie-talkie. I looked away, not seeking to challenge him.

Inside, I lined up behind the muhajiba women to pass through the metal detector. The first older woman set the metal detector off repeatedly and grew flustered. While the operator scowled, a short young man with glasses and hair pressed into a sleep formation pulled me out of line. He carried a walkie-talkie that seemed like an oversized toy in his small hand. Asking for my passport, he launched into a flow of questions in accented English.

"Why are you going to Israel?"

"To visit family friends."

"Where do they live?"

"Haifa."

"How long are you staying?"

"The weekend."

"Where are you coming from?"

"Amman."

"What are you doing in Jordan?"

"I am a graduate student. I study Arabic and economics."

"How long have you lived there?"

"Six months."

"Where do you live?"

"In an apartment in Webdeh."

"Do you rent the apartment?"

"Yes."

"Who do you live with?"

"No one."

"How much do you pay in rent?"

"Two hundred JD a month."

My answers were too short, and he kept motioning for me to continue, like he wanted me to speak for the exercise of speaking—a mannerism used by language teachers. He was testing my English while also judging my answers. He asked me about my research, and I gave a longer answer about increasing U.S.-Jordan trade and the general merits of free trade, in the hopes of boring him into submission. Citing trade statistics is a good way to change or end conversations. He was tough, though.

After five minutes, he sent me back into line and spoke quickly into his walkie-talkie. Looking over my shoulder, I saw the man in sunglasses from outside respond and exit the room. I turned back to the sounds of two older women setting off the metal detector. In a loud voice, a young uniformed female soldier called out in Arabic, "Come here, *haja*, come here."

Haja is a term of respect used for older Muslim Arab women that implies they have completed the *hajj*, or pilgrimage to Mecca. There was no way that the guard could have known whether the woman in question had completed the pilgrimage, but using the term was an attempt at showing respect. Any respect intended was lost in the guard's scowl and tone, though, which reminded me of an overwhelmed mother, at the Greyhound station, frustrated with her crying child.

The two women were whisked away by the guard to a curtained area for further inspection as I approached the metal detector. The guard ordered me to empty my pockets, take off my shoes, and remove my belt. When I handed her my passport, she recognized that I am American, and she said, "Thank you." A dark policewoman with a black gun in her belt told the guard in Hebrew that I was cute.

I was checking her out, too, and imagined that if she lived in Jordan, she would easily pass for a Palestinian. Despite how wide the chasm is between Israelis and Arabs, there are shared roots. This policewoman was likely an Israeli of Arab descent—maybe from Iraq or Syria. Were Israel never established, she may have grown up in an Arab country as the ultimate minority, a Jewish woman. However, with the creation of Israel, she had become an empowered policewoman with a huge gun.

I passed through the metal detector and sat down next to an older Arab man clutching a U.S. passport. At a windowed booth before us, an older woman and her niece spoke with a thin, light-skinned female border official who couldn't have been more than twenty-one years old. In Arabic, the border official asked the younger woman her uncle's name, her destination, and how long she would stay in Israel. Her tone, like that of her colleague at the metal detector, was one of frustration.

The interview did not progress smoothly. Although the border control official spoke Arabic, her mistakes and the Hebrew rhythm of her words made her difficult to understand. When the woman and her niece expressed their confusion, the official repeated her questions in a louder tone. The two ladies, intimidated, kept producing different folded papers that they hoped would appease the border control.

Amid their distress, a burly maintenance man with gigantic forearms and lamb-chop sideburns climbed a fifteen-foot ladder a couple of feet away and changed a ceiling bulb. The border control's partner—a blonde woman who was about the same age and was snacking on the Israeli equivalent of Cheetos—interrupted to ask her what she was doing for Shabbat. A teenage soldier in an oversize green uniform then came over and tried to flirt with the Cheetos eater. The sounds of laughter, and then other young soldiers with cups of coffee, spilled out of the office to the left of the booth.

The full names of the woman's father and paternal uncle were eventually confirmed, and the two ladies continued on. The man next to me approached the window, and the border control official looked through his passport. She asked in English, "How long do you plan to stay in Israel?"

"For as long as you permit," he replied in English.

"Do you plan to work?" she countered.

"If you like," he responded.

These answers would have been deferential in Arabic, but they sounded sneaky in English. The official, about thirty-five years his junior, exploded; she demanded to see all of his money in order to know how he would finance his stay. Under repeated questioning and much duress, the man requested a three-month visa. The border control official told him that it was impossible to stay in Israel for three months and that he could stay for one month as she stamped his passport.

The hall had filled up over the last few minutes and the blonde official opened her window and beckoned me forward. She flipped through my passport's Arabic stamp-filled pages, and I immediately asked her in English not to stamp it.

"Why don't you want an Israel stamp in your passport?"

"I want to be able to go back to Syria."

"Syria?!"

"Yes, you'll see the stamp right there . . ."

"Why would you go to Syria?"

"For tourism."

"For tourism!"

"Well, for research, too. I'm a student, and am doing economic research on, um, trade in the region and I, um, will have some interviews . . . in Syria . . ."

"Why are you going to Israel?"

"To v-visit family friends."

"Where are they?"

"On a farm outside of Haifa."

"How long will you stay?"

"The weekend."

"Have you been to Israel before?"

"Yes, a few times . . . but before." This was my second passport and there was no evidence of a previous trip to Israel.

She told me to write down my friend's name, address, and phone number and to sit down while she called him. She returned five minutes later and asked me the name of the farm that I would visit. I told her the Hebrew name.

"Your friend is Jewish?" she asked in surprised tone.

"Yes," I answered.

"And you are Jewish?" she replied, a puzzled look on her face.

She hadn't called Elad and had instead mistaken me for an Arab. Because my destination was Haifa, a mixed Jewish and Arab city, she had no way of knowing that my cousins are modern Orthodox Jews. Since I was coming from Jordan—where most of the border traffic is Palestinian—and had traveled throughout the Arab East, she had assumed that I was an Arab American. I glanced at all the Palestinians waiting behind me. With a sense of remorse for the abandonment of my fellow travelers and for the ending of our common experience, I answered, "Yes."

Crow's-feet emerged around her eyes, and her face relaxed. "How long will you stay in Israel?" she asked as she pounded documents with her stamp, beneath the window and out of my sight.

"The weekend. D-did you just stamp my passport?" I stuttered.

"No, have a nice trip. Shabbat Shalom," she said with a smile as she handed me my passport. The visa paper shoved between the front cover and the first page of my passport had an entry stamp on it valid for a three-month stay.

Tribalism reigns not only in the Arab East, but in Israel, too. Groups form layered alliances based on bonds of loyalty against shifting external enemies. Arab societies are rife with internal divisions, such as between Jordanians and Palestinians or Muslims and Christians, but it is outsiders—those who adhere to different and unfamiliar traditions—that constitute the clearest threats. There is an oft-repeated Arabic proverb that goes something like, "Me against my brother; me and my brother against our cousin; me, my brother, and my cousin against the foreigner."

The saying may be a cliché, but it is true. There is a social trust that exists in Arab societies that does not include foreigners. Palestinians and Jordanians may hate or dislike each other, but with America threatening war against Iraq, they'll put aside their differences to view the United States as a common enemy capable of worsening the status quo. Such is the case in Israel, too. In the world of stereotypes, Ashkenazi Jews discriminate against Sephardic ones, and there are a host of complicated feelings that involve the Russians and Ethiopians. But they are all Jews, and relative to the "Arabs," Jews aren't going to hurt other Jews. Tribally speaking, once it was clear to the border control official that I am Jewish, it also became clear that I was relatively harmless.

I spent another hour going through more metal detectors, having my bag searched, and waiting, but Israelis welcomed me once I was deemed kosher. A petite brunette who swabbed my bag for bomb chemicals chatted with me about the weekend. A pretty Ethiopian-Israeli border guard asked me what I was doing in Jordan and why I was studying Arabic. When I stepped out of the terminal and into the West Bank, it was 12:10 p.m. The Israeli border process, with minimal waiting in lines, had taken me three hours. Inside, my Palestinian travel partners continued without me.

Outside of the terminal, a throng of local drivers approached and asked in Arabic and then Hebrew where I was going. With the exception of hearing Arabic-accented Hebrew, the scene was similar to taxi stands in Egypt, Morocco, and Syria. There was the familiar line of Peugeot station wagons, a crowd of people bargaining and jockeying for position, and drivers barking out destinations. Avoiding one driver who sought to take me directly to Haifa in a "deluxe" car for $100 "cash money," I piled into a station wagon going to Damascus Gate in Jerusalem's Old City.

The driver packed the car with seven passengers, and we zipped through a wide and empty highway, past little hills with green buds, listening to Arabic Top 40 star Ihab Tawfik's new cassette. On the right, the sparkling white settlement of Maaleh Adumim sat between craggy hills and scattered shrubs. The thousands of plastic bags that litter roads throughout the Arab East were conspicuously absent. I mentioned to the older gentleman squished against me how clean and pretty it was, and he explained that Israelis "are very interested in the environment." On cue, the guy sitting shotgun lit his last cigarette and was ready to toss the box out the passenger's window when the Palestinian driver intervened and motioned for him to put the trash in the car's ashtray. Two minutes later, we pulled up to an Israeli checkpoint where a muscular soldier checked the driver's ID and waved us forward routinely.

As we approached the Palestinian villages on the outskirts of Jerusalem, passengers called out to the driver, requesting drop-offs at specific places. Over the next fifteen minutes, we made four stops in the winding alleys of two different villages. Each departing passenger called out *"Allah ya'atik al-afya"* to the driver. The crowded homes stacked on top of each other, the children running and playing in the dirt streets, the Arabic graffiti on the walls, and the garbage overflowing from the communal bins—it could have been any number of Arab villages in Jordan or Syria, but for the scattered Hebrew signs. Between the familiar colloquial Arabic and those Hebrew signs, I struggled to find my bearings.

The driver pulled into Friday afternoon traffic outside of Jerusalem's walled city. The streets were congested with Muslim worshippers returning home from Friday prayer and religious Jews heading home for the start of Shabbat. A few blocks from Damascus Gate, I called out *"Allah ya'atik al-afya"* to the driver and got out. Walking to the gate, I read for the first time the clusters of Arabic signs for stationary, clothing, and electronic stores that packed the street. When I lived in Jerusalem, the Arabic characters on the signs were meaningless symbols to me.

I stopped at a falafel stand that I frequented in 1996. The same older man, now with hair a bit more gray, sat behind the cash register, but he didn't recognize me. The others in the restaurant spoke Arabic and I was the only non-Arab there. I wished him *as-Salaam Alaikum* and ordered in Arabic. Had our Hebrew small talk seven years ago just been a courtesy? Was it always so Arab here, or had Israelis stopped coming to East Jerusalem? After finishing my falafel, I walked a few steps down the street, and in Arabic, changed $60 worth of Jordanian dinars to Israeli shekels.

Dressed in my Syrian coat, with my goatee and short dark hair, I blended into the Friday afternoon crowd. I walked past the green uniformed soldiers in front of Damascus Gate and turned into the Muslim Quarter. The Friday market inside Damascus Gate was a flurry of activity. Merchants hawked everything from toy dolls to green onions while casually dressed men and muhajiba women shoppers perused the market. Young children clutched their parents' hands and stared at the bustling activity. Next to a man selling olives and pickles, the voice of Amr Diab, a popular Egyptian star, blared from a cassette salesman's boom box. I could have been in any city across the Arab East. This was Jerusalem, though, a place that I thought I knew. Damascus Gate, the villages that we had driven through, the falafel stand, the money changer, it was all Palestine.

I descended further into the market, looking for some sweets to bring Elad's family. I found a shop brimming with pastries wedged between two clothing stores and asked the salesman in Arabic if his sweets were kosher. I explained that I was visiting a kosher home for Shabbat, and he rushed to show me that his pastry boxes had "kosher" written on them in Hebrew. I ordered two kilos of *ruggelach* and would like to believe that they were indeed kosher.

Ordering kosher pastries in Arabic from a Palestinian in the Muslim Quarter of Jerusalem's Old City was an optimistic moment. It left me scratching my head, though, as to how I could buy kosher pastries in Palestine, but not use the word "Israel" among the Jordanian-Palestinians I know in Amman, who consider themselves staunch supporters of the Palestinian struggle. On the seam between Israel and the Arab East, where lives and mutual interests overlap, some Palestinians are able to reach a coexistence with Israelis that angry members of the diaspora would find impossible to understand.

Leaving Damascus Gate, I was overwhelmed both by a wistfulness to visit my old haunts and a desire to explore a familiar but new place. Elad expected me in Haifa, however. I trudged up the hill, past the New Gate. I looked longingly to my left at Jaffa Gate and the last chance that it represented—at least on this trip—to wander around the Old City again. I sighed and turned right onto Jaffa Road instead, the street that leads toward downtown and the bus station.

The bustling masses, noise, and overall activity that characterized the Muslim Quarter and Damascus Gate melted away. Though I'd only been walking for ten minutes, I was now in West Jerusalem, and Shabbat was only a few hours away. A clean wide-lane street led into downtown Jerusalem's main artery. The bus stops were empty, and cabs zipped by, perhaps not wanting to stop for a dark man carrying a backpack and wearing a coat on a sunny day. As I neared Zion Square and an outdoor coffee shop on my right, Israelis, some wearing shorts, sat in the sun reading newspapers, chatting, and drinking coffee.

Remembering one of my favorite sandwich shops (yes, I'd just eaten a falafel sandwich), I ducked into a three-table place with a giant display counter filled with meats, side dishes, and spreads. A graying Israeli woman behind the counter looked at me skeptically. Summoning Hebrew from my deep reserves—I've actively repressed any Hebrew language instinct for the past six months out of fear of personal Armageddon—I smiled and said, *"Shalom, efshar likabel sandvich schnitzel veh marak adashim?"* Would it be possible to have a schnitzel sandwich and lentil soup?

She smiled back, and with a Russian-accented Hebrew said, *"Be-tahh, hamoudi."* Of course, sweetie.

Two hours later, on a bus heading north to Haifa, staring out the window at the Mediterranean Sea on my left, it occurred to me that it had been a trip without stamps. They didn't stamp my passport at the Jordanian border, the Israeli border, or on Jaffa Road at the invisible border that I never knew existed. I had left Jordan at the King Hussein Bridge, but it was only on Jaffa Road, over a bowl of lentil soup, that I entered Israel. In between, I crossed Palestine.

Some people will find this personal revelation threatening and label me an apologist or, worse, a self-hating Jew. After six months in the Arab East, I've learned to appreciate another perspective on history, and I'm not referring to the Palestinian perspective, but rather "people's history." Let me explain.

As Americans, a lot of us appreciate rules and adhere to what is official. Establishing a firm set of rules and then enforcing them is a way to try and ensure equality for everyone. U.S. history is about the evolution of our nation's struggle for equality—from the time that colonists revolted against the British Empire because they were being taxed without proper representation to the civil rights movement of the 1950s and 1960s. In a lot of ways, we take this American penchant for rules, forms, and officialdom and apply its logic elsewhere. Personally, I'm guilty of applying it to history, viewing history through the perspective of nation-states, rather than of people.

On the issue of Palestine, the United States does not officially recognize Palestine as an independent state, and for good reason: It isn't a state. There isn't a Palestinian government that rules independently over the Palestinian people and that has internationally recognized borders, embassies in other countries, or officially recognized documentation. Palestinians have always been ruled—at least officially—by Israel, Jordan, and the British, among others. The closest that Palestinians have come to living in their own independent state was in the mid- to late-1990s, when they lived under the governance of the Palestinian National Authority. With this historical background established, and given my American adherence to the parameters of national and international rules, my understanding of Palestine's existence was compromised. Because there is no history of Palestinian rule and there is no internationally recognized independent Palestinian state, I was unable to see Palestine as a place.

From the perspective of people and a people's history, though, existence and history do not depend upon official sovereignty and independence. To be sure, the actions of government institutions and the relationship between ruler and the ruled are key parts of any history. They influence the quality of a people's life; however, they are not exclusive components to a formula that determines a people's history.

The absence of functioning and sovereign government institutions that are internationally recognized do not prevent Palestine from existing as a fact on the ground, a place. There are Arabs who have lived for hundreds of years in East Jerusalem, Bethlehem, Ramallah, Nablus, and other places in the West Bank and Gaza. If we were classifying these people by nationality, we'd call them by the nationality they've chosen as a people—Palestinian. So what of the official name of the land that they live on? Why do we insist that it be called the West Bank or Gaza? In the breathing world of humans, it is Palestine, the place of the Palestinian people. Official stationery, passports, and voting rights at the United Nations will not change the history of Palestinian life. It will add a new and positive chapter, but it will not make Palestine exist for the first time. Palestine is already a place with a history and a people. The passports and papers will make it a state.

People I've met in Jordan, Syria, and Egypt generally use the Arabic word *Philistine* when speaking about Palestine. Some Palestinians use the terms *Gaza* and *al-Dufa*, or "the Bank," when referring to specific places in Palestine. Their affection for and familiarity with the place aside, these Jordanians, Syrians, and Egyptians naturally view Palestine as a place and are less inhibited by "official" mind-sets. Official things here don't necessarily carry the same credibility as they do for Americans. Governments aren't elected fairly or chosen. There isn't a history of government responsiveness or representation of people's aspirations or ideas in the Middle East. If the popular level of belief in Egypt is that the government is corrupt, there is no reason, on a popular level, for people to adhere to the government's official perspective on history, or anything else for that matter.

People's history is something that is told in homes. While to varying degrees people in Jordan, Syria, and Egypt may have ceded authority to their governments over ownership of the public domain or space, by no means have they relinquished authority regarding their sense of the truth. Families, villages, and tribes have their own history, which isn't necessarily the same as the history of the state. And from that perspective, it isn't that important to people's understanding of Palestine's existence that it isn't a country recognized by governments. They recognize Palestine's existence based on different criteria; they recognize a people's history of living in a place, with distinct traditions and customs, over a period of hundreds of years.

Now that I've seen the light, it's time for me to be judgmental. This trip without stamps and the shock of realizing that Palestine already exists in places like East Jerusalem, which I'd thought of as a part of Israel where Palestinians lived, has made it clear to me that to deny the reality of the existence of a place called Palestine is to be either uninformed or dishonest. A week ago, and certainly six months ago, I was uninformed. There is no reason to choose to be dishonest. At the same time, there is also no reason to stop appreciating the merits of Zionism—the idea that Jews should have (and need) their own state in their historic homeland.

For those challenged by the concept of Palestine as a place, admitting Palestine's existence does not mean that Israelis or Jews have lesser claims and can't live in a place called Israel. Israelis and Jews trace their "people's history" to a time of sovereignty over the land more than 2,500 years ago. But it is important to remember that the history of the Jewish people also runs through periods where they lived as a people in a place—as Palestinians do now—not under their own official rule.

For Palestine to become a state—while maintaining Israel's existence as a Jewish democratic state—compromises and agreements need to be worked out within international law, as they were with the creation and recognition of Israel in 1948. Undoubtedly, Israelis are going to have to relinquish sovereignty over some areas (within Palestine) that contain a majority of Palestinians, even though those places or cities are of emotional and historical attachment to the Jewish people's history. In the same way, Palestinians will have to relinquish claims to areas, cities, and villages inside of Israel—which are a part of their history and their homeland—that contain a majority of Israelis. The key, though, is that the existence of an official Palestinian state doesn't require the dismantling and replacement of the state of Israel. There are two people's histories that have intertwined in an awful conflict over the last seventy-five years. It isn't necessary that this conflict be settled in a winner takes all fashion. It is possible for there to be Palestinian bakers that sell kosher ruggelach.

Speaking of the ruggelah, they tasted good; my cousins and I had a nice visit. Even better, I'll return to Pittsburgh in a couple of days for the first time since July for a ten-day visit. I finished my semester last week and have a break before the start of spring courses. See you soon.

Love,
Ben

Letter 14

Pickaxes and Squeegees

February 26, 2003

Dear All,

The idea of evacuation has hung over my head since I arrived in Jordan last July. The reality has finally arrived.

The imminence of war with Iraq has been with me throughout this journey, from my informal "press conferences" with locals on U.S. policy to my "debate" with the leader of the anti-America protest in Aleppo. Evacuation has always seemed like a sensational concept, like something out of Hollywood—images of military helicopters taking off from the roof of an embassy building and crowded airports with worried Western faces clamoring toward the gate, their tickets in hand and roller luggage in tow.

There would be panic and fear at the uncertainty that lay ahead, but at the same time—strangely—I imagined there would be a feeling of relief akin to a snow day back home. The inevitable would become the reality; overplanning, contingencies, and speculation would give way to action with the routine canceled. My daily shuffle would be postponed indefinitely. I wouldn't have to worry about cramming in as much Arabic as possible or interviewing people for my research project, just the basics of getting to the airport and onto the plane.

Snow days are a warm memory. As a kid, I would jump on the bed, cheer in celebration, put on my long johns, and hit the streets for snowball fights and sledding. For some reason, I've associated the idea of evacuation from Jordan, a cancellation of the routine, with an unexpected snow day. In surreal fashion, as evacuation loomed on the approaching horizon, it snowed. It snowed a lot, at least eight inches, maybe even a foot. Unlike my warm and fuzzy memories, though, I don't feel the relief that I expected—knowing that the writing is indeed on the wall, and that I have no choice but to leave because of the impending war. Instead, Amman's snow has left me trapped inside my apartment feeling angry, frustrated, and guilty.

Three weeks ago, I received an e-mail from my fellowship sponsors that conveyed the inevitable: My personal race against time in Jordan had ended. The State Department had issued an "authorized departure" for nonessential personnel from the U.S. embassies in Jordan, Lebanon, Syria, and Israel. Translation: It was officially unsafe for me to remain in Jordan. I had to leave by the end of the month. Since last summer, when I started talking with people in Washington and seeking advice about my upcoming year in Jordan, I knew that this moment and the war were likely. One after the other, Middle East professionals and experts told me to "go now" to Jordan so that I could have a few months before the war, or that this would certainly be "an interesting time to be there," with war on the horizon.

So while "the war" has always been a part of my planning, the pressure that has built over the past few months has reached a point of almost being unbearable. Uncertainty and the fear of war are everywhere. For the last few months, my presence has served as an indicator for when war would come. As long as I kept showing up at the grocery store, pickup basketball games, Nai, or the university, people could believe that war was a threat, not a reality. The Americans would leave Jordan before war started. When I went to Morocco in January and missed a week of school, I didn't get a chance to tell one of my teachers. When I returned the next week, she was so happy to see me that she almost hugged me (she didn't, of course, because she is muhajiba and I'm a foreign man). She thought that I had left Jordan for good, suddenly, and that war was imminent.

Thankfully, my ordered departure from Jordan did not mean that I would lose my fellowship. I just needed to make alternative plans for continuing to study Arabic and completing my research elsewhere. After some e-mail consultations with my Arabic teacher from grad school and with some friends in Egypt, I decided that I would return to the place of departure for my Arabic language odyssey: Cairo, *Um al Dunya*, or mother of the world.

My flight for Cairo leaves tomorrow morning, and I've spent most of the last two days snowbound in my apartment, ruminating about the upcoming war. I did make it out of the apartment, however, to see how Amman and Jordanians were dealing with the snow. Generally, it rains here in the winter and can even dip into the low thirties. Every few years, it will snow, but Buffalo-type blizzards like this one are rare. I wasn't exactly prepared for a foot of snow. Two weeks ago, after the semester ended, I went home to Pittsburgh to visit my family and took my winter clothes with me. Given my pending relocation to the more southern climate of Cairo, and with winter mostly passed, I thought I would be okay; turns out that I was wrong. After looking out the window, I put on a few T-shirts and my remaining sweatshirts, slipped some socks on my hands for gloves, and confronted Amman's blizzard of 2003.

I live on a side street burrowed about three-quarters of the way up the Webdeh Hill. Since there are no ploughs, my little street was buried by the snow. I climbed up to the main road that is lined with my supermarket, the grocery store, and all the other shops. It was like an idyllic early morning Christmas moment: Stores were shuttered, cars were buried under fresh powder, and not a person was in sight. The entire neighborhood was immobilized. On my way to Abdali station and downtown, I turned a corner and found some kids playing in the snow and building a snowman. I looked like an easy target with my socks on my hands and my Syrian sports coat covering my gray sweatshirt with a hood, and one of the kids called out in Arabic, "Hey, uncle, want some?"

The blizzard of 2003, Abdali Station.

The blizzard of 2003, Webdeh.

The blizzard of 2003, King Abdullah mosque.

He and his six little friends then started throwing snow at me. But they didn't know how to pack it into tight snowballs like I do. White socks on my hands, sports coat and all, I took on seven Jordanian kids in a snowball fight. I had to represent the Pittsburgh Public Schools and the snow days of my youth. It was the snowball fight equivalent of a Chuck Norris movie where he defeats something like fifteen black-clad ninjas at once. One by one, I picked them off; spinning and pivoting, I rained snowballs down on their little heads, chests, and retreating rumps. We all laughed, and I fought back the urge to lift my arms in the air and chant "USA, USA." I'm not Rocky, and it isn't the time.

Instead, I wished them peace and made my way down the hill toward Abdali. The station's overhead structure had collapsed under the pressure of the accumulated snow. All that was left was a twisted metal sculpture, under piles of collapsed sheeting, covered in snow. I approached to take a picture and came across some soldiers trying to push their vans and other cars free. There was no traction, though, since the streets hadn't been cleared. A few guys had farmers' pickaxes and rubber squeegees that are used to clean floors and they were trying to dig out and clear a way. It was slow going. Eager to be of some assistance and to cast doubt on the opinion that Americans only bring destruction, I helped push cars for awhile. Somehow, I resisted the urge to announce that I was an *Amriki*. After thirty minutes, my sock-clad hands were frozen, so I returned home to warm up. There was nothing to do at home, however, but look out the window and ruminate some more.

Jordan has lived under a dark cloud for the past few months. At JFK last week, as I walked to my gate for my direct flight back to Amman, I passed a neighboring gate where the flight was headed for Spain. Men and women chatted loudly in Spanish, children ran and played, and it seemed as if there was music playing. At Gate 4, destination Amman, sat a collection of the most sullen and distraught-looking people I've seen outside of an emergency room's waiting room. The gate area was full of mustached men sitting quietly, waiting for someone's execution, perhaps their own. The tension was so palpable that I waited at Gate 5 for the boarding call.

The growing terror of war has led to rampant speculation here: Saddam will use chemical weapons on U.S. soldiers and winds will blow the fallout to Jordan; Iraqi refugees will flood the Jordanian border; Sharon will push Palestinians into Jordan from the West Bank; Saddam will use WMD on Israel, and Israel will retaliate with nuclear weapons; and thousands of innocents will be killed. With the exception of Palestinians being driven out of the West Bank, I've come to adopt these fears, too.

Already Jordan is feeling the economic effects of war. Besides the lack of tourism, industries that trade with Iraq—one of Jordan's chief trading partners and a source of free oil—have already suffered due to worst-case scenario speculation over the past few months. No one wants to think about a stoppage of free oil and what that will mean. This is a poor country already; it could get a lot worse very soon.

From my trip home to Pittsburgh, I got the sense that most people think that Saddam is responsible for this whole situation. The onus is on him to cooperate with weapons inspectors and to take action to avert war. The view from Jordan is completely reversed. The United States is responsible for causing an unnecessary crisis. There is deep sympathy for the suffering that the Iraqi people have endured over the past decade of sanctions, which were enforced by the United States. There is indeed hatred among many for the brutality of Saddam, but there is also fury at the choice of America and, in particular, President Bush to bring war.

Yesterday, on day two of the blizzard, it stopped snowing, but still there were almost no shops open. Some bulldozers had plowed through some of the busier streets, but not mine. Instead, the sun turned hilly Amman into a city of streams and rivers. I sloshed my way down to Abdali to say good-bye to Kholood and her uncle. I still didn't see any shovels, as men continued to dig their cars and driveways out with spades, pickaxes, and squeegees—a hopeless task.

Ammo and Kholood picked me up at the shattered bus station, its six-lane garage still a mess of twisted metal covered in snow. I thought we would go for tea, but we just drove around the block and stopped. Kholood sat in the front seat and she turned around to say good-bye and wish me the best. She was choked up and asked me what I thought would happen. "Would there be war?" she asked.

Of course I expected war since the U.S. government was making me evacuate the country. What could I say? As Kholood looked imploringly at me, I wondered what would happen to her, to Ammo sitting quietly beside her, to her mother, and to Bahaa, Ibrahim, Ramis, Na'el, and everyone else I've come to know here. What could I say? As I tried to muster an answer, Ammo began to yell at me in Arabic.

I have Ammo to thank for Kholood's continued work with me. After our discussion about me being Jewish, Kholood asked Ammo if it was okay to teach me Arabic. Ammo, a large, sliver-haired, and soft-spoken person, told her that she had to; it was a duty and an opportunity. Ammo has crooked knuckles that were broken by Israeli soldiers, and he is old enough to remember leaving his home in the West Bank, but he told Kholood that they had to learn to live and coexist with the Jews. Ammo moved in with his sister (Kholood's mother), his niece Kholood, and his nephew after the death of Kholood's father a year ago. As I've written previously, Ammo takes care of Kholood, chauffeuring her about, chaperoning her, and mentoring the youth of the science and technology club.

He now shouted, "What is he doing? This man is crazy, he is completely crazy! He is going to kill Iraqis and Jordanians and Palestinians. What for? For oil? He is going to destroy the economy. There will be unemployment and losses. Why? For what reason? For weapons? For oil? For Israel? He is crazy. Crazy! This 'cowboy,' he will kill us! He is a 'cowboy!' We don't want this!"

There was nothing for me to say. I could leave, but they had to stay and deal with the repercussions. There was no morning flight for them, just more waiting in their homes for the fulfillment of a menu of disasters. The tension is so thick here and fear has run away from reality, for everyone. I shook hands with both Ammo and Kholood, wished that God and peace be with them, and trudged with my head down, through the slush, back up the hill to my apartment.

Now that I am leaving, I find that people are looking at me strangely, with a little bit of jealousy and a lot of resentment. I felt it when I picked up my ticket for Cairo from the travel agent, when I was at the grocer last week, and also at the supermarket, where I drink coffee with the owner a couple of nights a week. It isn't so much their words but their body language and the look in their eyes when Randa, the travel agent, handed me my ticket, or when Hanna, the supermarket owner, shook my hand over coffee. No one blames me personally for what is going to happen, but there is a cruel irony that I'm the one who gets to leave and secure my personal safety, while at the same time, it is my country that is going to start this war and the chain of disasters that may befall Jordan.

My landlady, a very nice woman who lives downstairs with her elderly mother, took the news that I was breaking my lease well. She has a nephew in New York, and she travels abroad a lot. When I knocked on her door to tell her, she told me that she knew it was only a matter of time before I would go. The Portuguese couple next door is staying, though. I speculate that there is a feeling that I am insulting people by leaving.

In some ways, my departure can be interpreted as a statement about my lack of confidence in Jordanians to continue treating me with dignity. Hospitality is the rule here; people were shamed by Laurence Foley's murder. I don't worry about being singled out and attacked by Jordanians. And if I indeed don't fear Jordanians hurting me, then I must be leaving because I really do think that terrible things are going to happen. So, as I say good-bye to friends, I become this self-interested guy who either doesn't trust Jordanians to treat him hospitably or who is exercising privilege to escape impending doom while leaving others behind.

Given all of the emotions running through me, my personal feelings might be clouding my current judgment, but I'm struggling to figure out why Americans need this war right now. The immediacy of the threat cited by the administration isn't clear, and I am no longer able to defend U.S. policy in my long-winded impromptu "press conferences." While I would never admit it to my Jordanian cross-examiners, I find the Bush administration's rhetoric and decision-making irresponsible. We claim to act on behalf of a right and moral cause, but our arguments shift like Abu Alaa's sand in the desert. We swirl between Al Qaeda, disarmament of weapons of mass destruction, the suffering Iraqi people, and fighting regional aggression.

With the presence of U.S. soldiers in the Gulf, Saddam is contained. He does not actively pose a threat to Israel or Kuwait, so we can continue to support weapons inspections. Saddam's secular regime is anathema to the Islamist jihadi haters like bin Laden, who seek an Islamic state led by a caliph and governed by sharia; cooperation between the two parties seems highly unlikely. The jihadis want to unseat secular governments like Saddam's, not work with them. The United States is a target of their hatred and attacks because we offer support to other regimes, that they consider similarly heretical, in Saudi Arabia and in Egypt. Most important, though, bin Laden attacked us on September 11, not Saddam. It's been almost a year and a half since then. Why can't we catch him, and why are we diverting resources from that pursuit and from rebuilding Afghanistan?

After an incredible outpouring of goodwill following the 9/11 attacks, our Iraq policy and the manner in which we've conducted it have turned the world against us. On TV, I've watched coverage of protests from around the world against the Bush administration and America. How can it be that people aren't gathering in the streets to protest against Saddam's tyranny or bin Laden's killing of innocents, or to support global cooperation against the threats of weapons proliferation and terrorism? It seems as if both our tone and our substance have painted *us* as the global threat.

As an American, I worry about the repercussions for America of such a war. Attacking Iraq at this time and without international consensus will not make Americans safer; it will be another strike on the list against us and could serve as a recruiting tool for more people to descend into the "Arab Basement" and become America haters. The immediate threat to the United States is the proliferation of weapons of mass destruction and the transfer of WMD to haters like bin Laden. The British, French, Germans, Japanese, and Russians face the exact same threat. While Saddam is a cruel dictator and has a history of regional aggression, attacking him and Iraq is not a priority in dealing with this specific threat. If we disregard the United Nations and pursue this war, I worry about what we will face at home a few years down the road. How will attacking Saddam stop someone with a dirty bomb from getting into our country and blowing himself up in a mall in Cleveland or a hospital in Chicago? This war will not affect our current and persistent security threats, and it will bring us a future of international isolation.

I've heard the conspiracy theories about oil and the armchair psychoanalysis of the father-son Bush rivalry. I've also read about the desire to teach "the Arabs" a lesson in force. Syrians fear the Assad regime because of what it did to Hama. In the same way, there are those in Washington that think we can scare bin Laden and the other haters into not challenging and attacking the United States again. Perhaps Iraq is to be the example. The bottom line seems to be that the administration is choosing to go to war with Iraq. Whatever the exact reasons behind this choice, the war itself may set off a chain of events that include a chemical weapons attack, perhaps on U.S. soldiers or Iraqis or on Israel, and worse—a response with more weapons. I can only lamely hope that the casualties and destruction caused by our choice are minimal.

I could continue with my dissent, but it is futile, so I'll close for now. This is my last letter from Jordan, and I'm sad to be leaving. It is not so much because I will miss certain people here. While I do have friends and acquaintances that I care about, I will miss Jordan itself, my life here, and what I've been able to do these last seven months. I think back to my first few days and not being able to ride the bus or ask for the check at a restaurant. Yesterday, standing in six inches of melting snow, someone asked me for directions to downtown, and I delivered them in perfect Arabic. He didn't ask me where I'm from; he just said, *"Allah ya'atik al-afya,"* and marched on up the hill.

Aside from the professional goals I set for myself before coming here, I've discovered something special and personal. I've developed a deep affection for this country, this city, and its people—of whatever their origin of descent. I'm going to miss walking up and down hills, listening to *al control* call out the stops on the bus, sitting in Hashemite Square downtown, watching the sunset at the end of my block, and speaking Jordanian slang with my baker. Most of all, I'll miss being called *habibi* by strangers. The hospitality that I received here is greater than anything I could ever have imagined.

Jordan is going to miss me, too. Jordan may not miss me personally, but the departure of Americans and other foreigners is another cost of the war. Jordanians need Americans, the British, Italians, and even the French. There is something going on here; people are trying to develop their economy and to fight certain cultural and political battles. They need support and exposure to some of the things that foreign visitors offer. People like Ibrahim from Zarqa, or Bilal, a graduate student majoring in English who chases me around the university with a phrase book of American slang—they need international visitors to speak English with and to correct them when they use *Brady Bunch* words like "groovy."

Jordan needs relationships with the world, with unofficial ambassadors from America and other foreign countries who express an interest in Jordanian culture, invest in the country, visit Petra, provide diversity, and listen to political rants and respond by respectfully disagreeing. Who will teach the English classes at the British Council? Who will study Arabic with Kholood? And who will challenge the stereotype of an oversexed and violent America?

The Fulbright professors at Jordan University had to leave, too. How will their students finish their masters program in American studies without teachers? Maybe they will set up a satellite feed, but those students need human interaction with America, not isolation. They need Jack Davis in the flesh, not a picture of him on a TV screen. Jack is a professor from the University of Alabama at Birmingham who knew little about the Middle East but came here to teach American history on a Fulbright grant. He offers insightful lessons on Native American history and the civil rights movement to students whose lives are dominated by issues of honor and justice.

Under an overcast sky, I stood at the end of my street. I watched a city bus descend down the hill toward the center of town, its tires splashing through the running streams of melting snow. Life will go on here, but for me the sky will be a bit less blue. The United States has ratcheted up the pressure, our military is poised to unleash war, and it is time for me to say good-bye to a place that I've called home.

Love,
Ben

Part Four

The Beating Heart
of the Arab East

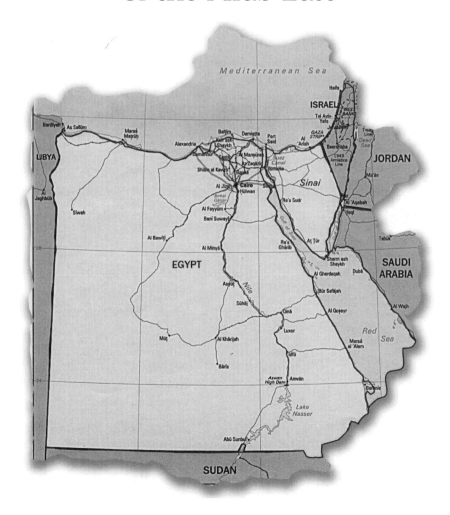

Letter 15

The Mother of the World

March 9, 2003

Dear All,

At 6:00 P.M., I stepped out onto my balcony for some air. I would say fresh air, but my undershirts turn brown if I leave them on the laundry line too long. This is Cairo, *al Qahira*, "the city victorious," home to roughly 20 million people and what seems like 10 million cars without mufflers. I imagine that there are a lot of everyday victories here, unless of course you are a delicate white undergarment, then you are always a loser.

Eight stories below my apartment's balcony perch, a jerky procession of cars, minivans, and buses honked their horns down the street while pedestrians young and old, slow and fast, male and female, played human "Frogger" between them. Abruptly, a 1970s Volkswagen minibus careened around the corner. Twisting off the side, hanging outside its door, was an eight-year-old boy, screaming, "Geeza, Geeza, Geeza" (the bus's destination), and waving his thumb and pinkie finger sideways à la professional wrestling great Jimmy "the Superfly" Snuka. A couple of middle-aged men wearing tucked-in, button-down shirts and slacks chased the van, waving their right hands in the same way yelling, "Geeza! Geeza! Geeza!" They passed a donkey-drawn cart carrying four little boys who were merging into traffic between two black-and-white Fiat cabs. What seemed like hundreds of car horns drummed a steady "beep, beep, beep" background beat as the van slowed to a roll and the men leaped aboard.

Across the street, on a dirt field, some forty-five children lined up for team handball practice. They took turns attacking the goalie and trying to score. Some cheated, throwing the ball at the net only after running past the lines traced out for them in the dirt. The goalie bounced the ball back to his attackers but refused to return the ball to the cheaters. A coach came over to show the players proper form and, at full speed, whizzed the ball past the little goalie.

Behind them, on a larger field dotted with grassy spots, boys in blue soccer uniforms lined up to run laps. After a couple of laps around half the field, the team began to sprint, and four boys imme-

Cairo, the view from the author's balcony.

diately separated themselves from the pack. From such a distance, the figures seemed like thoroughbreds the way they rounded the field's corners on a dime. Unexpectedly, one boy became Secretariat and left the pack to choke in a cloud of dust. There were no Winner's Circle moments, though, as the boys continued to jog laps below the evening smog.

Mounds of garbage line the outer concrete wall of the two fields. In the morning, a bulldozer, dump truck, and green uniformed men scoop it up and take it to whereabouts unknown. The clouds of dust and debris that float through the air during this process make me want to wrap a gas mask around my face. At lunch, less than ten feet from the garbage piles, a mother and three or four little children run a shiny silver lunch cart and sell *fuul*, a heavy mix of mashed fava beans and oil, to neighborhood patrons. At night, when it grows a bit chilly, the local bodega owner who sells candy, cigarettes, and cold drinks burns piles of trash and drinks tea around the fire with friends.

Some mornings, before the green men arrive, a shepherd leads forty or fifty sheep through traffic to graze in the garbage. Brown, dirty white, and black sheep mingle amid the refuse and nuzzle the plastic bags, empty cans, and rotting fruits and vegetables. After a spell, the shepherd drives them into traffic with whistles and a stick, and they too continue to whereabouts unknown.

This evening, children and cats were digging through the garbage mounds looking for something of value as an overloaded donkey pulling a garbage wagon approached. The young driver, a ten-year-old boy clad in a dirty gray *galabaya*, or traditional robe, stopped the donkey short, and with the momentum, three other boys flipped the cart on its side. The garbage swooshed down close to a pile as the donkey kicked for traction amid the loose dirt and the blows of the driver's whip. The donkey pulled the cart on its side until it flipped upright with the help of the three other boys and galloped off into traffic. The boys leaped on to the back of the cart, where garbage had sat only moments ago, and it bounced away. As that dump became a part of history, another donkey-drawn cart pulled up and hurled its load. This cart missed its mark by several feet, though I'm not sure that anyone else noticed. Certainly the donkey's groans received little attention. As the donkey struggled to right the cart, one of the boys punched him in the head while the driver beat his flanks with a long stick.

Like a thunder clap, the call to prayer accompanied by the wafting smell of fresh bread from the corner bakery eclipsed the cars' horns and the donkey's bellowing. Pulling away from the bakery was a young man on a bicycle, clad in navy galabaya. On his head, he balanced a five-foot by three-foot wooden bread basket. With both his hands on the handlebars, he maneuvered into traffic. Across the way at the *ahwa* or coffee shop, two men sat down in white plastic chairs that faced the street. The two friends joined others smoking water pipes and drinking tea. Passing traffic kicked up a cloud of assorted dirt, and they opened a backgammon board and started to play.

With the scent of fresh bread in the air, I realized that I was hungry and went downstairs to the restaurant next door to the bakery. I exchanged pleasantries with Abu Sayyid, my *bawaab* or doorman, freely this night, that is, without being shaken down for money by him, his wife, or his kids—all of whom live on the ground floor. In Cairo, nothing within reason costs a lot, but everything costs something. I frequently feel like an Egyptian guinea dispenser, spitting out filthy quarter and half guinea notes in response to neverending requests for *baksheesh*—a tip for services rendered, a bribe, or charity, depending upon the context.

I pay the bawaab to take down my garbage, though I'm pretty sure that he just throws it into the street, and to protect me at night. The sight of Abu Sayyid sleeping in the lobby, along with the sound of his jackhammer snoring, is enough to scare off Cairo's fiercest villains but only some of its countless stray cats. When I moved into my building last week with my two sixty-pound bags, neither Abu Sayyid nor his children were able to help me with my second bag. The bawaab attempted to pick one up, realized how heavy it was, pointed to his back, sat down on his cot, smiled, and said, *"Ma'alesh."* A distinctively Egyptian colloquial word, ma'alesh means something between "Oh, well," "I'm sorry," and "That's not important anyway."

Um Sayyid, the bawaab's wife (to me, the bawaabette), a round but sturdy-looking woman, promptly lifted my bag on to her head and followed me up the steps. Climbing the steps with my other bag, I heard her wheezing hard behind me, and it crossed my mind that she might die carrying my luggage. Impressively, she made it to the sixth floor before almost collapsing. She did find the strength to demand baksheesh, this time well deserved.

Once at the restaurant, a two-table shwarma and falafel joint with three rotisserie chicken spits out front, I found the lights off and a table barricading the entrance. Since nothing is ever closed here, I peered into the restaurant and saw that the staff was kneeling on prayer rugs. I waited outside until they finished praying and then went in and ordered two falafels. While a cook in his late twenties with missing front teeth made my sandwiches, we traded pleasant-ries in Arabic and had the following exchange:

"Where are you from?"

"Canada."

"Whose side are you on in the war?"

"No man in the world wants war. I want peace. We all want peace."

"And when there is war, what will happen?"

"God knows."

My last response, combined with pointing my right index finger above, past the exposed brown pipes protruding from the ceiling, pleased everyone there. We wished each other peace, and I left with my sandwiches.

Before stepping out onto my balcony, I had spent the day with my Arabic teacher from my graduate school in the United States. An Egyptian, Dr. Rashid has been stuck here with visa problems for two months and has missed the first six weeks of the winter semester. Ironically, it was only a little more than a year ago that the U.S. Department of Defense asked him to translate an Osama bin Laden video that was recovered in Afghanistan after the overthrow of the

Taliban. He provided a full translation within twenty-four hours. From the informal lessons my professor has given me as we wander around Cairo, drinking tea, reading book titles in bookstore windows, and discussing the dangers of crossing the street, it is clear that he misses his students and teaching, not to mention his wife and children still in America.

That day, we met at his friend's apartment on the shady, tree-filled island of Zamalek and decided to go downtown. To get there, we walked across the 26th of July Bridge, which spans the Nile, and passed two men running white paintbrushes over the filthy cement curb. The paint was white, but amid the noontime rush hour traffic, it went on gray as it mixed with the dirt in the air and on the ground. Two days later, I walked past the same spot, remembered the paint, and looked down. What I saw below me was so covered in dirt and looked so aged that it could have been applied ten years ago. I wonder what the inside of my lungs look like after a week and a half here and how they will look after several months. I also wonder whether those same two municipal workers would be back next week to paint the same spot or if they were now off painting whereabouts unknown.

My professor and I continued past the bridge and along the Cornice al Nil. Below us, kids swam in the Nile, while fisherman cast their lines and waited for a bite. Young couples—women with their heads covered and stylishly dressed men—smiled at each other on benches and strolled slowly along the tree-lined walkway. Vendors grilled corn, and hawkers offered rides on sailboats and party boats for as cheap as five Egyptian guineas, a little less than a dollar.

From the Cornice, it was on to Liberation Square, which sits between the American University in Cairo (AUC), the Arab League building, the Egyptian Museum, and the Mugamma—the dark and towering mother of all government bureaucracy buildings reputed for eating alive both Egyptians and *hawajja* in need of official documents. Hawajja is one of my favorite Arabic words. Translation: "white-skinned Western sucker who should be fleeced of all present and future monies." In some contexts, hawajja also means "sir," but it is only used for foreigners. Whenever I am addressed or referred to as hawajja, I know it is only a matter of time before I start dispensing guineas.

AUC's campus, a base of operations for many of Cairo's nontourist hawajja—namely, foreign students and faculty—is set behind an iron fence and tall green bushes that prevent Cairo's "bus riders" from intruding. Inside the campus, Cairo's well-to-do students and a collection of clever stray cats enjoy a paradise of green grass, shady trees, and air that seems just a bit more breathable. Most of AUC's students are well-off Egyptians; it is one of the region's premier universities, so there is a collection of wealthy Arabs from other countries and Orientalist and Arabist Lawrences. If AUC students were to take a field trip to Amman, they would very much enjoy spending a Thursday night clubbing at Nai. Though I am not a student at AUC, Dr. Rashid told me that if there was a war and I found myself in danger, I should go there. They had to let me in.

Once past Liberation Square and downtown, we stopped for a cup of tea. Dr. Rashid and I have had tea together almost every day. Yet whenever it is time to pay, we fight like crazy over the bill. We basically alternate paying every time and it is the other person's duty to give in after enough of a scene has been made. It's actually a fun ritual, especially since Dr. Rashid always teaches me some colorful Egyptian expression in the process of the argument. He had his tea and I had *sahlab*, a milk-based drink with coconut, raisins, peanuts, cinnamon, and bananas, if done right. Although it was about 85-degrees that day and I burned the top of my mouth on the hot drink, sitting in the shade, joking around, and drinking that sahlab were wonderful.

We spent the next two hours walking through markets that sold everything from toy divers that swim in the bathtub to batteries to bright green women's underwear, but we could not find the brown shoelaces that I coveted. Besides the difficulty we encountered on the shoelaces front, I remain stunned by the crowds of people that seem to be everywhere. Every open space is a closing gap between at least three people moving in what seems like four directions. Sometimes, when I'm walking down a street, talking to myself or practicing my pronunciation and I think I am alone, I'll look up and find two old women looking out a window, a bawaab sitting under a tree, and a kid crawling around under a car. It's maddening. The number of people here and their constant presence is so overwhelming that I've begun to grow numb to their existence.

The overabundance of people isn't just a problem on the street or in a bus. I've noticed it at restaurants and stores in relation to the number of people "working." There are five people standing around for every one real job. How many food runners are necessary at a fast-food restaurant? "Lingerer" and "loiterer" are almost official job titles here. I can see the application process:

"So, Mustafa, tell me about your experience."

"Well, sir, I've spent the last three years hanging around the bawaab and before that I had several good years of loitering down at the high school."

"Fabulous, get this man a uniform, you'll make an excellent lingerer!"

Joking aside, it's terrible to think that some percentage of these lingerers and loiterers have trade skills or university degrees that enable them to do something useful. They lack an appropriate opportunity, though. I wonder what is worse—a job lingering, or that position painting the same curb every week.

Swimming upstream against the currents of humanity, Dr. Rashid and I arrived at Khan al Khalili, the standard bearer for all bazaars in the Arab East. We made our way through tight alleys containing embroidered pillows, marble busts of Ramses II, gold painted hookahs, inlaid mother-of-pearl boxes and backgammon sets, and brass pots bigger than the Liberty Bell, but still there were no shoelaces to be found. By the time we sat down to rest in the square outside Al-Azhar Mosque, one of the most historically important Islamic learning centers in the world, I had been invited to look inside eighty-seven shops and offered "a special price that was just for me" sixty-four different times. Hawajja. My teacher made me ask at least fourteen different people selling shoes where we could find laces. None sold them, and all gave us bad information about who did. Evidently, in Egypt, "I don't know" is an expression only used by foreigners; I use it frequently.

While I looked longingly for a tea or juice vendor, my teacher explained that asking people for objects that "cannot be found" was a great way to learn and practice Arabic. Thanks. More important, I never realized what a luxury product shoelaces were; I had taken mine for granted. I told my teacher how they sold shoelaces in every drugstore in the United States, and he shook his head in wonder and disbelief.

"Aah, America, my home and native land of shoelaces!" I declared. Suddenly, visions of exporting shoelaces to Egypt danced through my head. I began to make up expressions in Arabic about how at the end of the rainbow we would find shoelaces, and then I noticed that everyone around me was wearing sandals.

In the end, we found laces near downtown on the way home. Our shoelace source had at least ten different varieties and was sporting a huge beard and a shaved head. I looked at him with great respect and exclaimed, *"Allah ya'atik al-afya!"* In Jordan, this expression goes far. Among other uses, it is employed to offer an especially heartfelt thank-you for a job well done.

But my bearded shoelace supplier just looked puzzled, and I could have sworn that Dr. Rashid was a little embarrassed. He smiled and exchanged a look with the vendor. I felt like a greenhorn immigrant who had tried to sound cool by regurgitating some TV slang, but instead had come up woefully short, along the lines of Bilal and his *Brady Brunch*–like phrase book in Jordan. Despite not being understood, I was happy to continue home with a pair of laces that cost only 15 cents.

Back on my balcony, a couple of falafel sandwiches later, I laced up and considered the day, my return to Cairo, and this city that is really more than a city. There is an Egyptian expression that once a person drinks from the Nile he is destined to return to Egypt . . . Well, it has been a week and a half since I returned to Cairo, my point of departure on this Arabic-language odyssey some two and a half years ago. I found Cairo both enthralling and tiring then, and I still do. That summer, I didn't know the difference between a donkey cart and my elbow. Short the oversized fanny pack, plaid pants, and the camera around my neck, I was without a doubt a hawajja. I walked around the city, sat in coffeehouses, played dominoes, drank tea, but mostly wondered what was going on around me.

I've changed a lot since then, though it is eerie how many things here seem similar or the same. Ahmed, the driver who picked me up at the airport in July 2000, was there to greet me again. This time, though, we chatted in Arabic and I found out that he has three kids. When I checked into my hotel, I bargained over the rate for my room and insisted upon holding on to my passport. Last time, because I couldn't understand anything, my passport and I were dragged to the duty-free store and coerced into buying a case of beer for the hotel. Hawajja.

I returned to the rotisserie chicken restaurant on 26th of July Street that I used to eat at a couple of times a week. The same cook was behind the counter, and the same waiter took my order. The waiter and I had our first conversation ever, and he asked me where I've been. I told him "Jordan" and that was that. What should I have said? "I've spent the last two and a half years learning how to answer that question."

After my meal, I walked past Shaky Hand, the elderly barber who massacred me that summer. In one of those "funny" foreign language miscommunications, he had understood my gestures and repetition of the word *fade* to mean that I wanted the sides of my head shaved clean. Shaky Hand was at least seventy then, and now looked fifteen years older. When I stopped in my tracks out of sheer amazement that he was still alive, he tried to pull me into his lair again. I saw a glint of recognition in his eyes, but that could also have been the hawajja shine that I give off every now and again, or maybe it was just his cataracts.

I hurried into the shop next door and instead was ripped off by a barber who had a mullet and gave me one, too. Why did I get ripped off? Well, there is no sign here that lists the cost of haircuts. Instead, you pay what you think is appropriate. He told me a sob story about his kid needing glasses; I understood it, and I gave him a bunch of guineas.

Despite still not getting good haircuts and spending a full day looking for shoelaces, it is empowering that my Arabic allows me to do things that I couldn't fathom doing before. Nevertheless, it is still very difficult to understand what is going on in Cairo. There is just so much motion, so many people, so much friendliness, and so much noise. Merely crossing the street is like living a "choose your own adventure" novel. At the same time, I'm just not sure that anyone is really going anywhere. My initial response to Cairo is that it has grown older, but not changed. If I lived here for ten years, it is very possible that I would be living a real-life version of *Groundhog Day*, where Bill Murray wakes up every day to the same day.

Still, with my new frame of comparison from having lived in Jordan and visiting Syria, Morocco, and Palestine, I understand that there is something in Cairo and among Egyptians that reeks of greatness. Egyptians have a certain sense of themselves that isn't tangible. There is a Cairene identity of confidence and complacency that I just didn't find in Amman. People, and not just poor people, live their whole lives in Cairo. The worlds created by Naguib Mahfouz, the Arab East's lone Nobel laureate writer are here. Foreign expatriates move to Cairo because of the city's history and spirit. I don't know many expats who have moved to Amman for its spirit.

Foreigners are assaulted with expressions of pride like, "Welcome to Egypt!" or "Egypt is the mother of the world!" I constantly hear about "7,000 years of history" and great civilizations. A Cairene will tell you that Cairo is the gateway to Asia, Alexandria is the most southern city of Europe, and Aswan is the entryway to Africa. In the last week and a half, the question that I have been asked most frequently is whether I think Egypt or America is better. My questioners indignantly want to know why I prefer America and are only satisfied by my answer that everyone loves their own home. As a national characteristic and stereotype, Egyptians take an almost European-like (in arrogance) stance about the greatness of their homeland. After spending so much time with the Palestinian-Jordanians of Amman, who speak in romantic terms about a village or a city that might no longer exist and where they would rather be, I'm shocked by Egyptian nationalism.

Such nationalism carries over to expression as well; Egyptian Arabic is the correct Arabic. Why does my teacher continuously correct my Jordanian slang? Why was he embarrassed when I said *"Allah ya'atik al-afya"* to the shoelace man? And why did Mr. Shoelaces not understand me? Well, the Arabic that I was speaking was inferior Arabic and not the Egyptian dialect. As sophisticated as I think my Jordanian and Palestinian friends are, an Egyptian street vendor looked at me like I was a back-road bumpkin when I spoke to him in the Shami dialect, the Arabic spoken in Jordan, Palestine, Syria, and Lebanon. Similarly, I don't hear English the way that I did in Amman. In Amman, speaking English was a sign of prestige and a demonstration of one's education. If I tried to speak English in my neighborhood here, no one would understand. I wouldn't be surprised if someone yelled at me (in Arabic), "Speak Arabic! You're in Egypt!"

Differences in language and national sentiment, not to mention economic conditions and needs, demonstrate once again that it is a mistake to lump all "Arabs" together. Ironically, it was Gamal Abdel Nasser, Egypt's president in the 1950s and 1960s and the country's greatest leader since the time of the pharaohs, who asserted that the Arab world was one nation—an Arab Nation—that had been divided by Western powers for Western gains. Though the premise of Arab nationalism and Arab unity were torn to pieces by events such as the Jordanian Civil War, the Lebanese Civil War, the Syrian occupation of Lebanon, the Iraqi occupation of Kuwait, and the historical and continued abandonment of the Palestinians, I still find that many in the media back home and in my e-mail inbox refer to the "Arabs" as a bloc. These countries are individual countries with some similar cultural traits, and of course with common human traits, but with their own dynamics and problems. Make no mistake, Egyptians are Egyptians first, not Arabs; *their* home is the center of the world.

Irrespective of whether Egypt is a politically deteriorating state and the murky questions surrounding aging President Mubarak, his son, and succession, Cairo projects greatness. This greatness is more historical and less dynamic and progressive in its character, but it still exists. The people, the poverty, and the personified identity of Cairo as the "mother of the world" are different from what I saw in Amman. Worlds upon different worlds exist here, and I'm just scratching the surface. Not to be mistaken, Amman is a complicated and interesting place, too—with its Palestinian dynamics, its relationships with Iraq and Israel, and its own daily stories—but it is nothing like Cairo. From language to culture to size to people, Cairo isn't just a city; it's a world, a complete world for many.

Hope you all are well—

Love,
Ben

Letter 16

Amid the Ambers of the Arab Street*

March 22, 2003

Dear All,

"Ali! Ali!"

In a dark dirt alley littered with food wrappers and garbage, Dr. Rashid called up to his brother's apartment. I looked up at the third-story apartment window, obstructed by the flutter of laundry, and then back down the alley. The only light came from the dim apartments above and from the open door across the way, where I heard the slapping of dominoes hitting a board. Dr. Rashid turned to me and said, "Ben, wait here, and I will get him."

He disappeared into the building's darkness and left me standing alone on what felt like the set of the movie *Black Hawk Down*.

---

*A version of this chapter appeared in the March 22, 2003 edition of the *Pittsburgh Post-Gazette* as "Beneath the Angry Arab Street."

To my right, two men passed each other in the dark, one going home, the other going out. They greeted each other with familiarity, and I once again felt as if I was wearing a wool sweater in August. I've never been to Baghdad, but I understand that there are streets like this one there—unpaved, without lights, and with cookie-cutter, block-shaped apartment buildings whose differences are indistinguishable to outsiders like myself. When Dr. Rashid emerged alone from the shadows of the dark building and announced that we could go, I exhaled in relief.

We went to Imbaba that night, a thickly populated and poor neighborhood deep in the bowels of Cairo, so Dr. Rashid could introduce me to his brother, Ali. Dr. Rashid was to return to America the next day, and introducing me to Ali was his way of continuing to take care of me. He also wanted to show me another flavor of life in the "mother of the world." Imbaba is in a part of Cairo that most expats and certainly hawajja don't visit. In 1992, the Egyptian government "lost" Imbaba to Islamic fundamentalists and had to take it back by force over several weeks. Families live in one- or two-bedroom apartments, in cinder-block or mud-walled buildings that don't have doorbells, and on streets that don't have names, much less lights. I wasn't the only one confused by Imbaba's maze of no-name look-alike streets. We had wandered down a few similar alleys before Dr. Rashid, who lived in Imbaba twenty years ago, found Ali's apartment. The apartment buildings that we passed differed from each other only by the color of the towels hanging on the lines above.

Once Dr. Rashid emerged from the building, armed with directions on where to find Ali, he guided us through the neighborhood's obstacle course. We picked our way through bustling crowds, donkey carts bearing fruits and vegetables, open-air trucks packed with people, honking taxis, and the ever-present minivans equipped with a boy dangling off the vehicle's side, screaming a destination. It was about ten o'clock at night, and making our way through Imbaba's streets was akin to walking against the grain of the New York Marathon starting line, except that the grain ran six different ways. Besides the traffic coming in and out of shops, crowds of men, age 15 to 85, sat outside coffeehouses watching television; playing cards, dominoes, and backgammon; drinking tea; and puffing on water pipes. Thousands of people were out and about, but it was just a Tuesday night in Imbaba.

We found Ali at an ahwa that looked no different from the sixty-three others that we had just passed. Wearing a black leather jacket, he had a full head of black hair and a face creased with laugh lines. He was sitting with three middle-aged men, drinking tea, and he smiled broadly at the surprise appearance of his older brother. He said good-bye to his friends and the three of us pulled plastic chairs up around a nicked, square metal coffee table nearby. Within ten minutes, the discomfort I felt in the alleyway was forgotten as I laughed, played dominoes with Ali, smoked a water pipe, and drank sahlab.

After a few games, we turned to the subject of American foreign policy and Iraq. We all had heard President Bush's ultimatum to Saddam, but people still did not believe that there would be a war. There was a widespread conviction, shared by Ali, that it was all a ruse, that Saddam is an American agent, that there are no weapons of mass destruction, and that this was just an assertion of American power to control oil markets and to protect Israel. Ali argued that the ultimatum was just a dramatic flair, a new bit of theater. The United States would maintain the status quo. We played and chatted for about an hour and a half, and Ali even let me win a game. When we got up to leave, it was past 11:30 P.M. I noticed that the number of people at the ahwa, out in the street, and honking the horns of the anything-on-wheels parade had at least doubled, if not tripled.

That was a week ago. Ali might know his dominoes, but he was wrong about the war. Since the war's start two days ago, my e-mail inbox has been flooded with messages of concern. Thankfully, the circumstances of the war have not turned my life into the apocalyptic opening scene of *Terminator 2*. While Egyptians may indeed be very frustrated with what is happening in Iraq, there isn't going to be a revolution or popular uprising. Since the war began, I'm struck by the way in which Cairo has maintained its plodding beat, and frankly, how I've been unable to do the same. Playing dominoes with Ali and Dr. Rashid in Imbaba was the last time that I truly enjoyed myself; the war is taking an emotional toll on me.

On the first morning of the war, I was unsure of what to expect but was determined to check Cairo's beating pulse. At 10:00 A.M., dressed in my Syrian coat, dark slacks, and a button-down shirt, I left my apartment and began to make my way downtown. Despite my fashion-wise attempt to blend in, I felt the eyes of my neighborhood burrowing into my back as I slipped past the garbage mounds and soccer fields. No matter what clothes I wear, this isn't Amman, where I can pass as a local. Tall guys don't melt into the Egyptian pot so easily.

At a little before noon, I crept up the steps of the Sadat Metro station, across from Liberation Square and in front of the American University of Cairo. Two crowds had gathered in the traffic circle that is the center of Liberation Square. One was colorful, checkered with people wearing red T-shirts emblazoned with the words "No to War," holding signs, and chanting slogans. The other, wearing black uniforms and visor-helmets, carried bamboo batons and stood in lined-formations blocking the square's outlets to the south and east. I followed two young muhajiba women across the street and advanced into the traffic circle.

A blossoming mob pumped their fists to the sway of a bellowing megaphone-enhanced voice and responsively shouted (in Arabic):

Liberation Square, March 20, 2003.

"God is greatest! Down with America!"

"Mubarak, Mubarak, where are you? Sheikh al-Azhar, Sheikh al-Azhar, where are you?"

Trailing the two muhajiba women, who wore skirts to their ankles and carried school notebooks, I scanned the crowd from the traffic circle's edge. Angry young men in sports coats and slacks—whose fashion choices I sought to emulate—took turns inciting the minions. Middle-aged women alongside balding, mustached men hoisted placards of Gamal Abdel Nasser and Iraqi flags. AUC students—some wearing Yankee caps backwards, others sporting Chicago Bulls jerseys, and many wrapped in black-and-white checkered, Arafat-style *kaffiyehs*—punched their fists into the air. Galabaya-clad *Sa'idis* or Egyptians from Upper Egypt, with patterned scarves and white beanies, bearded believers with prayer marks on their foreheads, and wrinkled ladies covered in black from head to toe rounded out the shapeless and expanding crowd.

The mosaic pulled together with calls for justice in Iraq and throughout the Arab East. The megaphone was passed among the protest's leaders. They called out, "Palestine is Arab! No to Zionist aggression! America is the terrorist! The voice of Egypt is free!" Then came a version of the popular refrain, heard at demonstrations throughout the Arab East. The crowd chanted again and again: "With our blood, with our souls, we sacrifice for you Baghdad!"

The choice of symbols and words were poignant. Revolutionaries, dreamers, and the antagonized masses were making appeals for a firm leadership that would command justice. While they demanded accountability from Egypt's political and religious leadership, President Mubarak and Sheikh al-Azhar, they toted pictures of the late President Nasser, the icon of Arab power and the symbol of the pan-Arab dream. In the 1950s and 1960s, Nasser projected power and was a popular hero for a people accustomed to being on the receiving end of imperialism. Despite the shattering of the pan-Arab dream in the 1967 Arab-Israeli War, Nasser is remembered for standing up to the West. Furthermore, protesters carried Iraqi flags, not pictures of Saddam. They pledged opposition to a war of aggression against the suffering Iraqi people, not support for a reviled dictator.

As seen on the news, the street was a wildfire. I wondered whether it would be contained or would consume itself in a fury. Overcoming my uneasiness, I pushed further into the crowd and found a different reality. Vendors sold cookies, pastries, and bottled juice. Six boys, age 10 to 15, played three-on-three soccer with an undersize kickball. Steno-pad-wielding reporters and vest-clad cameramen swarmed the crowd's edges, taking notes and pictures at a rapid-fire pace. I listened in on the students and the bearded men; they conferred about an engineering class, made calls on cell phones to friends, and admired a blonde reporter.

While a dirty city bus crammed with about a hundred passengers sat stuck in traffic fifty feet away, belching smoke, I realized that I was attending a spectator sport, not a budding revolution. I stared at the creased face of a middle-aged man pressed against the window of the bus; he shared a one-seater with another man. He was the one who should have been protesting—protesting a life stuck in traffic on a continual trip to nowhere. When Bus Man and people like him climb off the bus and join the protest, and when there are

Riot police in Liberation Square, March 20, 2003.

demonstrations in neighborhoods like Imbaba, then it is time to worry about uprisings and instability.

Despite the gathering's harmless nature, a tension that went beyond my own paranoia hung over the crowd and below the pollution. Bad mojo emanated from the second crowd, the hundreds of men-in-black riot police who locked their shields, held their bamboo batons at the ready, and hemmed the protestors into the square between the Egyptian Museum, the towering Mugamma, and the university. Hundreds of reserve troops peered out of the wire-mesh windows of steel-drum blue trucks parked throughout the square. These trucks have been fixtures downtown for as long as I've been in Cairo, and I walk past them frequently. I've yet to decide, though, whether the Tasmanian Devil is on the inside or outside. Are the surly-faced police kept behind wire-mesh windows for their own protection or for the protection of the general public?

While I checked out the police from across the square, a pair of bearded men carrying the black, white, and red Iraqi flag led several hundred slogan-hurling and Nasser-placard-toting protesters into the protest from the direction of an eastern side street. They headed directly toward my position next to the pastry man, and I retreated against the wave of Egyptians behind me and toward the riot police, hoping that they would protect me against the rowdy new arrivals.

Just as a closer look at the "mob," which I had now become a part of, had revealed something else, a closer look at the riot police yielded a clearer picture, too. I've seen peaches with more facial hair than some of the police. The oldest of the troops couldn't have been more than twenty-one years old, and several soldiers held their friends' hands behind their shields. Same-sex hand-holding is common behavior among friends here, but I've never seen it practiced among riot police. This unit's commanding officer, a scowling man with a hooked nose, screamed at his charges to stand up straight and to contain the oncoming crowd. Unfazed by the new arrivals or the troops' supposed authority, three little boys threw pebbles at the riot police and taunted them for being wimps.

The boys in black pulled it together, however. With their over-size, pot-like helmets rattling away, casting the image of an army of bobblehead dolls, the riot police met the new arrivals head-on. Batons lifted into the air, the bobblehead army began to beat and drag off a couple of protestors who had not realized that this was only a show. Having had my fill of the protest, I walked across the square to McDonald's to use their first-class facilities and to eat lunch.

Finding a clean bathroom in the Arab East is a problem. Most falafel and shwarma joints don't have them—just a sink for washing up—and I'm frequently far enough away from home base that I've learned to keep a mental list of "safe houses." Western hotels, like the Amman Hyatt, where I would take hot showers in the lobby bathroom's sink, are gold. Of course, it is advisable to dress presentably and to have some idea where the bathrooms are hidden so as not to end up squirming around the lobby like a nervous hawajja at an antiwar protest.

Western fast-food restaurants like McDonald's and KFC are typically very good safe houses. Even the fake Western restaurants, like the *Mo'amen* chain, have a spotless toilet tucked away on the second floor somewhere. I frequently enter such restaurants in a hurry; wish several lingerers "peace," "good morning," or "good evening," as appropriate; and act as if I am late and looking for a friend. Sometimes, I'll even ask if they've seen him, "a short Russian guy, dark clothes, wearing a hat . . . named Boris," and I run upstairs to check.

I like to think that I get away with this sort of thing because of my quick-thinking and wit, but I know that my access to Cairo's nonpublic restrooms has more to do with being a Westerner who is expected to spend money. I have no idea where Egyptians who do not enjoy such privilege relieve themselves when they are away from home. There aren't a lot of options.

McDonald's was packed that day, and after not finding Boris or any of the *Rocky and Bullwinkle* characters in the bathroom, I decided to stay for lunch. At home, a trip to McDonald's is an act of desperation. It's late, I'm on a road trip, Shoney's is closed, and it is either Mickey D's or Waffle House. In Cairo, McDonald's is an oasis amid a desert of food options that make Ramadan-fasting a healthy and welcome respite. All orders are made to order. A burger and fries might take ten minutes to prepare, but they are always hot and always fresh (well, relatively fresh since they probably arrived in a cardboard box from somewhere). Moreover, McDonald's is air-conditioned, plays popular Arabic and English music, and has a staff of about twenty-five people who remain poised to wipe the slightest soft drink condensation from any table.

What this means is that McDonald's is a cool place for young wealthy Egyptians to hang out. That day, due to the peak in anti-American feeling, I expected that the McDonald's staff might have reason to linger a bit more than usual. I was mistaken. The place was full and the staff was running about, serving Big Macs and Cokes. The AUC crowd of wealthy Egyptian students did not deny themselves their Mickey D fix. In Gap shirts and Calvin Klein head scarves, they chatted away, flirted, and ate fries at the bastion of American consumerism. Nothing had changed. I even recognized several of the protesters from outside. They were taking a lunch break.

After lunch, on my long walk home, I passed through the protest again. There was nothing new to report, except for several hundred more people hollering "Down with America" and waving more of the same signs and banners calling for justice. More remarkable to me was my walk along the Nile. A young man, less than sixteen years old, and wearing worn, dirty, and paint-spotted clothes, was meticulously adding a fresh coat of green paint to the iron fence of one of Cairo's sports and recreation clubs. He was oblivious to all around him, the noise of the day, and the fact that he would never have the opportunity to use the private club. He continued about his work in both heroic and stupefying fashion.

I stopped to watch the paint dry and considered this everyday warrior who represented all that is right and wrong here. His steady nature and willingness to continue painting the fence on that day were inspiring. At the same time, his tacit refusal to demand more from the Egyptian government was maddening. Perhaps as a result of my disgust with the protest that was more photo-op than political statement, the inspiring eclipsed the maddening. On the verge of tossing an *"Allah ya'atik al-afya"* his way, I caught myself. Who was I to offer Paint Boy moral support? And why would he ever welcome it from me on that day.

I reluctantly moved on as I realized that others passing by had stopped to stare at the Anglo watching the boy painting the fence. A little further along the road, walking alongside the fence of that same club, I stopped again. This time, though, it was to shake my head as a foursome of overweight Egyptian golfers teed up. Such a stark contrast and disconnect between people in the same society and in such close proximity is hard to process. If Paint Boy is going to continue working in the face of the protest down one street and the golfers down another, and if those "ketchup eating" golfers aren't worried about a mob of "bus riders" storming the putting green and demanding an equal share, and if protesters are taking lunch breaks at McDonald's, then what does all of that equal? Despite what you see on the nightly news, Cairo is not going to burn.

Still, even though revolution and chaos are not imminent here, it is a mistake to put a check next to Egypt and to ignore what is going on in the everyday worlds of Cairo and other Arab East cities. There is more to the "Arab Street" than the angry throngs of people that fill American TV screens. A closer look, beyond the superficial reports of CNN, Fox News, and al Jazeera, reveals Egyptians' deep resentment at having the ins and outs of their everyday life made more difficult by a forced acknowledgment of weakness.

A walk through my neighborhood, or really a day in my everyday life here, reveals people's angry frustration with the unjust use of power, and in this case, the abuse or misuse of American power. Yesterday, I passed Um Sayyid in the lobby where she was washing the floor with a rag. As I've mentioned, she lives with her husband, the doorman, and children in the lobby's back rooms, and probably earns less than $75 a month. We used to happily exchange pleasantries, but in the last few days, she no longer looks me in the eye and only minimally acknowledges my "good mornings." At night, when I pass her and her young children sitting on the stoop, conversation stops. Her oldest son, Sayyid, a student at Cairo University, dropped by my apartment the other day to check on me. We went up to the roof, and he showed me some puppies that were to be trained as police dogs. In a year or two, Sayyid will enter the Egyptian army to do his service. While we played with the puppies, he asked me point blank, "Why does America want to kill Muslims?"

I avoided the falafel and shwarma restaurant downstairs for four days, and after eating there four or five times a week for a couple of weeks, I was missed. When I stopped in yesterday, the cooks demanded to know why I hadn't come to see them. Salah, a middle-aged cook I'm friendly with, was especially hurt by my disappearance. He kept pressing me as to why I hadn't come to visit, and finally I told him that I was upset because of the war. I haven't really wanted to engage with anyone, not just them. He shook his head and told me that he was upset, too, but then in an almost angry tone asked me, "Is there anything that I can do? Is there anything you can do? Do I want children to die? Do you? No, so we have to continue together."

He put his arm around my shoulder, and I felt myself choking up. While I struggled for the words to respond to Salah's kind gesture, Muhammad, another cook who is a few years older than me and missing some teeth, announced that he hates Americans and would like to kill them "because they have no mercy."

I've avoided my grocery store, too, ever since the president issued the ultimatum. I usually stop in every other day to pick up some vegetables or cheese, and the grocer and I have established a friendly repartee. Last night, though, I ran out of food in my apartment and had to go shopping. The grocer asked me where I've been, and I told him that I haven't been feeling well. He wished me good health and then asked me for the first time where I'm from. I looked over his head at the thirteen-inch TV screen where American missiles were ripping apart Baghdad. A crowd of shoppers stood nearby watching the news like it was a state funeral.

With my eyes cast toward the floor, I nodded my head toward the TV. Though I've lied to cabbies, strangers, Salah, and the other cooks, I just couldn't continue. Agree or disagree, those were my fellow citizens on that TV fighting a war that they were told would make our home safer. I looked up and the grocer was staring at me with his mouth open. "Bless you, may God provide for you, you are Iraqi?" He asked.

"No, the other," I responded.

His face became even more disbelieving. He bit his lower lip, grimaced, pulled back, and shook his head as if to retreat from a bad smell. I feared that he was going to attract the attention of the wake behind him. Instead, he handed me my change and with tired resignation in his voice asked, "What are you doing here?"

"I'm a student."

"You speak Arabic very well."

At the language institute where I study, it is more of the same. I have four hours of class a night with a small and friendly group of assorted liberal Europeans. My Egyptian colloquial teacher used to laugh all the time and good-naturedly tease me about being an imperialist before the war started. She doesn't laugh at all anymore and certainly doesn't tease me. To her credit, she remains very professional and does her best to continue calling on me and correcting my mistakes. Sa'id, my Modern Standard Arabic teacher, is also very professional and doesn't say a word about the war during class. Our ten-minute coffee breaks, however, are something out of an Ari Fleischer press conference from hell that could be an amusing *Saturday Night Live* skit if I didn't have to play Fleischer.

Sa'id peppers me with questions from the theater of the absurd while the Europeans make anti-Bush jokes. He asked me yesterday, "Ben, which country will America invade next, Syria or Iran?"

Things deteriorated further when the group began making its own guesses and Sa'id led them in a vote. The Europeans can't figure out why I keep declining their invitations to go to late-night dinners and jazz clubs. To them also, the war is just a spectator sport and a topic of conversation. For me, though, it is my life. Here, I am America. While in public I may lie to some Egyptians about being a Canadian, there is no escaping the private doubt that I feel over this American decision to go to war and my guilt and fear for the war's potentially destructive and catastrophic consequences.

Instead of drinking Egyptian beer with liberal-minded French and German women, I watch nonstop coverage of the war on Egyptian state TV and visit Al Jazeera's website several times a day to try and calculate the news. I've now learned the Arabic words for "convoy," "reinforcements," and "hostages." Between reports on the Nile Channel News, the network repeatedly shows a pair of montages. The first includes muhajiba Arab women shopping in a market and smiling children playing in a school yard; it fades out with the word "Iraq" floating across the screen. The second montage is composed of U.S. and British sound bites transposed against President Bush's smirk and protesters demonstrating around the world. It ends with the phrase, "No to war, when the world says no."

If life here were an action movie, the United States would be the bad guy who gets killed in the end. The mixture of contempt, anger, and frustration that lurk below the surface here are now focused squarely upon the U.S. government. America has supplanted the Egyptian regime or any other local surrogate as the poster child for injustice and abusive power. *The New York Times* reported that the U.S. administration's answer to the lowly perception of America across the Middle East is liberation. America will be loved in the Arab East when Marines liberate the Iraqi people and are showered with rice. Maybe Um Sayyid will once again smile in my direction. I hope so, but I think that there is a better chance that such a smile would be as deep as a puddle.

I suspect that Operation Iraqi Freedom will become another bullet item on the list of grievances held by the people of my neighborhood and neighborhoods throughout the Arab East—a list that is headlined by U.S. sponsorship of regional dictators and lopsided support for Israel. It really angers and frustrates people here—and in Jordan (I can't help but think of Ammo's outburst as we said good-bye at Abdali before I evacuated)—that we have chosen to disrupt the status quo despite the prevailing local sentiment against war. The U.S. decision to attack Iraq serves as a vivid reminder of our power over life here, no matter what the people's wishes.

Dictatorial Arab regimes long ago sent their people scurrying to the privacy of their homes. We might think that we are liberating them from their plight, but I speculate that many people here believe we are instead shaking the foundations of the lives they've carved out for themselves, under the terms that these regimes have offered. Life is hard in its own way here; there is no reason for people to believe that our actions are going to make it smoother or easier. Instead, there is a palatable fear that we will make everything more difficult. The behavior and policies of the regime are an accepted evil of society. Our addition to people's troubles, though, is an unwelcome and resented burden.

The United States has the chance to offer something unique to the people of the Arab East. Ideally, we would choose to offer concrete education or economic opportunities and reasons for hope—like advances in technology and medicine. That is the historic appeal of America. Some of you back home will argue that we are offering liberation and freedom, the greatest forms of hope. The view from Cairo is different, however. All the Egyptians that I've met or spoken with view the war with Iraq as an unjustified mission with the potential for devastating human and financial costs. In the face of such perceptions and in the context of such a one-sided relationship, the United States' potential to earn credibility in this region, and overcome its history of pursuing policies of self-interest, such as protecting oil, might be an impossible dream. I'm not planning on things changing the moment that U.S. tanks enter Baghdad and take down Saddam.

So, if there isn't going to be a popular revolution against the Egyptian government in Cairo, why does the imposition of U.S. power on Paint Boy, the grocer, and my teachers matter? They seem like—and probably are—harmless individuals. We have demonstrated to the powerless that they indeed are powerless, and 99 percent of these individuals will continue with their daily lives and accept their fate. Their struggles and emotions will not impact our daily lives in Pittsburgh, Chicago, and Detroit.

Beyond the question of whether we, as Americans, want to take such a callous approach to the world, there is the more complicated question of the threat that that remaining one percent pose to our security and interests. My doorman's son Sayyid is a friendly and gentle guy, but he is also young and somewhat easily influenced. He studies economics and could grow up to be a successful engineer. It would be nice to look at the U.S. relationship with the Sayyids of the world in a proactive way—where we help them gain the best education and enable them to make the most substantial contribution to their societies. This isn't possible, though, given limited resources and other more prioritized interests (like taking care of our own American Sayyids). But we can't just ignore the Sayyids of the world. There are young men here, perhaps the same age as Sayyid and students as well, that are disaffected and insulted. They are vulnerable to the America haters scooping them up and leading them, with promises of glory and honor, down into the Arab Basement.

We need to make sure that we are not inspiring these young men of the Arab East to see merit in the recruitment speeches of the America haters. Maybe Mohamed Atta, the Egyptian who flew the jet into the North Tower of the World Trade Center, was always an America hater at heart. But what if fifteen years ago he was a young, impressionable, and insulted kid who stumbled into the wrong hands? In that vein, how many young men have we just further embarrassed or emasculated and taught that all the United States understands is force?

On my way home last night, I walked by the Macy's-like Omar Effendi department store, where large televisions tuned to al Jazeera filled the display window. Clustered around the glass were Little Caesar's and McDonald's delivery boys. On the television, Saddam's irregulars, dressed in dark clothes and checkered *kaffiyehs*, shot automatic weapons into the air and pandered to the camera crew. They looked a lot like the Palestinian militants who star on Al Jazeera in a similar fashion. I saw these warriors' reflection through the eyes of the awe-struck delivery boys. The irregulars represented a powerful image of what it means to be a man. What lasting impression will such images of this war leave throughout the Arab East?

As these and other Hollywood-style depictions and sound bites are presented in the Arab media, the image of the United States is literally being transformed into an entity much like the Arab East's pariah, Israel. It is only a matter of time before the United States is labeled an "occupier," too. Perhaps the Arabic news outlets will begin to refer to the U.S. military as the "U.S. aggression forces" the way that the Israel Defense Forces have been dubbed the "Israeli occupation forces." Once Americans lose our common thread of humanity with the people of the Arab East, as has already happened with Israelis, we will face our greatest threat.

The killing of any American, like the murder of Laurence Foley, will be justified and accepted on a popular level as an act of retribution. It doesn't take many America haters like Mohamed Atta—angry and shamed individuals who seek to prove their strength against power—to change our world and our future. I don't think that Sayyid personally would ever fall into such a category, but what other fuels have we just ignited that will later explode?

These days, I'm stuck between two worlds. My heartburn of the soul arises from my steadfast belief in Americans' positive intentions, my nuanced understanding of life here in the Arab East, and my dire apprehensions for the future of the American-Arab relationship. In the end, perhaps the White House is right and the only way to ensure America's security is to show other nations that we are to be feared. This might be easier to deal with an ocean away in the "City on the Hill," but here, in the "City Victorious," I'm left feeling anything but triumphant.

Love,
Ben

Letter 17

Salah al Fuli and the Fall of Baghdad

April 10, 2003

Dear All,

In this age of satellite television, there are some things that just cannot be ignored or covered up, even in an authoritarian society. Egyptian TV did indeed cover the celebrations and looting in Baghdad. Beyond the historic images, though, deciphering what the fall of Baghdad means here is complicated.

A lot of the insight I have gained during this past year has been through individuals' stories. In this fashion, the stories of Salah al Fuli and Walid will provide a better understanding of what is going on in Cairo. Salah al Fuli works as a cook at the falafel and shwarma restaurant next door to my apartment building. He's there seven days a week, twelve or thirteen hours a day. From my eighth-story balcony perch, I can frequently catch a glimpse of Salah diligently tending to the rotisserie chickens on their outdoor spits. Salah is thirty-three years old, but the lines under his eyes, his receding hairline, and the ever-present beads of sweat above his brow combine to make him look ten years older.

I pass the restaurant at least once a day, and if I don't greet Salah and my other friends there, Ahmed Bedoui and Muhammad, they take great offense. A "head nod" sort of guy at home, I've learned more about hospitality this past year, including the importance of acknowledging people a bit more warmly. The extra time it takes isn't really any skin off my nose. Generally, nothing more than the standard "Hello, how are you? Where are you going? When are you coming home?" exchange is expected.

Usually waiting for me inside the restaurant's front entrance is Ahmed Bedoui. He stands over a cauldron of bubbling oil, slapping falafel mix into patties and then floating them into the sizzling oil. When the falafel is ready, he fishes each patty out of the cauldron with a metal spatula with slits that allow excess oil to drip free. The wafting scent of the fresh falafel, called *tamiyya* in Egypt, is irresistible and attracts a flock of customers to the restaurant's entrance. When Ahmed sees me among the customers from his perch above the bubbling oil, he calls out, *"Banga! Banga! Salah! Salah! Banga hina!"* or "Benja! Benja! Salah! Salah! Benja is here!"

When I moved here from Jordan, I introduced myself to the guys at the restaurant as Benja. Since the J is pronounced as a hard G in the Egyptian dialect, and because "Benga" sounded too much to them like *bonga* a bong in Egyptian dialect, Ahmed and Salah call me "Banga." If Salah isn't tending to his case of rotisserie chickens out front, then following Ahmed's announcement, he emerges from the back kitchen and we go through our routine of pleasantries. While our conversation is the same every day, it is the courtesy of stopping by that is important to him and Ahmed.

It takes me several minutes to get out of my neighborhood every day as I greet both my doorman and the bakery people in a similar way. Like I said, it isn't such a big deal, but the "head nod" part of me is reluctant to take my clothes to the neighborhood launderer, whose shop is located next door to the restaurant. Patronizing the launderer would mean waking up five minutes earlier in the morning to greet more people.

Over the last few weeks, my relationship with Salah and his falafel-making shadow Ahmed has progressed to the point where I have tea with them four nights a week at a local ahwa after they finish work and I finish class. Salah and Ahmed enjoy a great degree of pride from their friendship with the neighborhood Canadian (me). They always insist on paying the bill and grow offended whenever I try to pay. The two of them would sit and drink tea with me the other three nights of the week as well, if I obliged. While I enjoy our time together and speaking with them in Arabic, by nature of my Americanism, I fear commitment and need some personal space. So, I come home late the other nights of the week, at a time when I know they will have already left work.

On the issue of being the neighborhood Canadian, I met Salah the day that Saddam was issued his prewar ultimatum. That wasn't the best day to be an American in the Arab East. Under an eager

Salah al Fuli at the schwarma stand.

Ahmed Bedoui cooking falafel.

barrage of his questions, I claimed to be Canadian—the alternative nationality of choice for most Americans abroad who aren't bilingual—and told Salah that Toronto was our capital. I skirted questions about the Canadian government and its visa policies by changing the subject to Celine Dion, whose music is wildly popular in the Arab East. This was also a bit dicey, though, since I have not seen *Titanic*. Since then, I spent some time looking at the Canada page on the CIA's *World Factbook* website. I am now well-versed enough to say that Canada is a country of 32 million people, our capital is Ottawa, and we have ten provinces. It is very cold, and by the way, did you know that Celine Dion is Canadian?

In this same conversation, my restaurant friends told me that there is another "Canadian" living in the neighborhood. As they described to me exactly what building and floor he lives on, and then talked about the Russians also living in the neighborhood, I began to wonder how many people know exactly which building and what floor I live on. I also questioned whether this other guy was a "Canadian" like me or a real Canuck. The number of Canadians in the Middle East has increased by a multiple of seven in the last three weeks; mysteriously, most Americans have disappeared. If I were a Canadian, I'm not sure whether I would be proud or indignant.

Anyway, sometimes Salah, Ahmed, and I play dominoes, but mostly we talk over cups of sugar with a little bit of tea on top. The conversations themselves are ridiculous; aside from the occasional questions about work and visas in Canada, these sessions mostly consist of Salah performing. About 40 percent of the time, the laughter is at my expense. Most jokes focus on my language deficiencies and the fact that I have yet to visit Cairo's zoo—mysteriously, this has become a very big deal. I really don't mind being the butt of Egyptian jokes, and anytime I get in a good one-liner, it's worth ten of Salah's quips. The group rewards me with high fives, similar to *Seinfeld*'s David Puddy, though stylistically in Egypt, they are a cross between low fives and a handshake.

A couple of nights ago, Salah explained to me, Ahmed, and Muhammad, another cook, how he could understand animals. With pantomime and sound effects—he does a great lion impersonation—he demonstrated how he cured animals of their various ailments. We then got to talking about cars, and he told me that he owned a BM-Carro. In Egyptian colloquial Arabic, a *carro* is a donkey-drawn cart, and BMWs, according to Salah, are the nicest and most expensive cars in Egypt. Hence, a BM-Carro is a "luxury" donkey-drawn cart. Salah spent twenty minutes explaining the nuances and dangers of driving a BM-Carro with whipping pantomime, clucking noises, and a detailed description of the fear of having a donkey shit on you, all to the howls of the peanut gallery.

Frequently, I wonder about Salah's mental state. I actually had begun to reconsider whether spending four evenings a week with him and Ahmed was the best use of my time. Later that night, though, as we parted ways, he pulled me aside, put his hand on my shoulder, looked me dead on, and told me that it was important to laugh because it cured the heart. I thought about his day and what was waiting for him tomorrow and the next day, and I realized that I had underestimated Salah.

On another night last week, Salah and I had tea alone and I took the opportunity to ask nosy questions. After calling his wife from a pay phone, he told me that he hadn't gone home for two days. Instead, he slept at the restaurant, which is open twenty-four hours, and covered someone's shift. Salah earns about $5 a day, paid in cash at the end of every shift, and works every day because he needs the money to support his family. His mother's brother has twenty-three children by two different wives. Salah, on the other hand, has two small children but does not want any more kids because he won't be able to provide for them. With pride, Salah emphasized that he has worked as a cook "specializing" in shwarma, other meats, and fish for seventeen years, and in seven different countries.

On politics, Salah explained that Egypt is poor because every minister puts public money into his own Swiss bank account. There is no way to fix the situation, as power itself is the problem. He told me about life in pharaonic times and how the people were "heretics, Jews" that worshipped the pharaoh. Life was "undeveloped" without computers and television, but that if you wanted to marry a woman, you just asked permission and married. To get married today, you have to buy an apartment, furniture, and a television. Yet, he believed that life is better today than it was a few thousand years ago. In addition, Salah doesn't like Americans because they are insincere. When I return to Canada, though, he wants me to call him every week, but knows that I will forget him.

Salah refused to acknowledge that he has a dream or greater aspirations. But, when I asked him whether he would like to own his own restaurant, a wistful look briefly crossed his face. He would build a three-story glass restaurant that served different foods on each level, not like the one where he works, gesturing to the four-table place crammed between the bakery and cleaners. The restaurant would be "respectful," with "big chairs," he explained as he sat up straight, pulled his chin in to his neck, and brought his eyebrows together properly. His posture slipped, though, with a realistic and knowing shrug, as we drank tea in white plastic outdoor chairs set up in a parking space fifteen feet away from the garbage piled against the soccer field walls. Fittingly, at that moment, a car pulled into the space next to where we were sitting.

That conversation was why Salah and Ahmed need to laugh about BM-Carros. It was about the face of poverty and knowing that there will be no rapid change because the system is not built for such change to occur. Life is hard in a different way here, but that certainly doesn't mean that it is empty, two-dimensional, or lacking spirit. I don't mention all this so that you will pity Salah and start a "Make a Wish" fund for underprivileged Egyptian cooks, but to offer a better idea of what people's perspectives are for judging world and regional events.

Walid, whom I met at a friend's house last week, is a dark-skinned, crooked-toothed, baby-faced Egyptian student. Though he was born in Egypt, Walid is not legally Egyptian since his father and mother were born in the Sudan and immigrated to Egypt. Citizenship in Egypt and in most other Arab countries is determined by the citizenship of one's father. Because of Walid's legal status, his university bills fluctuate based on the changing relations between Egypt and the Sudan. Over dinner, Walid explained that he was in favor of the war in Iraq because he hates Saddam, but if he were an Iraqi, he would "defend his homeland and fight the Americans."

When we left my friend's apartment, we passed a young man in the hall. Walid called out to him happily, and they exchanged kisses. On the street, Walid explained that the man he greeted is Iraqi. He used to call his brother in Baghdad every day to check on his family, but he cannot get through anymore because of problems with the phone lines. I asked Walid if his Iraqi friend knew his position on the war. He looked at me incredulously and laughed, "Do you think I am crazy? I don't want to die."

What I understand from Salah and Walid is that language differences alone are not the reason why Americans don't understand what is going on in the Arab East. A prominent American newspaper columnist suggested that to reach the Iraqi people and to convince the Arab Street of the United States' benevolent intentions, General John Abizaid, the deputy commander at U.S. Central Command and an American of Lebanese descent, should conduct war briefings in

Arabic. The gap in understanding between Americans and Arabs, however, is not the literal lack of comprehension that results from two different people speaking two different languages. A team of translators will not solve our problems.

The language difference between Arabic and English only compounds the cultural gaps that separate the United States and the Arab East. Americans do not understand the Arab East because we fundamentally do not grasp the fact that people here hold a disparate world outlook that includes different perceptions for what is possible and varying preferences for the colorful shades of gray. In contrast, we Americans love the stark tones of black and white. But life here isn't like an old Wild West film where the cowboys wear white hats if they are good and black hats if they are bad. With the exception of the *kufi*, those knit religious beanies, no one here really wears hats. In the Arab East, it's not hate Saddam, love America; it's more like hate Saddam, hate Bush. It isn't as simple as "Iraq is liberated and America is now good." The more common line of thinking is, "Great, Saddam is gone, but now there is looting, dead civilians, and a huge foreign army occupying an Arab country."

As for the often-repeated American rhetoric of "liberation" and the intent to form a "decent" and democratic government, people here can only respond with skepticism at best. From my position of watching a bulldozer pick up garbage piles fifteen feet away from where I drink tea with Salah and Ahmed, it is hard to have faith in Donald Rumsfeld's and Paul Wolfowitz's intentions when they say that under Ahmed Chalabi—one of the prominent exiled Iraqi opposition leaders—Iraqis will, metaphorically, get those three-story glass restaurants or whatever it is they aspire to. Since that outcome is beyond the realm of possibility, it raises the question for me as to whether Rumsfeld and Wolfowitz are being deliberately misled or whether they are the ones doing the deliberate misleading. Expecting the Salahs of Iraq—i.e., the poor and working class—to put faith in any government, much less an installed foreign government, is not just a mistake; it is beyond comprehension. They already feel that the whole system is rigged against them, and now, providing for their family just became more difficult.

With all of this in mind, I find it difficult to look into people's hearts here, in Damascus, or in Amman, and to know whether they want to pull the statues and posters of their leaders down as well. But it is easy to see that people are deeply insulted by America's presumptuous attitude, and they are highly skeptical of America's intentions when American soldiers do arrive with tanks to pull those statues down themselves.

Instead of jubilation in Cairo, Saddam's fall has been met by an annoyance that borders on disgust, confusion, and relief. The "shock and awe" was that Saddam and his regime seem to have disappeared with a whimper, not a poetic stand that would have added to the annals of Arab and Muslim resistance to foreign aggression. The fall of Saddam was instead the fall of Baghdad—one of the Arab East's great cities and a center of Arab history and culture—to a foreign force. It was another blow to Arab pride. On the other hand, had the people of Baghdad sacked this regime, it would have been perhaps the greatest of Arab moments.

Part of this annoyance was the confusing mixed signals that emanated from Baghdad before and during the war. The wartime press conferences held by Iraq's creative minister of information, Mohammed al-Sahaf, and the prewar demonstrations of support for Saddam in Baghdad, led many to expect more from Iraqi fighters and civilians. If Saddam was to be toppled, Iraqis would at least fight the invader with honor. One Egyptian state TV commentator rhetorically questioned the thousands of Iraqis who had publicly pledged their lives for Saddam and who now beat his likeness with their shoes, the ultimate insult. On the air, he frustratingly asked, "Why did they chant those slogans?"

The surprising powerlessness of the region's toughest tough guy who dominated his people but wouldn't fight the big bully was also a source of confusion and disgust. Some people here, perhaps thinking of their home lives and their children and the damage wrought upon Iraq and its people, asked why? If Saddam was just going to give in, couldn't he have done so earlier and avoided this war? And in regard to that "big bully," a new nervousness has been created by the demonstration of American military power and the popular disbelief that surrounds U.S. claims and goals. Sa'id, my teacher who has now become more of a friend, observed that if America did that in Iraq, they could conquer Egypt, too. With complete seriousness, he then asked me if America was going to invade Egypt.

There is relief here, as well. It comes, though, with the perception that the killing of civilians in Iraq will now end. The death of Iraqis and of other civilians was met with great outrage. Given local assessments of American intentions and tactics, as well as the non-stop news coverage of the war, it is impossible for most people to believe that American fire did not deliberately target the Jordanian al Jazeera journalist and the European journalist who were killed in Baghdad two days ago. Their deaths were the dominating detail of the early reports of the fall of Baghdad.

My colloquial Arabic teacher, a bubbly woman who makes an effort to laugh as much as possible, congratulated me on "my" victory in the war and added that she hoped all of the killing would now end. A beautiful thing about Arabic is that there is a response to most expressions. So I gave the customary response, which literally translates to "May God bless you in this way, too"—in other words, "May you, too, one day, defeat Iraq in a war." We both laughed.

As the American story in Iraq continues and experts refer to the dangers of the Arab Street, think of the millions of individuals like Salah al Fuli and not the thousands that are at the demonstrations broadcast across the world. Or think of Walid and the deep shades of gray that make up opinion here. American optimism is a national virtue, but we really should enjoy this moment right now. It is as good as it is going to get for us. Already, there are reports of hospitals that can't function because of looters, not to mention a lack of water. The question never really was about who would win, but about what we would do after our victory, and that question remains.

Happy Holidays this week.

Love,
Ben

Letter 18

Beauty and the Beasts

May 17, 2003

Dear All,

The last two Fridays, I traveled to two of Cairo's different worlds. Last night I visited beauty and the Friday before, the beasts. Beauty came in the form of a Christian Egyptian wedding I attended until 2:00 A.M. As for the beasts, I went camel shopping at the Bir'ash market thirty-five kilometers outside of the city.

I maneuvered my way into the wedding and the secret world of beautiful Christian Cairenes through a friend from graduate school who is a diplomat posted at the U.S. embassy. One of her Egyptian co-workers in the visa office was getting married, and the bride invited all of her colleagues and friends, Egyptians and Americans alike. Sita, my friend, in turn, invited me. Judging by how beautiful the bride looked, not to mention her Egyptian co-workers from the visa office, I now believe that the reason people line up outside the embassy is for the chance to talk with them; obtaining a visa to enter the United States is secondary.

I can't confirm that all Christian Cairenes belong in *People* magazine; however, Coptic Christians do make up about 15 percent of the population here in Egypt. There are some Christian government officials, but the number of Coptic officials relative to Muslim ones is nowhere close to the percentage of Copts in Muslim-majority Egypt. From a few different conversations, it would seem that Egypt's Copts are generally made to feel like second-class citizens and are persecuted in different ways, both officially and unofficially. Official discrimination comes in the form of numerous laws and regulations. For instance, to build a new church, Copts must attain the Egyptian president's approval; to make even the smallest of repairs to an existing church—from a leaky roof to a broken toilet—approval must be granted by the provincial governor. In contrast, there aren't any special approvals necessary for either the construction of new mosques or the repair of existing ones. Further discrimination occurs through the state education system and school curricula, which deemphasize Copts' role in Egyptian history and culture. There is official legal discrimination, too, with laws relating to marriage, divorce, and religious conversion influenced by Islamic law.

Unofficial discrimination comes in various social forms, from harsh words to the extreme of physical attacks. Converts to Christianity, especially those who have converted from Islam, deal with continual harassment from security forces and Islamic groups alike. Opportunities for all types of harassment of Christians are plentiful since every Egyptian's religion is listed on the individual's identity card. So, even if a Copt has a religiously neutral name, whenever he or she presents his or her identity card, whether to a police officer or government official or for purposes relating to work, there is the possibility of some form of abuse.

From a conversation that I had with a furniture-parts factory owner at the wedding, I learned that one of the responses to such discrimination is reverse discrimination. He explained that he only hires Christian upper staff and management. Making sure to protect one's own first and foremost, he tries to hire mostly Christian labor, too. So it would seem that even Egypt, the Arab East's one true nation-state, according to Tahseen Basheer, is not immune to aspects of tribal culture.

The wedding, which started at about 8:30 P.M., was held at a grand white-columned church. Hundreds of people packed the church, all the way to the rafters and the wraparound balcony. The crowd was well dressed and brought together the most diamonds assembled outside of a South African mine. Even the glamorous and wealthy couldn't keep from sweating, or "glistening," though. It was over 100 degrees here yesterday, and the church didn't have fans. Luckily for Sita and me, we happened to sit behind a fan that was being used to keep some computer equipment from overheating. The couple had arranged for a PowerPoint presentation that included photos from their childhood, lyrics to songs and hymns, and their wedding vows.

The ceremony was beautiful and lasted more than two hours. According to what I can only assume is local tradition, the groom waited at the altar for the bride for at least forty-five minutes. Once the bride was escorted down the aisle, the bride and groom sang a duet, the bride's sister sang a song, and four different priests made speeches. The wedding was conducted in a combination of "cultured" colloquial and Modern Standard Arabic, which is much easier to understand than the street dialect that Salah and my friends at the restaurant speak. A personal highlight of the ceremony was when one of the priests warned the couple about the devil, and he wasn't talking about me or America—a nice change of pace.

I gave up my fake Canadian citizenship a few weeks ago when I was busted trying to pass as a Mexican at the Khan al Khalili bazaar. Being from Canada, and having to regularly reference Celine Dion and *Titanic*, had gotten tiresome, so when a smooth-talking hookah salesman tried to hustle me into his shop, I claimed to be from *Mexiq* to avoid English altogether and bypass his stand. The problem was that he started speaking to me in Spanish, and all I could do was reply in Arabic. He then said in English, "Oh, you're really American. It's okay, you can be here, don't worry."

Until then, I'd been slowly reclaiming my American citizenship out of a feeling that I had to live with the social consequences and criticism of the war. Still, in select places, I have continued to hide my nationality. At the Khan and in other markets, I avoided telling vendors that I am American, assuming they would overcharge me either for being rich or for other political reasons. However, I took the hookah salesman's outing of me at the Khan as a sign. So, a few minutes later, over a negotiation for a pair of new undershirts, I successfully tested out the American-identity waters and haven't looked back.

After the wedding ceremony ended, the bride and groom stood on the church steps and greeted the hundreds of guests. Only close friends and family were invited to the reception afterward, but somehow, I ended up there, too. It was held at a private club and didn't start until about midnight. Except for the Arabic-speaking MC, it was similar to American wedding receptions. There was the introduction of the couple, their first dance, the "father of the bride" and "mother of the groom" dance, and a long buffet filled with delicious (Arab and Egyptian) foods.

The PowerPoint presenters set up shop at the reception, too, and played old music videos of the couple. As children, the couple had made Christian music videos, so there were some terrific clips of the bride and groom, with big hair and wearing Jordache fashions, performing on 1980s-style sets. It was like a Menudo-does-Egypt tour. Apart from the music videos starring the bride and groom, almost every song the deejay played was in English. Celine Dion was featured prominently.

It will never cease to amaze me how popular Celine Dion and Mariah Carey are in the Arab East. The toughest, most angry-looking characters, who may even be in a mid-sentence diatribe about some political grievance, turn into crooning softies when Celine Dion comes on the radio. I've been listening to a lot of Arabic Top 40 lately, and have noticed that every song is about love and contains some combination of the words *salaam*, *hub* (love), *habibi*, and *Allah*. The literal translations to English of some of my favorites hits are "Where is she?" and "I miss you." Romance, honor, and true love . . . maybe Mariah Carey's appeal isn't such a stretch after all.

The wedding was really enjoyable. It was a universally "human" event, and I managed to avoid all political and most religious discussions the entire evening. There were some funny moments, too. The most entertaining part of the wedding reception occurred during the groom's speech. In the midst of a heartfelt thank-you to his family and friends, the groom thanked, in English, the American embassy consular staff for making his wife so happy. One of the American consular officers, who had loosened up considerably after his Sprite became a vodka and Sprite, stood up and, using his limited vocabulary, waved his arms and yelled, *"Visas l'kulkum!"* or "Visas for all of you!"

Happily, I found the same kind of freedom from political and religious conversations at the Bir'ash *sou' al gaml* or camel market. Instead of having a political conversation about donkeys (President Mubarak is derisively referred to as a *humar,* or donkey, under people's breath here), we talked about camels.

Shopping for camels is an early morning activity, so I picked up Sita (a good shopping partner) at a quarter to 7:00 last Friday. We took a cab to Imbaba, the former home of the camel market, to catch a minibus to the new camel market in Bir'ash. Imbaba is where Dr. Rashid took me before the war to meet his brother. I'd returned a few times with Salah and Ahmed Bedoui to drink some tea and smoke a hookah, but only late at night after they had finished work. Each time, I was a lone white face amid thousands of Egyptians passing by and shopping. Dirt roads, teenagers flying through traffic on mopeds, packed covered trucks that serve as taxis, donkey-drawn carts hauling green onions or cabbage, the deafening noise of shoppers and hawkers set to Arabic Top 40 music, and the checkerboard of hundreds of ahwa and fuul joints together form Imbaba. The neighborhood is a sensory-overload experience of Egyptian life.

Calling Imbaba part of the "developing world" is a stretch of the term—it is unmistakably located in the third world. At 7:00 A.M. on a Friday morning, Imbaba was quiet, though, which made its landscape, rather than its people, prominent. By the light of day, I saw that the main road was paved and lined with dented coffeehouses, food stands, and dust-covered stores. Dirt roads branched off of the main road and wound into neighborhood mazes of cement-block-style apartments. In the middle of the paved road, a long stretch of garbage piles separated traffic. Dogs darted in and out of the piles, and men of all ages drank coffee and smoked water pipes. Nearby, as children and flies hovered about, women sat on the ground and sold greens or sugar.

Imbaba is an "English-free zone," making it a welcome delight to me. As I mentioned before, some expats come to Cairo for cultural reasons, and others live here for professional purposes, working for branch offices of multinational companies. Between the two sets, there is a vibrant expat life here, conducted in English, in the form of hotel-bar karaoke, salsa dancing at TGI Fridays, dinner parties, and politically active conversation. At times, I welcome the opportunity to take a step back and eat pizza with fellow American grad students. Most of the time, though, I try to seek out cultural immersion in an English-free zone—the reason I moved my life first to Jordan and then Egypt. Imbaba is just such a refuge, and I was excited to go to the Bir'ash market for a morning of full Egyptian immersion.

Without a problem, Sita and I found our minibus to Bir'ash amid the gawking hookah smokers and tea drinkers. The forty-minute ride cost only 20 cents but was worth at least a hundred times that. Along a bumpy, unpaved road, the scenery changed as we passed water buffalo and donkey-pulled carts. Urban sprawl melted into farmers tilling lush green fields under a bright blue sky. At 7:30 on a Friday morning, I wondered if those farmers ever took a day off, or if every day was basically the same, give or take a few moments.

The minibus dropped us at a walled-in compound surrounded by various spare parts and dirty plastic bags blown against the wall. From the entrance to the market, we got our first glimpse of the camels inside. There were hundreds of them of all sizes and weight. Most of the camels had their front left leg bent at the knee so that their ankle and quad could be tied together and they would be unable to run away. The result was that the camels hopped spastically around the compound. In a chicken-and-egg scenario, it was unclear to me whether they were hopping about because they were tied up and being beaten by their handlers with long sticks, or whether their handlers tied them up and beat them to keep them from hopping around.

If Imbaba is the third world, we had just stepped into a portal from a different time. Most of the younger handlers and older owners

The Bir'ash camel market.

wore colorful full-length galabayas and some type of kaffiyeh, or head covering, to protect them from the sun. The majority were dark skinned, had heavy mustaches, and came from southern Egypt or Sudan. Owners mingled among the camels, negotiating prices and inspecting product. Sita and I wandered among the swarms of flies, island-hopping camel crap and attracting considerable attention as I took pictures. Owners, traders, and camel handlers were all friendly to us and their disbelieving stares became warm, surprised smiles when I wished them good morning and asked them how they were.

They were stunned that I was an American who could speak Arabic. There was one dealer who refused to believe that I'm American and insisted that I was Lebanese. This has happened before, especially in Egypt, where people can't imagine a non-Arab being able to speak Arabic. So, it is a common assumption that any foreigner who can speak Arabic and who doesn't look Egyptian must be from Lebanon or Syria—countries that have a full mix of blonde and redheaded Arabs. This guy was persistent, so I just admitted that my grandfather was from Lebanon rather than argue with him all morning.

Camel traders at the Bir'ash camel market.

From a couple of different conversations, I found out that the camels were brought by flatbed trucks from the Egyptian southern city of Aswan and as far south as Sudan. Most of the camels were about two years old, but we also saw a baby, born three months ago. It hardly had a hump, leading me to ponder the awkwardness of camel puberty. The camels ranged in price from $600 to $2,000, depending on size and condition. Some are bought for work, while others are eaten. If I wanted a camel, I didn't necessarily have to pay in money. There were offers to put together a package of camels in exchange for Sita's hand in marriage.

There was also a pack of camels without their front legs tied that were the best-behaved camels in the compound. This past week, when I've had trouble sleeping, I think about whether they were drugged or whether they were smart camels that didn't want to be beaten. I tried to convince one camel beater named Ahmed that he was better off reasoning with the camel and explaining to it the consequences of misbehaving. I attempted to clue him in to the teachings of Salah al Fuli, Egypt's ambassador to the animal kingdom, but he didn't understand my liberalism and just laughed. I think he was a neoconservative.

One camel dealer asked, "Do you come here every week?"

I replied, with a straight face, "No, I just need to buy a gift for a friend before I go home to America." He nodded knowingly–commiserating that gift shopping for the right camel can be difficult.

This is the Cairo that I love, one of the English-free zones that are so rich with life and that have not been hit by the tidal wave of foreign influence. One of the joys of studying history and languages is in imagining life in other times and places. The beauty of travel is that one gets to actually visit these places and sometimes even to go back in time. In visits to places like Bir'ash and Imbaba, I find ways of life that I've never seen before and that do not exist in the Western world of speed, efficiency, and practicality. I had a glass of the best lemonade of my life in Bir'ash. It came from a giant tub of squeezed lemons and water, in which floated a solid block of ice. Forty flies circled overhead, but it was perfect. Snapple will never invent anything so good.

A few blocks from my apartment in Cairo, there is another place that belongs to the Cairo I love as well. In the orangish hues of dusk, after the day's summer heat has subsided, I step out of my building and walk a few blocks east. City life surrounds me. People buy eggs and vegetables at outdoor stands that edge into the street, children fly kites from the roofs of cars, men puff away at water pipes in white plastic chairs that face outdoor TVs playing Egyptian soccer matches, and couples drink freshly squeezed mango and guava juice. There is so much smiling, so much contentment, and so much activity and life. As I walk through these streets, an older Egyptian woman sitting in her window might guess that I'm a foreigner busily on my way somewhere, but I already have reached my destination. Sometimes, I feel part of a beautiful film. I visualize pulling the camera back into a boom shot from above. I trace my path past the watermelon wagons and the piles of onions and peaches, through the outdoor markets, across the city, and underneath the warm evening glow.

There is so much color and flavor to this Cairo. In its most humble and common settings, the city is never more beautiful or more alive. It would be criminal to put a Safeway here, a supermarket that would sell onions, eggs, *and* plums. Or worse, a Starbucks—that green, sterile mermaid that would swallow the outdoor coffeehouses where I drink thick Arabic coffee and play dominoes with three old guys in galabayas who pound the board with their tiles and yell at me for being too slow. Already, Liberation Square downtown is littered with a KFC, Pizza Hut, and McDonald's. It is ironic: I can't imagine that a place called "Liberation Square" was ever intended to become a home to Western fast-food chains.

Maybe the efficient and the eternal as well as the modern and the traditional can coexist in Cairo indefinitely. Egypt is a place of conflicting and contrasting worlds living on top of each other: pollution-belching traffic and fresh peach stands; McDonald's $2 made-to-order McNuggets and Ahmed Bedoui's 10-cent fried tamiyya sandwiches; elegant weddings with PowerPoint presentations and the camel market of Bir'ash with its fresh lemonade. In a few months, when I come home, I know that there will be many questions about safety and the character of the people and life here. What will be hardest to explain is the beauty and vividness to parts of life that are otherworldly and from a different time.

The time for those explanations will come soon. It's been ten months since I arrived in Amman. I remember my second evening in Jordan, when I didn't know a single person in the country. I sat in a public square near the Nef and watched children run and play as their parents relaxed on benches, ate seeds, and drank tea. It was a full moon that night, and after a day of not finding a place to live, I studied the moon's bright white light and questioned what I was doing. I felt alone and far from home. Since then, I've marked every full moon that has passed. At some point, though, the full moon's meaning flipped in my head. I went from counting down the months that I've been away to now fidgeting that another month has passed. It is hard to believe that only a few months remain before it is time for me to come home.

Hope you all are well.

Love,
Ben

Letter 19

Amman Dreaming

June 11, 2003

Dear All,

"Why do I like America?" my barber's wife asked me.

"Why?" I answered, not knowing what to expect. Could it be the fall of Saddam's statue and our liberation of the Iraqi people? Did we win a heart or perhaps a mind?

"Because the American people have freedom—the government went to war, but the people had protests in the streets," she explained as I sat next to Na'el, my favorite barber in the world, in his Amman home.

Who says you can't ever go home again? I returned to Amman for two weeks to visit six factories and to conduct interviews for my research project. I also went cruising with the water-delivery guy, returned to Nai for some nightlife, drank coffee with the neighborhood East Banker "Godfather" and his compatriots, and went to lunch at my barber's house. Along the way, I had the opportunity to assess from up close the impact of the war, the double-edged benefits of peace, and the current prospects for democratic processes in Jordan.

I was thrilled to return to my home in the Arab East and to find that everyone's worst prewar fears had not come true. Amman was neither overrun by Palestinian or Iraqi refugees, nor laid to waste by the fallout of a chemical weapons exchange. That's not to say that there still isn't a lot of uncertainty about the future. In fact, Abu Alaa's shifting sands of the Middle East and the man in the street's feeling of powerlessness over the future never seemed more apparent. Referring to U.S. intentions for Iraq and the rest of the region, acquaintance after acquaintance asked me, "What do you think is going to happen here now? What will happen to us?"

My home in Webdeh was exactly as I left it, except that instead of snow on the window sill, spring sunshine poured through the white curtains. When I picked up the key, I joined my landlady and her mother for a glass of tea with fresh mint, and we discussed the situation in Jordan and Iraq. Both women expressed disgust and anger toward Saddam, as well as fear and uncertainty about the future. Al Jazeera has given prominent coverage to the mass graves being unearthed in Iraq, and my landlady's mother, a sweet woman who has difficulty walking and sits in the screened-in porch all day with her Bible at her side, declared that "Saddam is the devil."

Zein, my landlady, seconded this sentiment but expressed greater concern about Al Qaeda. The recent bombings in Saudi Arabia and Morocco hit home for Jordanians. A week before my trip to Jordan, Al Qaeda terrorists bombed three gated residential compounds for foreigners in Saudi Arabia and five sites in Casablanca. In Saudi, they killed thirty-four people, including two Jordanians, and at least forty-one people were killed in Morocco, too. There is popular indignation over the killing of innocents. "They were just living there; they didn't do anything," Zein said, commenting on the Jordanians killed in Saudi Arabia.

If militants targeted Arabs in Saudi and in Morocco, both monarchies and American allies, then they could do the same in Jordan.

Perhaps with this in mind, Zein then asked me, "What will happen to this region? What is America going to do?"

She had been planning on opening a travel agency and had postponed starting the new business in the fall due to the situation with Iraq. She now wanted to know whether I thought it was a good time to open the business.

Obviously, I don't have inside information about what the Bush administration plans to do. I can only guess as to whether the White House will now use the fear of American power to push for peace between Israelis and Palestinians or threaten the dictatorship in Syria with invasion, too. It is clear, though, that people here don't feel in control and that they are waiting for their fate to be determined by outside powers—by Americans and the America haters alike. This point was reinforced throughout my neighborhood visits, as I cobbled together pieces of the puzzle that I had missed while living in Egypt.

I wandered to the end of my street to check out my view of the city. As I stood in the empty lot below Amman's clear blue skies and listened to the forgotten sounds of chirping birds, the water-delivery man, Mahmoud, drove by. I waved him down and we exchanged greetings. Mahmoud is twenty-two years old and drives a blue van around Webdeh delivering purified drinking water. He is saving his money to get married in a couple of years. He asked me where I'd been and then wanted to know what Cairo was like.

"Lots of crowds and pollution, not like here," I said. "All you hear are the cars and the people; there aren't any birds." He smiled and invited me to ride with him while he finished his deliveries.

"What's happened here? What's been the biggest result of the war?" I asked.

He paused for a second and replied, "Everything is more expensive now. No more oil from Iraq, so gas is more expensive. Taxis are more expensive. The bus is more expensive, and the shared taxis are more expensive, too."

"How much more?"

"They changed the meter on the taxis. The bus is 17 qirsh, and the shared taxi is 11 qirsh." There are 100 qirsh in a Jordanian dinar (JD), and a dinar is equal to $1.41. So the bus still costs less than a quarter and the shared taxi 16 cents, but these were overnight increases in the cost of living of at least 10 percent. Jordan is a poor country, and if "bus riders" faced an immediate 10 percent increase in the cost of living across the board, then they are struggling financially.

Mahmoud made his last deliveries, and we chatted some more about his plans for his wedding in a couple of years. When we drove into the Webdeh traffic circle on the way back to the water store, it was impossible not to notice that the little park inside the circle looked like a used-car lot. There were green, red, white, and blue banners everywhere. "What happened? What's all this?" I asked.

"Elections. We have parliamentary elections in a couple of weeks." They were campaign banners.

"Really? Who's going to win? Are you going to vote?"

Mahmoud smiled at my excitement, looked over at me, shook his head, and said, "Nah, it's not important." We pulled into the van's parking space, arranged for him to drop some water off at my place on his way home, and said good-bye.

I crossed the street, stepped into the traffic circle, and read the hanging campaign signs. There were slogans on each, next to the candidate's name. While some banners actually spoke to issues such as corruption and the newfound financial difficulties resulting from the war, my earlier crash course in Jordanian politics came rushing back. Campaign banners reflected the world of strife between Jordanian-Jordanians and Palestinian-Jordanians. One candidate, a Palestinian-Jordanian (i.e., a Jordanian of Palestinian descent), declared that "the nation is for everyone," while an East Banker or Jordanian-Jordanian candidate, in thinly veiled language, proclaimed that he would offer, "Help and support for all those who participate in building the Nation." Other candidates played the anti-Israel card, with slogans like, "No to normalization with enemies," and "We support the *intifada,* and its continuation is a religious and national duty."

Still other candidates sought to burnish their images as representatives who would fight against the widespread corruption found in government. Campaign banners claimed the "Dignity of the citizen is first," and "Your vote is the weapon against corruption," and my personal favorite, "With your vote, you forbid gibberish."

Some would-be parliamentarians sought to appeal to people by speaking to the newfound economic hardships that bus riders face as a result of the war with Iraq. One declared that he would restrict "price increases of basic resources" (like gasoline), while another contender claimed that he was for a "rich standard of living and a tax cut." That one sounded familiar.

Intrigued by the thought of democratic elections in a monarchy, I crossed the street to visit my friend Hanna, the owner of my supermarket, to find out more. Before my forced evacuation, I drank coffee with Hanna one or two evenings a week as his supermarket was closing for the day. He is a Christian East Banker, who I think of as the neighborhood "don" for Jordanian-Jordanians. In the supermarket, there are portraits of King Abdullah II, the crown prince Hamza, the late King Hussein, and the late King Abdullah I, Jordan's first king. Hanna is fiercely patriotic and loyal to the royal family. In the past, he has expressed concern about corrupt officials, mostly of Palestinian descent, he explains, who offer King Abdullah policies that only benefit themselves and not the country. In the evenings, friends join Hanna for coffee and conversation. Their conversations fluctuate between laugh-filled joking, which I usually don't understand, and political talk, which I can mostly figure out.

When I arrived at the supermarket, Hanna was already having coffee with two friends. He welcomed my return and insisted that I join them. We launched straight into the issue of Iraq and what was going to happen now, in both Jordan and Iraq. Like so many others would during my visit, Hanna asked me what America was going to do, as if by nature of my nationality, I was privy to classified information. Hanna told me about some of the new business coming to Jordan as a result of the war. For one thing, Jordanians were now driving aid workers, journalists, and Western entrepreneurs into Baghdad. These trips are dangerous, and drivers frequently speed down the desert road at 120 mph to avoid attacks. Later during my stay, I ran into Fayez—my friend from my days at the Nef —and he told me that Issa was one of these drivers.

Pointing to the traffic circle and the signs outside, I asked Hanna about the elections and if he was going to vote. Nodding his head, he replied, "Yes, it is important, a duty." He then grew upset as he described how the Palestinian-Jordanians are campaigning by identifying themselves with the villages they had come from in Palestine, rather than with Jordan and Jordanian issues. He had parked outside of a rally for such a candidate the week before and sat in his car, listening to the speech. He came away very angry and concerned for the country. He complained that "they sit in government-built buildings, they receive government benefits, and they criticize everything in the government. They are not loyal to Jordan first."

"Al Ordon Awalan," or "Jordan First," is the national slogan, and it appears on billboards all over the country. Yet the meaning of the slogan is open to interpretation, and the national ad campaign has proven controversial. I believe that government spin mavens intended to make a domestic statement that on *all* issues—even pan-Arab international ones, such as those dealing with Iraq or the peace process—the Jordanian leadership will put the homeland's interests and the citizens' interests first. Given the context of tensions between East Bankers and Palestinian-Jordanians, though, the slogan has been perceived to mean that citizens of Jordanian roots come first and that citizens of Palestinian ancestry are second-class. This sensitive issue actually resulted in a melee several months back at the university between East Banker and Palestinian-Jordanian students. I wasn't there (this was before my evacuation, though), but I heard from a few people, including my language partner Ibrahim, who was there, that Jordanian-Jordanian and Palestinian-Jordanian students faced off and that, at one point, the East Banker students chanted, "We love Sharon," to antagonize their counterparts of Palestinian descent. A giant fistfight ensued, with security guards involved, too. In the *Jordan Times*, the incident was written up as an anti-Israel and antiwar protest, with no mention of the "We love Sharon" chants, given popular hatred here for the Israeli prime minister.

No sooner had Hanna finished sharing his thoughts on the elections when a candidate showed up to pay his respects. A tall, thin, and balding man with a thick mustache, the candidate came into the supermarket with his little boy and shook all of our hands. Hanna beamed with pride over the visit and explained to me that the candidate came from an important family in the south—which I took to mean that he was an East Banker of Jordanian ancestry.

Over my two-week visit to Jordan, I noticed pictures of candidates plastered all over Amman and banners hanging on streets throughout town. I asked everyone I spoke with about the elections to gauge their interest and level of intended participation. Granted, most of my contacts and interviewees are of Palestinian ancestry, but students, intellectuals, cabbies, vendors, and businessmen agreed: The elections were nothing but a sham meant for external consumption.

Ramis, my friend who owns the ceramics factory, explained to me that the system is gerrymandered. Districts are not drawn based on proportional size but rather nationality. There are many little districts for the areas with East Banker majorities, while there are only a few districts for the larger urban areas like Amman and Zarqa, which are densely populated by Jordanians of Palestinian descent. Such district lines ensure Jordanian-Jordanians an overwhelming majority of the number of seats in parliament. In addition to the gerrymandering, another problem is that candidates don't represent issues but rather their tribes. Voters make their choice based on family allegiance; issues such as health care or education don't come into play. Furthermore, people I spoke with were dismissive of the entire purpose of the voting exercise since the parliament is generally considered a rubber stamp for the king.

Ramis explained that the best thing to do was just to stay away from politics entirely and to concentrate on making money. It seems, though, that the elections are one way to make money. I spent a day at Ramis's ceramics factory learning about his business. After lunch, one of his contemporaries—a young managing owner from another factory—visited and they talked about candidates buying votes by the busload at 5–10 JD a head. The two joked about putting a bus of voters together. Of much greater interest to Ramis than the elections, however, were my thoughts on what was going to happen here. He is concerned for his business and potential new obstacles that may prevent him from exporting ceramics to Europe.

One person who is optimistic about the future is my favorite teacher from the university, Khalid. Khalid taught our current-events class, where we would read newspaper articles and then discuss the news. It became quite clear from our discussions that Khalid is the master of the conspiracy theory. In the fall, when Minnesota's Senator Paul Wellstone died in a plane crash before the midterm elections and then the Republicans won control of the U.S. Senate, Khalid was convinced that something untoward was afoot.

I bumped into Khalid on the bus ride home one day. We got off the bus together at Abdali and went to his cousin's stationery store, where we drank juice and talked politics. Like everyone else, Khalid wanted to know what the United States was going to do in the region next. When I in turn asked Khalid, a Jordanian citizen of Palestinian descent, about the elections, he waved his hand and explained to me that the elections were not important.

Instead, Khalid explained to me why he was optimistic about his future. He believed that President Bush was now strong enough to force peace between Israelis and Palestinians. Once a Palestinian state would be established, the Jordanians of Palestinian descent would either go to Palestine or stay here. East Banker Jordanians would be forced to recognize the Palestinian-Jordanians who stayed in Jordan as equal citizens. Not only that, but Khalid expected that he and other descendents of Palestinian refugees who stayed would receive a financial settlement from the international community for choosing not to go back to places like Jaffa. Then, he continued, once there was a Palestinian state, it would form a federation with Jordan. The federation would be governed by a Palestinian prime minister and a Jordanian prime minister, under the leadership of the Jordanian king. He smiled and wiped his hands together as if finishing up a meal.

Randa, my travel agent, was a bit more cynical, especially regarding the elections. While I served as a personal indicator for many as to when war would come, Randa didn't need me. She was already in the know because she handled several airline tickets for Western diplomats' spouses at the end of January. She, in fact, told me that war was coming before my fellowship sponsors sent me the evacuation e-mail. Randa is of Palestinian ancestry, but her husband is from a prominent East Banker family. I stopped in to see how things were going, and she told me that business was booming, with many people coming to Jordan since it was the gateway to Iraq. As for the elections, she offered trenchant analysis.

"Life isn't just food—you can't just feed us *mansaf*," she said. Randa had been to a campaign event the week before and all that the candidate provided was mansaf—the Jordanian national dish of lamb, rice, and yogurt. There was no talk of real issues. Randa was most interested in hearing something about education and unemployment problems and found the event a ridiculous charade.

Neither my barber nor his wife thought much of the upcoming elections, either. The return to my favorite barber, Na'el, was an emotional moment for me. The only enjoyable part about the haircuts I've received in Egypt has been nicknaming them afterward. There was the "half mullet," the "plucked chicken," and most recently, "helmet head." After "helmet head," I decided to wait for my return to Amman for my next haircut. As I entered the barber shop, Na'el expressed genuine happiness to see me and gave me five kisses—one on my right cheek and four on the left.

In Jordan, the first two kisses are a given, but the number that follow afterward depends on how happy the person is to see you. I've seen some people give seven or eight kisses, each person alternatively taking the initiative and upping the ante, kind of like a "Can you top this?" battle of who is happier to see whom. I've grown to appreciate the "kiss hello" aspect of the culture. I used to equate it to childhood visits to Brooklyn where my dad's aunts would take turns squeezing my cheeks and shrieking, "*Boobileh,* you're such a big boy!"

After explaining where I had been and professing my happiness to return to Amman, where my Cairo cough, sneeze, and athlete's foot all disappeared in two days, Na'el and I talked about his family, the differences between Egypt and Jordan, the work of Egyptian barbers, and how much we missed each other. At the end of the haircut, Na'el invited me to come to his house for lunch the next week.

A week later, I sat in Na'el's living room, playing with his two sons, ages three and one, while his wife cooked us lunch. I brought Na'el some sweets and a postcard of the Statue of Liberty on which I had written in Arabic, "My friend Na'el—the best barber in America and Jordan, with peace and friendship," and signed "Benja." Signed postcards from home never fail to impress as gifts—sentimental gestures go a long way.

This lunch was a little different from other meals I've had at people's homes because it was just the two of us. On other visits, I ate with big groups of families, usually just the men. Since Na'el's

Na'el.

kids are small, they were taken to another room, and Na'el's wife, Um Wasem, who wore a head covering in the house because I was visiting, did not join us until we had coffee and dessert. Over *maqlubeh*, Na'el and I talked mostly about how much he could make per haircut if he had a shop in the United States and what he would have to do to go about opening a shop. He lost interest as I sketched out the expenses for him.

Over coffee and baklava, Um Wasem bombarded me with personal and political questions. Neither she nor Na'el speaks English, and I was the first American to visit their home. I answered all of her questions, and in return, I learned that Um Wasem, who is probably in her late twenties, is the oldest of ten children that all live in Zarqa. I also found out that she considered the elections "empty talk." Na'el showed his agreement by nodding his head and telling me that it was all "theater." Um Wasem was much more interested in talking about America than Jordanian politics.

"Why do I like America?" she asked.

"Why?" I answered, stumped.

"Because the American people have freedom—the government went to war, but the people had protests in the streets, real protests. We saw it on al Jazeera, in New York and in San Francisco— hundreds of thousands of people. Here, no one agreed with the war, but we couldn't protest. We have no voice." We didn't speak about my impression of the protests in Cairo, but it seemed that Na'el's wife shared my view about their lack of seriousness.

This point about Americans' freedom of speech was made by others, too. People fundamentally disagreed with the war but had no way to express themselves. They greatly admired how Americans voiced their opinions against government policies. It is ironic that we were supposed to win respect in the Arab East through a display of our force but, in fact, we gained respect as a democracy by the activities of those who were derided as "unpatriotic."

American voices of protest were heard in Egypt as well. Just the other day, I watched a TV program that was a debate on whether to boycott American films and American products. There was full

agreement among the different guests that Egyptians should boycott American goods, but they did not all agree that American films
should be boycotted. Among people here, Hollywood won credibility
with Michael Moore's speech at the Oscars, as well as Tim Robbins's
and Susan Sarandon's comments.

With thoughts of local elections and the impact of war swirling
in my head, I set up an interview with Adnan Abu Odeh, a pioneering
figure in Jordanian politics. Of Palestinian descent, he rose to the
prominent position of political adviser to King Hussein. He also
served as minister of information and permanent representative to
the United Nations. He wrote an excellent book, *Jordanians, Palestinians, and the Hashemite Kingdom in the Middle East Peace
Process*, that I read in grad school, and that piqued my interest in
Jordan.

Over homemade cookies, fresh lemonade, and tea, Abu Odeh
and I spent two hours in his sitting room speaking about Jordan, the
United States, and the future of the region. His thoughts on the big
picture and the region's persistent trends—the conflict between
tribalism and state formation and anti-Americanism—were incisive.
To Abu Odeh, the fall of Saddam and the occupation of Iraq revealed
the failure of the Arabs to build true nation-states following the colonial period. He contended that in Iraq and most other Arab countries, "The rule of law is weak, there is no political participation,
and there are no real institutions—just structures. Educational sys-
tems do not promote critical thinking, a key component to a responsible citizenry."

He lamented, "I had thought that Iraq was a nation-state, but the
institutions turned out to be false." The country descended into a
tribally based state of affairs so quickly, where "everyone turned
inward to take care of his own, while public concerns receded."

Abu Odeh later continued on this point, saying, "The Iraq War
was an earthquake. We learned that there are no citizens in the Arab
world, just residents. . . . There is no effective political opposition in
the Arab world . . . and there is no leader on deck, waiting in the
wings."

"Well, what role can popular pressure play in the development of real nation-states?" I asked.

Abu Odeh warned that I shouldn't expect change from bottom-up pressure that would emanate from the grassroots and push national leaders to respond. "The masses do not play a part in political life," Abu Odeh explained. "They have accepted a role as recipients of dictates . . . a policeman lives inside each person, guiding his steps. . . . The American action in Iraq is like a theater. We are all waiting for the second scene, the restructuring of Iraq and a new Middle East." His words implied that people here did not see an active role for themselves in determining the future—a notion enforced by the many friends and acquaintances who asked me about what the future would bring for them, for Iraq, and for the entire region.

"What about Jordan?" I inquired. "Where is Jordan in the process of state-building?"

"For Jordan, the creation of a Palestinian state will be the moment of truth. Palestinians in Jordan will demand their rights and will no longer accept second-class status because it would be permanent. Jordanians will have to adjust to this reality," he stated matter-of-factly.

A shroud of uncertainty hangs over Jordan regarding the issues between Palestinian-Jordanians and East Bankers and the impact the creation of a full Palestinian state will have on domestic affairs within the kingdom. While many East Banker Jordanians may like to believe that the majority of Palestinian-Jordanians and Palestinian refugees will return to Palestine where they will be Palestinian citizens, this is not likely the case.

There could be a political solution worked out for Palestinian refugees residing in Jordan that would include compensation or resettlement in other places (including, possibly, the West Bank or Gaza), but it is highly improbable that Palestinian-Jordanian citizens will leave Jordan in mass. First, Israel will never agree to such a population transfer as part of a final peace settlement. Second, for Khalid and many other Jordanian citizens of Palestinian descent, such as Na'el or Ramis, who have strong emotional ties to Palestine, their homes and livelihoods remain in Jordan. Once there is a Palestinian state, it will become indisputably clear across the Jordanian landscape that citizens of Palestinian descent are Jordanians of Palestinian heritage, rather than simply Palestinians living in Jordan. If these Jordanians of Palestinian descent actively choose to stay in Jordan, and to remain loyal Jordanian citizens after a Palestinian state has been established, it seems unlikely, as Abu Odeh pointed out, that they would tolerate second-class status.

My conversation with Abu Odeh eventually moved to the topic that has struck near to my heart this entire year. "What impact will the war with Iraq have on anti-American sentiment?" I asked him.

"It is the American presence in Iraq that will determine the Arab attitude toward America," Abu Odeh responded. "What happens in Iraq will perpetuate how people feel, one way or the other, as far as the image of the United States [is concerned]," he predicted. "America has put itself into the fray and made itself a tangible actor." Previously, America was criticized for the actions of proxies that we support—namely, Israel and the Egyptian and Saudi regimes. Now, Abu Odeh explained, Americans are frontline participants.

"Do you think Iraq will become more important than the Palestinian issue?"

"In Jordan, no; in other countries, though, it may."

Given Jordanians' physical and emotional proximity to Palestine, I can't imagine another issue supplanting the Palestinian struggle in importance to Jordanian-Jordanians and Palestinian-Jordanians alike. In other neighboring Arab countries, however, I can see how American actions in Iraq could dictate the ebbs and flows of American policy critics' ire. Iraq has become the center of attention on satellite news stations, and policy critics across the Arab East will become intimately familiar with our failings in Iraq as these shortcomings are broadcast daily throughout the region.

While the negative impact that our involvement in Iraq will have on anti-Americanism is clear, it is more difficult to see how the war in Iraq has the potential to have a positive influence on American policy critics' rebuke. Given the extreme popular distaste across the Arab East for any sort of occupation (a result of Israeli and colonial history), the chances of winning "hearts and minds" as a result of our actions in Iraq are slim. It is possible that President Bush will turn a new page in Middle Eastern history and support the creation of a democratic state in Iraq that does not threaten its neighbors, and that treats its citizens fairly, enabling them to pursue their own opportunities. Yet that's very hard to visualize, given Iraq's history, the history of its neighbors, and the context of the Hoover Dam-like obstacles that the Iraqi bus rider counterparts of Na'el, Salah, and Fadi must face in their daily struggles.

My conversation with Abu Odeh, and for that matter all the others I've had since my return to Jordan, reinforced for me the importance of context and perspective in viewing events in the Middle East. It's possible that, at this very moment, a White House or State Department spokesperson is praising "free elections" in Jordan. While this could be political spin, one could also honestly look at the superficial layer of banners and signs, skip the gerrymandering, and conclude that democracy may not be spreading its wings here, but it is at least stretching them. Or as massive amounts of foreign money truck through Amman on the way to Baghdad, Jordan might demonstrate some nice statistical economic growth, and someone might conclude a year from now that the economy grew due to the war. But who accrued those benefits? There will surely be some ketchup eaters that make it big, but what about the bus riders now paying 10 percent more to get to work and then return home?

Major issues are just so much more complex here than the thirty-second highlight coverage they receive at home. From up close, heart-wrenching, smile-inducing, and above all, colorful details both complicate and clarify the picture. Over this past year, I've tried to apply idea after honed idea to the complexity of real life and found that after close examination, things aren't quite what they seem.

For example, my exposure to the Palestinian diaspora of Amman gave me a new perspective on the realities of the Arab-Israeli conflict and the meaning of the "right of return" for refugees. I see now that while Israel and the West have assumed that refugees are not returning to former villages and homes, no Arab leader in Palestine, Jordan, Lebanon, or Syria ever shared such information with the refugees, who in many cases live in poverty and without equal rights. Their hope for deliverance isn't improved government policies or educational opportunities but a return to their home in Palestine. They have a tower of expectations, perhaps in this case not realistic, that still needs to be dismantled and then renovated into something new.

There are other examples of the sharper perspective offered by proximity and context. Life in Amman taught me about the different streams of anti-Americanism. There is big difference between American policy critics who appreciate American popular culture, business practices, and political governance and the nihilists or haters who indeed seek to kill us and our allies for how we have interceded in their lives, supporting the ruling regimes in their countries and contributing to their own state of powerlessness and feelings of lost honor.

Furthermore, living in both Egypt and Jordan has allowed me to see the distinctiveness of Arab cultures within the Arab East. From language to history to economic opportunities to religious practice, daily life is different in every place. There are common traits that all humans share and common features related to living in a Muslim majority culture, being a part of Arab history, and living in post-colonial authoritarian ruled societies. However, it has become clear to me that each place that I've lived in or visited this year—from Morocco to Syria—has its own culture and norms, too.

My best example, however, of the importance of context in understanding events comes from my research project on three-way trade between Jordan, Israel, and the United States. As a result of the peace agreement between Jordan and Israel, the United States extended free trade status to Jordan for goods produced in specified industrial zones, as long as the finished good contained a certain percentage of Israeli input. The main goal was to build relations between Jordanians and Israelis by creating constituencies that benefited tangibly from peace. These qualified industrial zones (QIZs) have had a positive impact on the Jordanian economy, notably increasing exports to the United States, bringing in foreign investment, and creating tens of thousands of new jobs. My idea was to study these successes more closely and gather lessons learned so as to recommend applying this type of policy elsewhere in other Arab and Muslim countries.

In conducting my research, I visited six different factories throughout Jordan and spoke with owners, managers, and laborers. I also met with government officials, academics, and other experts in Amman. Most of the factories produce garments and textiles purely for export to the United States. Roughly 70 percent of Jordanian workers at these factories are women, and many are religious women working their first jobs. In one very clean factory, muhajiba women sat at sewing machines chatting away and sewing Victoria's Secret underwear.

A site manager explained that many of these women are unmarried villagers in their early to mid-twenties and that their salary, in many cases, is the family's only cash income. The manager also told me that proving to be a wage earner has increased the marriage prospects for many of these women. At the same time, a lot of them have achieved a taste of independence because of their new jobs. How so? They have bought cell phones and can receive their own phone calls for the first time. On the peace-building front, at the industrial zones in the northern city of Irbid, Jordanians and Israelis truly work together in joint ventures producing garments and electronics.

These are "smile-inducing details," and the points about the female workers and the macroeconomic successes characterize the stories that have thus far been written about QIZs. There are also "indigestion-inducing details" that muddy the idyllic picture but that also clarify whether to replicate this policy elsewhere.

Through my work, I learned that a large part of the QIZ success story can be attributed to investments made by Asian garment and textile companies exploiting Jordan's special access to the United States prior to January 2005, when worldwide quotas on multifiber garments (a category of textiles) will be lifted. Because of their abundant cheap labor, factories in China and a handful of other Asian countries have the ability to dominate the textile market. The present quota system prevents these textile giants from exporting an unlimited amount of goods to the United States and other Western countries. However, because Jordan is granted an exception to these quotas through these industrial zones, there are no limits on the amount of Jordanian textiles that can be exported to the United States. As a result, Chinese and other Asian entrepreneurs have opened factories in Jordan to take advantage of the loophole.

Since Jordan is not an industrialized country with a skilled labor force, the Asian entrepreneurs must either import labor or train locals to work in the factories. Because the Asian factory owners aim to take the utmost advantage of this loophole before it closes in 2005, many foreign-owned QIZ factories employ foreign workers already experienced in textile production instead of spending the time to train new Jordanian workers. There is also, of course, the issue of whether Jordanians want to work in textile factories owned by foreigners. Accurate numbers on foreign labor are tough to come by, but the statistics on domestic labor, as provided by the Jordanian Ministry of Labor, state that 56 percent of the workers who produce garments in QIZ factories are Jordanian. Anecdotally, in my tour of one of the QIZ complexes, I visited the kitchen area that provides ninety meals a month for 3,500 workers. The kitchen is actually comprised of four separate units; there are two large kitchens for preparing Chinese and Sri Lankan food, and two smaller ones, one of which is for the preparation of Middle Eastern food.

Many of these foreign workers produce cheap garments, like underwear, and do nothing to create a unique Jordanian market niche worldwide. Once export restraints imposed by quotas disappear for the Chinese, it remains unclear whether owners will close these factories in Jordan or whether the factories will even be able to remain competitive in an open market. For this reason, Asian-owned companies with no emotional investment or long-term stake in Jordan are not concerned with developing specialized local industries (like a Jordanian line of Muslim women's conservative dress or shoes) or a labor force that will remain competitive into the future.

So the QIZs will succeed as long as there is this special window of opportunity, but then could fall flat unless steps are taken to develop a domestic labor force that can produce goods that sell in a competitive market. Foreigners could pack their businesses up, depart Jordan, and leave a legacy of disappointment and unfulfilled expectations.

Regarding the goal of building peace between Jordanians and Israelis, with the exception of the joint business ventures between Jordanians and Israelis in the northern city of Irbid, it doesn't make economic sense to include an Israeli input in textile products. Israel can't provide inexpensive cloth or other necessary inputs to the textiles that make up the bulk of QIZ exports. So, to attain the minimum Israeli 8 percent content, factories generally scrounge about for ways to include Israeli extras. For example, with the production of suits, factories buy Israeli-produced pins and belts and put them in the shipping package. Through this sort of input, the supply of unnecessary extras, businesses achieve the qualifying amount. I was told that these extras are frequently thrown out when the product arrives in the United States. So the Israeli contribution becomes the equivalent of an 8 percent tax (still cheaper than the costs of exporting to the United States from somewhere else). I can't imagine that this was the sort of cooperation that U.S. policymakers had in mind when creating this policy.

This U.S. policy has yielded some nice macroeconomic successes for Jordan. The QIZs have increased business for spillover industries like transportation; increased employment for Jordanian women, whose unemployment rate is off the charts; and created some new peace-building connections. It is not, though, the unqualified success touted by both the U.S. and Jordanian governments. The bottom line is that the QIZ policy has created an economic distortion with high expectations that are not quite grounded in a longer-term reality.

Given the stakes—if these zones fail it will impact the U.S.-Jordan relationship and the popular perception of peace—I wonder how U.S. officials who make the policy and those who make the public statements view the QIZ problems. Perhaps they have their own context, and choose to look only at the bigger picture of trade issues or U.S.-Jordan relations for the sake of having to make key decisions. Sometimes all the excruciating and human details—the color—only make it more difficult for policymakers to make cold-hearted decisions based on national interests. Or, in contrast, I wonder whether our leaders choose to see what it is that they want to believe, be it with the case of the QIZs or Jordanian elections or other regional issues, like the peace process, the war on terrorism, or Iraq.

My point is that context is important. It isn't a lie to talk about the fantastic short-term successes of the QIZs—particularly the new jobs and the empowerment of women workers. However, it is disingenuous to only assess the QIZs within a short timeframe and not to look at their future and the realities of the full picture. From a closer and more intimate proximity, there is always a different, more colorful, and more complicated view on offer.

Overall, the trip back to Amman was fantastic. Aside from all the personal connections and the visits with friends, the experience was, in a way, like a Jordanian final exam. While I'm still not an Arabic Jedi master, my skills have improved; I'm kind of like Luke Skywalker after Darth Vader cuts his arm off at the end of *The Empire Strikes Back*. I need some more training, but I can do some neat tricks. I returned a blank CD at the bootleg DVD market, convinced a waiter to seat me in a closed restaurant, yelled directions out of a moving cab to a passing driver, and discussed labor issues with an official at the ministry of labor. Still, I'm not yet where I want to be, and the intensive two-month course that I just started at the American University in Cairo should do me some good.

Hope you all are well—

Love,
Ben

Letter 20

The Oasis

August 15, 2003

Dear All,

By the light of the full moon, I dipped a grainy piece of dark pita into the communal bowl of steaming lentils. To my right on the red straw mat, Omar held his young daughter. Sitting on my left, his cousin Ali rocked his two-year-old son to sleep and spoke in a mix of Berber and Arabic to his one-eyed uncle. As I ate those lentils in Egypt's Western Desert, under the crimson glimmer of Mars on the horizon and just a few sand dunes away from the Libyan border, I paused to consider how far I had traveled to reach that moment.

The past year has flown by, including the three weeks since I finished my intensive summer language program at AUC. After classes ended, I traveled to Egypt's most eastern and western reaches—Basata, a primitive, organic beach on the Red Sea in the Sinai Peninsula and the Siwa Oasis in the Western Desert. I also took trips to Tel Aviv, Jerusalem, and the Sultanate of Oman. Within a twenty-minute time frame in Jerusalem's Old City, I told security officers in Hebrew that I didn't have a weapon and Christian-quarter merchants in Arabic that I didn't have any money. In Oman, a friend from graduate school and I spent two days driving through villages, over sand dunes, up stark mountains, and along deep blue sea coasts.

This past year has been about chasing dreams in Arabic, and I've traversed the region, doing my best to leave no Middle Eastern stone unturned. More than magic Arabic beans, I've sought a real piece of common ground between Americans and Arabs, one that transcends the failures of the U.S.-Arab East relationship on the world stage. From my spirited defense of American music one fall night in Aleppo to the sweltering early April afternoons in my Cairo apartment, where I watched coverage of the Iraq war, I've devoted myself to this quest.

As my days here have grown numbered, I've found myself engulfed in a sense of panic. Struck by an irrational guilt that I hadn't seen and done it all, I asked myself what T. E. Lawrence, a.k.a. Lawrence of Arabia and role model to Anglos in the Arab East, would do? As a reminder, Lawrence was the British archaeologist turned soldier who fell in love with Arabia, its traditions, and its people, ninety years ago. During World War I, he served as an adviser and liaison to Emir Faisal, the great-great-uncle of Jordan's King Abdullah, in the deserts of modern-day Saudi Arabia, Jordan, and Syria. I concluded that Lawrence would have advised me to seek my own answers in the desert's majesty. The dazzling stars above and the warm whipping sands below have eased many a troubled soul and even halted the rolling waves of time. I had hoped that the desert's purity would be conducive to my putting together the pieces of this yearlong jigsaw puzzle journey.

Carrying my small backpack, I departed Cairo early one morning and headed to Egypt's Western Desert and the Siwa Oasis, famous for its natural springs, 300,000 date palms, and 70,000 olive trees. The eleven-hour ride from Cairo taught me why people die in the desert. Peering beyond the bus's polyester, turquoise curtains, I looked for signs of life but saw only the beating sun pouring down on rock-hard sand. Besides an occasional truck, there was no other traffic. Rest stops were cement-block remnants from a time when sandstorms and cockroaches ruled the world.

As the desert's perils were clear, so was its wonder. Siwa was a shocking flame of green in the reds and oranges of the desert's early evening light. In contrast to Cairo, where I've sat in traffic jams at 1:00 A.M. on a Tuesday, the oasis was village-like in character. The people's Berber features and my dinner of vegetable couscous pulled me back to southern Morocco. While I spoke with people in Cairene Arabic, it was Berber dialect that I heard spoken around me. Unlike the mobs in Cairo that gregariously shout "Welcome to Egypt!" to foreign faces, in Siwa, when people heard my Cairene accent, they asked, "Are you Egyptian?" and declared, "Welcome to Siwa!"

With the setting sun, the town's mosques produced a chorus of competing calls to prayer. On bicycles and donkey-drawn carts, Siwans commuted home and to their mosques. Fully covered women, wearing blue-blanket shawls atop their head coverings, sat in the back of carts driven by dutiful sons.

After dinner, I walked through the oasis, greeting men outside of their homes in the traditional Muslim fashion. One round father of seven children drew me in with his questions. I told him about Pittsburgh, its steel industry, and the Steelers. His blue eyes and bearded face emitted friendly confusion. At the end of our conversation, I glanced at the donkey and mud-wall home behind him and wondered what it was like for this man to sit on his stoop and hear a tall white guy talk about a place called Pittsburgh, its three rivers that run through downtown, and its football team's storied Steel Curtain defense. If I ever meet an English-speaking alien from Saturn, who tells me about his favorite rings, I guess I'll know.

The next morning, I walked three miles through the oasis's fields to Cleopatra's Pool, a natural spring. Boys in donkey-drawn "taxis" followed and harassed me, seeking to cash in on the pressures of the desert sun. Rebuffing their offers for a ride at a "special price," I passed olive trees, palms, and ditch diggers. With a temperature of 110 degrees and climbing, my mouth filled with a cotton-ball taste, and I questioned my decision not to fork over the equivalent of $1 for a ride. Was I truly principled or just that cheap?

With my attention focused on the glimmering salt sea on the horizon, beyond the cracked red ground before me, a young boy with a big smile and budding Afro riding a nicked gray bicycle pulled up beside me. His name was Musa (Moses), and he led me to Cleopatra's Pool. On the way, we chatted about Siwa, his family, and why I was walking in the desert in the middle of the day. Once we arrived at the spring, Musa rode off to go to work with his father in a field, and I dove into the pool's bubbling water for a swim.

Twenty minutes into my walk back to the hotel, I turned to see a giant yellow bulldozer bearing down upon me. Lunging for the side of the road was unnecessary as the young driver, a smiling guy named Issa (Jesus), stopped to offer me a ride. I climbed into the cab, Issa slid over, and we shared his seat. A three-mile walk in the desert at the height of a summer day turned into a ten-minute ride filled with laughter about sharing an eighteen-inch seat with a foreigner who was silly enough to attempt walking through the desert at midday. The moral of this story: When lost in the desert, keep an eye out for Muslim prophets' namesakes riding bicycles and driving bulldozers.

Late that afternoon, I embarked on an overnight trip with two guides, Omar and Ali, to the nearby Great Sand Sea, a chain of dunes, ten to fifteen stories tall, that are blown back and forth across the Western Desert. Usually such a trip is done with other travelers, but there weren't a lot of tourists in the Middle East this past year. An even more select few travel to the desert in August, and it's only the T. E. Lawrence wannabes who wish to sleep there.

Our first stop was Well Number 1, a freshwater spring and a splash of green amid sandy dunes. While I floated on my back and did my *Jungle Book* impersonation of Baloo, Omar and Ali lounged with the well-keeper, who dangled a string attached to a stick over the spring's edge. Moments before we left, the well-keeper pulled a whopper from the spring and became a fisherman. The sight of Ali in his off-white robe holding down the enormous bug-eyed fish flopping in the sand while the fisherman removed his hook was absurd. In the fish afterlife, what kind of abuse would that fish take from the salmon and tuna for having the luck to be caught by a well-keeper in the desert?

From Well Number 1 we cruised up, over, and down the Great Sand Sea's waves. Bouncing along in Ali's 1982 Toyota 4X4 was like riding an old wooden roller coaster without a safety belt. We climbed an especially high dune and parked to watch the sunset. Omar collected driftwood for a fire. I don't know how the driftwood got there—it was just there, like the fish in the well. Over a fire and glasses of Siwan tea, we watched the blazing red sun descend below the horizon. An equally deep red full moon rose behind us, and a desert wind from the north splashed us with sand.

Omar and Ali told me about their village and asked me if I would like to sleep near there. Excited by the prospect of an experience beyond the boundaries of tourism, I agreed. We drove at dusk over dunes and across roads to a spot between their village and the Libyan border. Our destination was a large tent abuzz with activity, lit by the glow of the full moon. Ali explained that for three days every year, his family slept in the desert so that its older members could undergo rheumatism treatments, submerging their bodies in the sand for twenty to thirty minutes for a few days in a row.

A group of twelve men sitting on a red mat welcomed me and invited me to join their dinner. Ali introduced me to his uncle, the family patriarch, as an American who spoke Arabic and was studying in Cairo. Adult cousins and brothers joked, ate, and played with their children. Behind the tent, away from the sight of strangers, wives and mothers prepared food and kept their own company. Spellbound, I sat cross-legged and barefoot, ate some chin-wetting watermelon, and listened to the family speak in a mix of Berber and Arabic.

Suddenly, from somewhere over my left shoulder, a voice called out:

"Allahu Akbar! Allahu Akbar!"

"Ash-hadu alla ilaha illa-llah!" ("I bear witness that none is worthy of worship but God!")

After hearing it five times a day for a year, in seven different countries, I have developed affection for the adhan, the call to prayer. This adhan, deep in the silence of the Western Desert, was one of the most beautiful that I've ever heard. I turned to see the silhouette of one of the cousins atop a sandy rock hill. He called out

Sunset in the Western Desert, with Omar and Ali.

through cupped hands for Muslims to gather and pray. The men stood, walked over to the hill, formed a horizontal line behind the cousin, and completed their final prayers of the day. Dressed in their light-colored robes, lit by the shocking full moon against the waves of the desert, the family presented a striking picture of religious devotion.

After prayer, conversation resumed, with discussions ranging from what company made the best four-wheel-drive vehicle to the objectionable personalities of city folk such as those living in Alexandria and Cairo. Omar asked me if I preferred the city or the desert. It's gotten to the point where I now hear Cairo's honking horns in my sleep. I had no problem gesturing to the stars above and the desert hills to my back and telling the group that the desert was beautiful.

The group was also curious about American culture. Ali wanted to know whether it was true that an American could live with a girlfriend for a year or two and not marry her. To drawn and pity-lined faces, I explained that traditions differed across the country but that this was indeed the case. Unbelievably, the topics of war in Iraq, the war on terrorism, and American support for Israel did not make appearances that night. They seemed of little relevance to the time and place. War in Iraq, like the *Sex and the City* life of Americans in New York, could have been as far away as another planet.

However, the next morning, while I played with my guides' children, Omar's son asked me why America "made war on Iraq." When I opened my mouth to respond, I realized that that cotton-ball taste had returned. I am well versed in delivering such arguments in Arabic, English, and Hebrew. No matter what language I used, however, there was nothing that I could say to that boy, in that wonderful place, that would enable him to understand why my country had chosen war. I began to sputter something about weapons of mass destruction and Saddam's tyranny, but as I looked into his earnest face, I was unable to finish my sentence.

I've written about tribalism in past letters, from my experiences traveling with my mom to my conversation about state formation with Abu Odeh. My travels of the past few weeks have further bolstered my feelings on the subject. When I entered Siwa, I left Egypt. True, there are Egyptian soldiers around the area, but it is tribal custom that rules Siwa and its surrounding villages. It's illegal for Siwans to cross the border to Libya, yet a border never seemed more artificial than when Omar explained that his family had lived in their village for the past 100 years, since the time they came from the nearby area that is now Libya. In Basata in the Sinai Peninsula, where I watched the sunrise from my bamboo hut and looked out on Israel, Jordan, and Saudi Arabia, I couldn't imagine a place less under someone's sovereignty. In both places, Basata and Siwa, people asked me whether I came from "Egypt," not from "Cairo." While Cairenes certainly think of Cairo as Egypt, others in Basata and Siwa viewed Egypt as another place that did not necessarily include their homes. In Oman, it was the same. Villagers asked me and my friend if we had come from "Oman," referring to the capital city of Muscat and implying that we were now somewhere else.

It isn't just names and dialects that indicate divisions between people within these different countries. There are real divisions that

Waking up in the Western Desert.

cut across both national and ethnic lines. Unquestionably, Siwa has more in common culturally with Berber areas in Morocco than it does with Cairo. Viewing the Arab East as a composite whole is to miss important details and to shortchange the region. Lumping together a forty-year-old from Siwa and a forty-year-old from Muscat because they share the same religion and speak dialects of the same language could very well be useless.

The people of these countries don't necessarily group themselves with their fellow countrymen of different cities, let alone with Arabs from other countries. The exception, of course, is when there is an outside enemy. Nothing brings people or tribes together like an outside enemy. In the face of a national or regional threat, every Siwan would immediately become an Egyptian. Just as Jordanians and Palestinians inside of Jordan became "Arabs" in opposing the common threat that war in Iraq posed to their joint welfare.

When U.S. leaders consider policy questions, such as how to conduct a campaign to "win hearts and minds" in the Muslim world, it would be helpful if they realized that this isn't math, where there is one right answer for everyone. There are many right answers, and clearly a lot of wrong ones, too. U.S. policymakers shouldn't be like Mohammed, my friend from the Farfara Oasis who asked me for the secret formula that would enable him to convince Western women to sleep with him. There are no magic bullets. Attempting to use a cookie-cutter mold based on a few common regionwide traits in order to carve out solutions is not likely to succeed, and could instead lead to further misunderstandings. Moreover, there are places and people that the United States should try to learn from rather than seek to change. Is it really appropriate to offer a democracy blueprint to the people of Siwa? Perhaps. I certainly believe that everyone is entitled to make their own choices, as is the case in a democracy. But I'm also sure that Omar, Ali, and their family have something to offer us in America as well.

That night in the desert, as I lay between Omar and Ali, wrapped in a blanket that they had brought for me, I looked at the ghostly sky above and enjoyed a moment in which I realized how unquestionably worthwhile it had been to study Arabic. After living on the frontlines of anti-American sentiment for a year, it was fulfilling to be welcomed in such an unassuming way, to such a pure place, whose distance from my home cannot be measured in miles. In addition to all the other places I traveled to this year, and the generous and difficult people I met because I could speak Arabic, Arabic took me to this magnificent place in the desert, an oasis in every sense of the word, and earned me a degree of fellowship.

By the time you read this letter, I'll be home, *in sha'Allah*. See you soon.

Love,
Ben

Epilogue

That next morning, I woke up in the Western Desert between Ali and Omar and began my journey home. We returned to Siwa, and I caught a bus that broke down in the desert a few times but eventually made it to Cairo. I got on an Egypt Air flight and stepped away from my life on the Arab Street with warm feelings for the people I met and the culture of hospitality that I enjoyed. Speaking and hearing Arabic every day made me smile. And while I was also happy to return home to my family, friends, and the start of the Steelers' season, I was sad to leave behind the ahwa nights, the smell of fresh bread, the bouncing beats of Arabic Top 40 music, and the life that I'd carved out among people I couldn't have imagined, in places I never would have guessed I would go.

Reflecting on my experience against the backdrop of increasing "anti-Americanism" that we face from both policy critics and haters, it is logical to ask, why was I able to have such a rich, meaningful, and positive experience? I entered a world that many people in America regard with fear and distrust. I did have an impact on the people that I met, but at the same time my own opinions were influenced, too.

First, I was lucky. For the most part, I met good and hospitable people. A cynic might allege that Fadi, Salah, Bahaa, and the others who filled my life may have had ulterior motives—to find a wife, to come to the United States or Canada, or to learn English—but everyone holds ulterior motives to some degree. I did: I wanted to learn the culture and the language. I wanted to persuade people that my home isn't a terrible place; that America has many qualities that in fact make it a wonderful place. In a parallel way, a lot of the people

I met and lived among in Jordan and Egypt felt the same way. They wanted Americans—and in some cases Canadians—to see them as people, not as angry caricatures. They were eager to engage in conversations, to speak and be heard, and to develop deeper relationships.

One of my favorite people that I met in Amman was Sundos, a slight eighteen-year-old muhajiba freshman at Jordan University. One October day during the break between Arabic classes, as I was drinking coffee with a French classmate in our building's crowded cafeteria, a young student in a white hijab and denim jilbab tentatively approached. In a quiet voice, she asked my classmate Veronique for help with her English essay. Veronique told her in Arabic that she was French, gestured toward me, and said that I could help, since I was American. I introduced myself and invited her to sit. Unsure, she sat down hesitantly and told me her name, Surdos. For the rest of the break, we then worked on her essay about what she did over the summer.

Over the next couple of weeks, Sundos found me during breaks or after class. She would shyly say a few words to me in English or show me a homework assignment that she had completed. Throughout the fall, we became friends. As I'd walk through campus between classes, I'd hear a little voice call out, "*Ya'atik al-afya* . . . Benja!" My favorite expression can be used to say "hello," too. Sundos would emerge from behind a tree, or be sitting on a bench, or hurrying to catch up with me. A couple of different times, I met her friends, too. We would sit on a bench under one of the university's towering trees and talk about family or life in America. When my mother visited, we happened to run into Sundos outside of the library. I introduced her to my mom as one of my friends, and Sundos beamed with pride at what I hadn't realized was an honor.

One time, in the late fall, Sundos asked me if I would teach her to use the Internet. She had heard about it, but had never been online. So we made arrangements after class one day to meet at a computer lab. It was a lesson in more than the Internet, however; Sundos had never used a computer. First I showed her how to log in with her student ID, and then how to double click with the mouse.

In a combination of Arabic and English, I did my best to explain the concept of the Internet. We went to Yahoo and clicked on "music," then navigated to "news." Sundos sat next to me in the lab, in her denim jilbab and with a silver necklace of the map of historic Palestine around her neck, transfixed, as I tried to explain how the different pages of the Internet worked. We then clicked on "e-mail" and set up an account for her. Her address was a derivation of "hebrongirl." Sundos's family was from Hebron in the West Bank.

A few days later, I started receiving a stream of electronic greeting cards. They were all from "hebrongirl." Some were pictures of boy bands like NSYNC and others were cards that simply thanked me for my friendship. It is possible that the Internet has only been a source of entertainment for Sundos these last few years, which of course still has value. I'd guess, however, that there is a better chance that Sundos has also made it a means to communicate with and explore the world beyond her home. It is even possible that using a computer could one day serve her as a source of employment and empowerment.

So, yes, I was lucky in that I met good people. But the other reason I succeeded was because even when I was ducking for cover, I knew that there was a role for me to play and I was able to fill the part. I was representing America. I might not have been a diplomat, a soldier, or some other type of paid and official representative, but that doesn't diminish the value of my contributions. I knew that I was an unofficial ambassador. All the conversations I had while in the Middle East, all the people I met, all the times that I felt like I had to speak for America and our foreign policies, I always believed that I was representing my family, my friends, the city of Pittsburgh, and indeed my country. And so, in addition to my sense of self-deprecating humor and persistent idealism, I went about my day-to-day routine with a degree of responsibility and the best of intentions.

Thinking this over now, I'm reminded of my interview with Adnan Abu Odeh. Just a few months after the fall of Saddam, he told me, "What happens in Iraq will perpetuate how people feel one way or the other as far as the image of the United States. . . . America has put itself into the fray and made itself a tangible actor."

He was right. We inserted ourselves as actors on the ground in Iraq, and by all accounts, the colossal and public mistakes like Abu Ghraib have eclipsed on the macro level the individual achievements of American soldiers, engineers, and diplomats who work in anonymity with Iraqis to try and build a secure environment and representative government in that country. At times, those official U.S. ambassadors, or really representatives, do get to bask in the prestige of representing our country. Mostly though, in the Arab East, they shoulder the burden of having to officially represent some pretty difficult positions. Often, they cease to be individuals first and instead become the faces and figures of much criticized U.S. policies.

But Abu Odeh's assessment wasn't complete. It discounted the unofficial ambassadors who long ago inserted themselves as actors into the script. Unofficial ambassadors have served American interests in the Arab East for more than a hundred years. They've traveled and lived in the Arab East as archaeologists and journalists, Arabists and Orientalists, professors at the American University of Beirut and study-abroad students in Cairo, oilmen and entertainers—the list is endless.

Unofficial ambassadors won a "battle for hearts and minds" before we labeled and kept track of such a thing. They are the appeal of America incarnate: experts, dreamers, and explorers. Today, in the face of extreme animosity and distrust of America, we need to enlist our unofficial ambassadors; we need to increase their number and enable their potential impact. Unofficial ambassadors are America's greatest assets: scholars or Fulbright professors like Jack Davis, who teach their fields of expertise; study-abroad students who bring enthusiasm and curiosity; participants in international visitor programs who offer technical or specialized knowledge; authors, artists, and entertainers who travel through the region presenting their work or performing; Peace Corps volunteers; Doctors Without Borders and other professional do-gooders who contribute their time, patience, and efforts; the technocrats and practitioners that make up the development world and fill unmet human needs; and the so many other unofficial ambassadors who make the difference for America by delivering seeds of hope. Along the way, they maintain our humanity to the people of the Arab East.

As long as the face of America to the Arab East is attached to the body of an official representative in a suit or a uniform, the "battle for hearts and minds" will be about policy choices, rather than people. Right now, amid the daily images and realities of Iraq, Palestine, and Lebanon, such a battle over policy choices is something that we may be able to defend, but it is not one that we can win—no matter what our views and intentions. So there has always been an important place for unofficial ambassadors in U.S. foreign policy, and there is an even greater need for them today. America does well to have people who will form individual relationships with the Kholoods, Ibrahims, and Um Samers of the world, relationships that will build capital and influence change and opinions over time.

Living as an unofficial ambassador, without protective security restrictions on my movements, policy guidelines prohibiting my contacts, and official responsibilities dominating my time, I was able to interact positively with the everyday people of the Arab Street. While unofficial ambassadors can't take actions that address the real issues of debate that surround U.S. policies, they are able to do some pretty useful things on a micro level that make people's lives better, happier, and more promising—such as teaching them how to use the Internet. Moreover, if they like, they can also sit for hours at an ahwa or in a salon, listen to complaints, and try to explain the rationale behind various U.S. policies. Or they can even agree that a policy is shortsighted or being implemented badly. On a government-to-government level, such dialogue is fundamental to maintaining relationships between countries. On an unofficial level, too, there is infinite value to such discussions. And as I learned, it is an experience that reaps its own rewards.

Benjamin Orbach
www.BenjaminOrbach.com
Washington, D.C.
September 2006

Glossary

All words are Arabic unless indicated otherwise

Abu—father of

Adhan—the call to prayer

Ahwa—coffee and coffee house

Allah ya'tik al afya—"may God give you strength in your work," used differently throughout the Arab East; in Jordan and Palestine, it is commonly used to graciously ask a cab driver to stop the car.

Allahu Akbar—God is greatest

Amriki—American

Asl—genealogical roots

Baba—Dad

Baksheeh—depending upon the situation, a tip for services rendered, a bribe, or charity

Bawaab—doorman

Caliph—political and religious leader of the Islamic community, but not considered a prophet. The Caliphate was abolished in 1924 by Mustafa Kemal Ataturk the first president of the Republic of Turkey.

Falafel—also *tamiyya* in Egyptian dialect, deep fried ground chick peas and spices formed into patties or balls and served in pita bread with vegetables and sauces

Fuul—a heavy mix of mashed fava beans and oil

Galabaya—a traditional robe worn by men

Habibi—my friend

Hajj—a title of respect used for a man that has completed the pilgrimage to Mecca

Hawaja—a foreigner, "sir," depending upon the context

Hijab—head covering or head scarf

Hookah—water pipe filled with sheesha (flavored tobacco), also called a nargila

Hub—love

In'sh'Allah—God willing

Intifada—uprising; specifically refers to the Palestinian al-Aqsa intifada, or second intifada, against Israeli military occupation. The al-Aqsa intifada started in September 2000.

Jihad—struggle or holy war

Jilbab—traditional covering worn by women over their clothes

Khaffiyeh—man's traditional headdress

Kufi—skull cap

Ma'alesh—an Egyptian colloquial word that means something between "oh well," "I'm sorry," and "that's not important anyway."

Muhajiba—covered, referring to a women who wears the hijab

Mujahideen—holy warriors

Niqab—woman's face covering

Ruggelach—(Yiddish) a type of Jewish pastry

Sahlab—a milk based drink with coconut, raisins, peanuts, cinnamon, and bananas

Salaam—peace, hello, and goodbye

Salaam Aleykum—peace be upon you, a common greeting and goodbye

Servees—shared taxi

Shabbat—(Hebrew) the Sabbath, Saturday

Shalom—(Hebrew) peace, hello, and goodbye; the equivalent of Salaam

Shami—adjective referring to "Greater Syria" (modern day Syria, Lebanon, Jordan, Israel, and Palestine), also the dialect of Arabic spoken in these countries

Sharia—Islamic law

Shwarma—grilled or roasted meat, usually lamb but also beef

Um—mother of

Acknowledgments

There are many people for me to thank for their help and support in completing this labor of love. Kholood, Bahaa, and Ammo; Fadi and Marwan; Hazim, Ramis, and Rasha; Na'el and Um Wasem; Hanna; Sundos; Sami and Suzette; Salah and Ahmed; Kassem; Omar and Ali; and Sa'id are friends who welcomed me, a stranger, into their lives and homes and showed me the meaning of hospitality. I've written about them to share what they taught me. I've given some of them pseudonyms only to protect their privacy, never to hide my gratitude. Thank you.

My "support staff" of readers was invaluable in making sure that I got things right and wrote what I meant. In the places where I came up short, I have only myself to blame. Christina Parisi, Jim Bessent, Andy Ambraziejus and the AMACOM staff were not only terrific but patient. My agent, Maryann Karinch, has been a stalwart advocate and guide. Suzanne Murray was a valuable editor; Barak Barfi offered sharp insights from the very beginning, when I was just writing the "Benja Letters." Fred Neumann, Maggie White, Assaf Moghaddam, Rula Awwad, Soner Cagaptay, Jane Ring, and Bob Murray all read advance chapters and offered me their expertise. Ashley Kushner, Jonathan Schanzer, Frank Delaney, Deepti Rohatgi, Peter Bergen, Jared Schwartz, Afshin Molavi, Maria Hawilo, Larry Kerr, Reem Mohammad, and Ed Orbach headline a group of friends and colleagues too long to list that offered encouragement for which I am grateful.

This work would not have been possible if not for the years of studying the Middle East and Arabic that preceded my decision to go to Jordan. In this regard, there are so many people to thank who took an active interest in my academic development at the University of Michigan, Hebrew University, The Washington Institute for Near East Policy, Middlebury College, and Johns Hopkins University. I would be remiss if I didn't thank Fouad Ajami, Megan Ring, Kassem Wahba, Rob Satloff, Haldun Solmazturk, Patrick Clawson, W. Andrew Achenbaum, Ahmed K., and Michelle Zimney. I offer my gratitude to Elizabeth Veatch and the David Boren Fellowship, as well as to the Center for Arabic Studies Abroad. Their support made this experience possible.

Special thanks go to Kyle Stelma, Karim Sadjadpour, John Baskerville, Dalal Hassan, Raad al-Kadiri, and my brother Gideon Orbach. They are expert colleagues and great friends who reviewed full versions of the manuscript, challenged me with their thoughtful observations, and bolstered my efforts with their enthusiasm.

Most of all, I'd like to thank my parents. I'm not sure that I would have completed this book without their patience and support. They offered criticism and encouragement throughout the process, in an honest way and always at a DSL-like pace. Their efforts and consideration make it hard to believe that they have full-time jobs, aside from being the founding members and boosters of my unofficial fan club. For everything, thank you, Mom and Dad.